JOCK OF THE BUSHVELD

JOCK OF THE BUSHVELD

BY

SIR PERCY FITZPATRICK

ILLUSTRATED BY

E. CALDWELL

 MASKEW MILLER LONGMAN

Maskew Miller Longman (Pty) Ltd
Forest Drive, Pinelands, Cape Town

Offices in Johannesburg, Durban, King William's Town, Polokwane,
Bloemfontein, representatives in Mafikeng and Nelspruit
and companies throughout southern and central Africa.

website: www.mml.co.za

First published 1907
New edition reset 1948
Twentieth impression 1991
New edition 1999
Fifth impression 2006

ISBN 0 636 01116 X
ISBN 978 0 636 01116 8

Printed by Creda Communications

RK7234

Dedication

It was the youngest of the High Authorities

who gravely informed the Inquiring

Stranger that

"JOCK BELONGS TO THE LIKKLE PEOPLE!"

That being so, it is clearly the duty, no

less than the privilege, of the

Mere Narrator to

Dedicate

THE STORY OF JOCK

to

Those Keenest and Kindest of Critics, Best

of Friends, and Most Delightful

of Comrades

THE LIKKLE PEOPLE

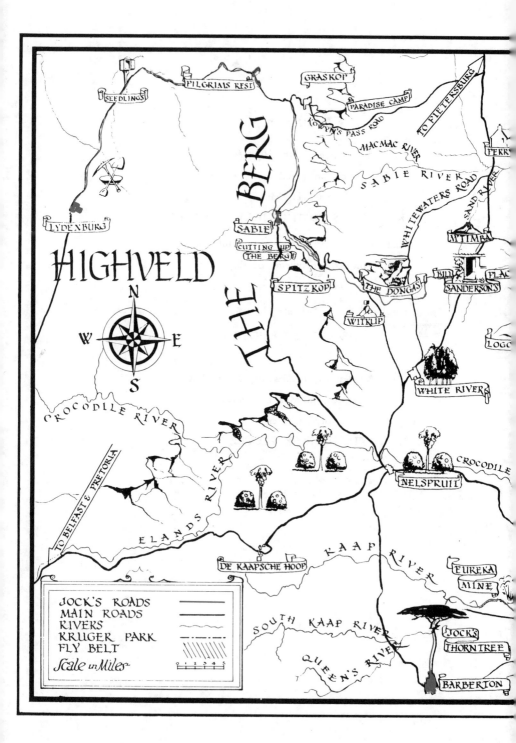

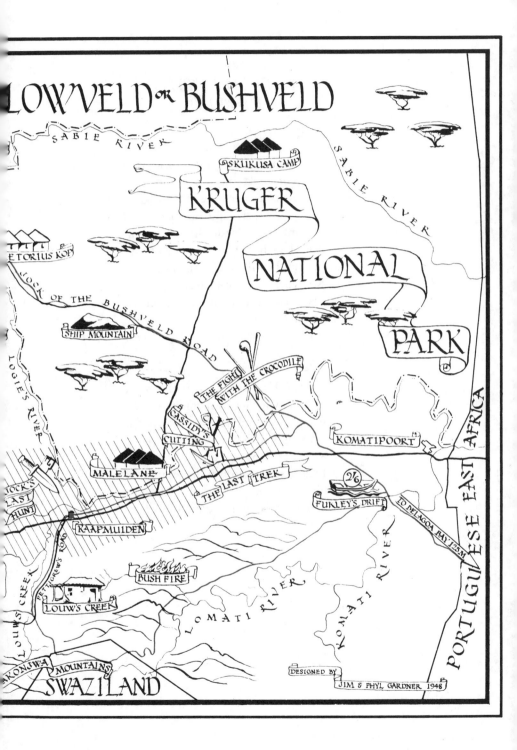

COMPLETE EDITION

'It is indeed by way of being a classic among animal stories, and the story of Jock, the bull terrier who shares his master's life in the veld, in the gold rush and in big game hunting, is as fresh and exciting as ever. Few books have been so fortunate in their illustrator, and E. Caldwell's delightful drawings so liberally scattered throughout the book give it an added delight.'

The Times Educational Supplement

'It's as fresh now as when it was written. FitzPatrick wrote this book originally for his own children—and it's a great children's book—but it isn't only children who've kept it alive in the bookshops all this time. In *Jock of the Bushveld* he recaptured all the ardours and thrills and sights and sounds of his days of adventure.'

B.B.C. Radio

PREFACE

"Sonny, you kin reckon it dead sure, thar's something wrong 'bout a thing that don't explain itself."

That was Old Rocky's advice, given three-and-twenty years ago—not forgotten yet, but, in this instance, respectfully ignored.

It happened some years ago, and this was the way of it: the Fox of Ballybotherem having served three generations—in his native Tipperary, in Kaffraria, and in the Transvaal—seemed entitled to a rest; and when, in the half-hour before 'lights out,' which is the Little People's particular own, the demand came from certain Autocrats of the Nightgown: "Now, tell us something else!" it occurred to the Puzzled One to tell of Jock's fight with the table leg. And that is how the trouble began. Those with experience will know what followed; and, for those less fortunate, the modest demand of one, comfortably tucked up tailorwise, and emphasising his points by excited hand-shakes with his toes, will convey the idea: "It must be *all true!* and don't leave out *anything!*"

To such an audience a story may be told a hundred times, but it must be told, as Kipling says, "Just so!" that is, in the same way; because, even a romance (what a three-year-old once excused as "only a play tell") must be true—to itself!

Once Jock had taken the field it was not long before the narrator found himself helped or driven over the pauses by quick suggestions from the Gallery; but there were days of fag and worry when thoughts lagged or strayed, and when slips were made, and then a vigilant and pitiless memory swooped like the striking falcon on its prey. There came a night when the story was of the Old Crocodile, and one in the Gallery—one of more exuberant fancy—seeing the gate open ran into the flower-strewn field of romance and by suggestive questions and eager promptings helped to gather a little posy: "And he caught the Crocodile by the tail, didn't he?" "And he hung on and fought him, didn't he?" "And the Old Crocodile flung him high into the air? High!" and, turning to the two juniors, added "quite as high as the house!" And the narrator—accessary by reason of a mechanical nod and an absent-minded "Yes"—passed on, thinking it could all be put right next time. But there is no escape from the 'tangled web' when the Little People sit in judgment. It was months later when retribution came. The critical point of the story was safely passed when—Oh! the irony and poetic justice of it—it was the innocent tempter himself who laid his hand in solemn protest on the narrator's shoulder and, looking him reproachfully in the eyes, said "Dad! You have left out the best part of all. Don't you remember how . . ."

And the description which followed only emphasises the present writer's unfitness for the task he has undertaken. In the text of the story and in the illustration by my friend Mr. Caldwell (who was himself subjected to the same influence) there is left a loophole for fancy: it is open to any one to believe that Jock is just beginning or just ending his aerial excursion. The Important People are not satisfied; but then the page is not big enough to exhibit Jock at the top of that flight—of fancy!

From the date of that lesson it was apparent that reputations would suffer if the story of Jock were not speedily embodied in some durable and authoritative form, and during a long spell of ill health many of the incidents were retold in the form of letters to the Little People. Other Less Important Persons— grown-ups—read them and sometimes heard them, and so it came about that the story of Jock was to be printed for private circulation, for the Little People and their friends. Then the story was read in manuscript and there came still more ambitious counsels, some urging the human story of the early days, others the wild animal life of South Africa. Conscious of many deficiencies the narrator has left two great fields practically untouched, adhering to the original idea—the story of Jock; and those who come into it, men and animals, come in because of him and the life in which he played so large a part. The attempt to adapt the original letters to the symmetry of a connected story involved, as one might have known, endless trouble and changes, necessitating complete rewriting of most parts; and the responsibility and work became still greater when, after a casual and unforeseen meeting, my friend Mr. Caldwell accepted the suggestion to come out to South Africa and spend six months with us in order to study the game in its native bush and to know the conditions of the life and put that experience into the work of illustrating "Jock."

The writer is well aware that, from the above causes and one other, there are grave inequalities in style and system, and in plane of phrase and thought, in different parts of the book. For this feature the 'one other' cause is alone put forward as a defence. The story belongs to the Little People, and their requirements were defined—"It must be *all true!* Don't leave out *anything!*" It has been necessary to leave out a great deal; but the other condition has been fully and fairly complied with; for it is a true story from beginning to end. It is not a diary: incidents have been grouped and moved to get over the difficulty of blank days and bad spells, but there is no incident of importance or of credit to Jock which is not absolutely true. The severest trial in this connection was in the last chapter, which is bound to recall perhaps the most famous and most cherished of all dog stories. Much, indeed, would have been sacrificed to avoid that; but it was unthinkable that, for any reason, one should in the last words shatter the spell that holds Jock dear to those for whom his life is chronicled—the spell that lies in 'a true story.'

Little by little the book has grown until it has come perilously near the condition in which it might be thought to have Pretensions. It has none! It is what it was: a simple record, compiled for the interest and satisfaction of some Little People, and a small tribute of remembrance and affection offered at the shrine of the old life and those who made it—tendered in the hope that some one better equipped with opportunities and leisure may be inspired to do justice to it and to them for the sake of our native land.

CONTENTS

FULL·PAGE·ILLUSTRATIONS

THE BACKGROUND

OF the people who live lonely lives, on the veld or elsewhere, few do so of their own free choice. Some there are shut off from all their kind—souls sheathed in some film invisible, through which no thrill of sympathy may pass; some barred by their self-consciousness, heart hungry still, who never learned in childhood to make friends; some have a secret or a grief; some, thoughts too big or bad for comradeship. But most will charge to Fate the thoughtless choice, the chance, or hard necessity, that drew or drove them to the life apart; they know the lesson that was learned of old: "It is not good for man to be alone."

Go out among them, ever moving on, whose white bones mark the way for others' feet—who shun the cities, living in the wilds, and move in silence, self-contained. Who knows what they think, or dream, or hope, or suffer? Who can know? For speech among that hard-schooled lot is but a half-remembered art.

Yet something you may guess, since with the man there often goes—his dog; his silent tribute to The Book. Oh, it's little they know of life who cannot guess the secret springs of loneliness and love that prompt the keeping of a trifling pet; who do not know what

moves a man who daily takes his chances of life and death—man whose "breath is in his nostrils"—to lay his cheek against the muzzle of his comrade dog, and in the trackless miles of wilderness feel he has a friend. Something to hold to; something to protect.

There was old Blake—"mad, quite mad," as everybody knew—of whom they vaguely said that horses, hounds, coaches, covers, and all that goes with old estates, were his—once. We knew him poor and middle-aged. How old to us! Cheery and unpractical, with two old pointers and a fowling-piece, and a heart as warm as toast. We did not ask each other's business there; and, judging by the dogs and gun, we put him down as a 'remittance man.' But that, it seems, was wrong. They were his all.

He left no letters—a little pile of paper ash; no money and no food! That was his pride. He would not sell or give away his dogs! That was his love. When he could not keep them it seemed time to go! That was his madness. But before he went, remembering a friend in hospital, he borrowed two cartridges and brought him in a brace of birds. That was old mad Blake, who 'moved on' and took his dogs with him, because they had always been together, and he could not leave their fate to chance. So we buried him with one on either side, just as he would have liked it!

There was Turner, who shot the crocodile that seized his dog, and reckless of the others, swam in and brought the dog to land.

2

There was the dog that jumped in when his master slipped from the rock, and, swimming beside him, was snapped down in his stead! And there was the boy who tried a rescue in the dark—when a rustle, yelp and growl told that the lions had his dog—and was never seen again.

So it goes, and so it went, from year to year: a little showing now and then, like the iceberg's tip, from which to guess the bulk below.

There was a Boy who went to seek his fortue. Call him boy or man: the years proved nothing either way! Some will be boyish always; others were never young: a few—most richly dowered few—are man and boy together. He went to seek his fortune, as boys will and should; no pressure on him from about; no promise from beyond. For life was easy there, and all was pleasant, as it may be—in a cage. 'To-day' is sure and happy; and there is no 'to-morrow'—in a cage.

There were friends enough—all kind and true—and in their wisdom they said: "Here it is safe: yonder all is chance, where many indeed are called, but few— so few—are chosen. Many have gone forth; some to return, beaten, hopeless, and despised; some to fall in sight outside; others are lost, we know not where; and ah! so few are free and well. But the fate of numbers is unheeded still; for the few are those who count, and lead; and those who follow do not

think 'How few,' but cry 'How strong! How free!' Be wise and do not venture. Here it is safe: there is no fortune there!"

But there was something stronger than the things he knew, around, without, beyond—the thing that strove within him: that grew and grew, and beat and fought for freedom: that bade him go and walk alone and tell his secret on the mountain slopes to one who would not laugh—a little red retriever; that made him climb and feel his strength, and find an outlet for what drove within. And thus the end was sure; for of all the voices none so strong as this! And only those others reached him that would chime with it; the gentle ones which said: "We too believe," and one, a stronger, saying: "Fifty years ago I did it. I would do it now again!"

So the Boy set out to seek his fortune, and did not find it; for there was none in the place where he sought. Those who warned him were—in the little —right; yet was he—in the greater—right too! It was not given to him as yet to know that fortune is not in time or place or things; but, good or bad, in the man's own self for him alone to find and prove.

Time and place and things had failed him; still was effort right; and, when the first was clear beyond all question, it was instinct and not knowledge bade him still go on, saying: "Not back to the cage. Anything but that!"

When many days had passed, it was again a friend who met him, saying: "Common sense is not

4

cowardice. You have made a mistake: repair it while you may. I have seen and know: there is nothing there. Come back with me, and all will be made easy." And answer, in reason, there was none; for the little truth was all too plain, and the greater not yet seen. But that which had swelled to bursting and had fought within for freedom called out: "Failure is the worst of all!" And the blind and struggling instinct rose against all knowledge and all reason. "Not back to the cage! Not that!"

And the heart that had once been young spoke up for Auld Lang Syne: the old eyes softened and dropped: "God speed you, Boy—Good-bye!" And as the mail-coach rumbled off the Boy put up his head —to try again.

The days passed, and still there was no work to do. For, those who were there already—hardened men and strong, pioneers who had roughed it—were themselves in straitened case, and it was no place for boys.

So the Boy moved on again, and with him a man in equal plight, but, being a man, a guide and comfort to the Boy, and one to lead him on the way. Hungry, they walked all day; yet when the sun went down and light began to fail the place where work and food and sleep should be was still far off. The mountain tracks were rough and all unknown; the rivers many, cold and swift: the country wild; none lived, few ever passed, that way. When night closed in the Boy walked on in front, and the man lagged wearily,

5

grumbling at their luck. In the valley at the mountain foot they came at midnight upon water, black and still, between them and the cabin's lights beyond; and there the man lay down. Then the Boy, turning in his anger, bade him come on; and, dragging him out upon the further bank, had found—unknowing —some little of the fortune he had come to seek.

Still morning brought no change; still was there no work to do. So the man gave up, and sagging back, was lost. And the Boy went on alone.

Rough and straight-spoken, but kindly men and true, were those he came among. What they could they did: what they had they gave. They made him free of board and bed; and, kinder still, now and then made work for him to do, knowing his spirit was as theirs and that his heart cried out: "Not charity, but work! Give me work!" But that they could not do, for there was no work they could not do themselves.

Thus the days and weeks went by. Willing, but unused to fend for himself—unfit by training for the wild rough life, heart and energy all to waste, the little he did know of no value there—the struggle with the ebbing tide went on; it was the wearing hopeless fight against that which one cannot grapple, and cannot even see. There was no work to be done. A few days here and there; a little passing job; a helping hand disguised; and then the quest again. They were all friendly—but, with the kindly habit of the place: it told the tale of hopelessness too well. They did not even ask his name; it made no difference.

6

"COME ALONG O' ME"

Then came a day when there was nowhere else to try. Among the lounging diggers at their week-end deals he stood apart—too shy, too proud to tell the truth; too conscious of it to trust his voice; too hungry to smile as if he did not care! And then a man in muddy moleskins, with grave face, brown beard, and soft blue eyes, came over to him, saying straight: "Boy, you come along o' me!" And he went.

It was work—hard work. But the joy of it! Shovelling in the icy water, in mud and gravel, and among the boulders, from early dawn to dark. What matter? It was work. It was not for hire, but just to help one who had helped him; to 'earn his grub' and feel he was a man, doing the work of his friend's partner, 'who was away.'

For three full weeks the Boy worked on; grateful for the toil; grateful for the knowledge gained; most grateful that he could by work repay a kindness. And then the truth came out! The kindly fiction fell away as they sat and rested on the day of rest. "The claim could not stand two white men's grub" had fallen from the man, accounting for his partner's absence.

It was the simple and unstudied truth and calm unconsciousness of where it struck that gave the thrust its force; and in the clear still air of the Sunday morning the Boy turned hot and cold and dizzy to think of his folly, and of the kindness he had so long imposed upon. It was a little spell before his lips

would smile, and eyes and voice were firm enough to lie. Then he said gently: If he could be spared— he had not liked to ask before, but now the floods were over and the river turned perhaps it could be managed—he would like to go, as there were letters waiting, and he expected news.

Up the winding pathway over rocky ledge and grassy slope, climbing for an hour to the pass, the toil and effort kept the hot thoughts under. At the top the Boy sat down to rest. The green rock-crested mountains stood like resting giants all around: the rivers, silvered by the sun, threaded their ways between: the air was clear, and cool, and still. The world was very beautiful from there.

Far, far below—a brownish speck beside the silver streak—stood the cabin he had left. And, without warning, all came back to him. What he had mastered rose beyond control. The little child that lies hidden in us all reached out—as in the dark—for a hand to hold; and there was none. His arms went up to hide the mocking glory of the day, and face buried in the grass, he sobbed: "Not worth my food!"

Science tells that Nature will recoup herself by ways as well defined as those that rule mechanics. The blood flows upward—and the brain's awhirl; the ebb-tide sets — and there is rest. Whatever impulse sways the guiding hand, we know that often when we need it most there comes relief; gently, unbidden, unobserved.

8

The Boy slept, and there was peace awhile. Then came faint echoes of the waking thoughts—odd words shot out, of hope and resolution; murmured names of those at home. Once his hand went out and gently touched the turf, reaching for the friend and comrade of the past—one who knew his every mood, had heard his wildest dreams described, had seen him, hot-eyed, breathless, struggling to escape the cage; one to whom the boyish soul was often bared in foolish confidence; one who could see and hear and feel, yet never tell—a little red retriever left at home; and the Boy stirred and sighed, for answer to the soft brown eyes.

No! It is not good for man to be alone.

A wisp of drifting cloud came by, a breath of cooler air, and the fickle spirit of the mountain changed the day as with a wand. The Boy woke up shivering, dazed, bewildered: the mountain of his dreams had vanished; and his dog was not there! The cold driving mist had blotted out the world. Stronger and stronger grew the wind, driving the damp cold through and through; for on the bleak plateau of the mountain nothing broke its force.

Pale and shaken, and a little stiff, he looked about; then slowly faced the storm. It had not struck him to turn back.

The gusts blew stronger, and through the mist came rain, in single stinging drops—portents of the greater storm. Slowly, as he bent to breast it, the chilled blood warmed, and when the first thunderclap split

9

overhead, and lost itself in endless roars and rumblings in the kloofs and hills around, there came a warmth about his heart and a light into his eye—mute thanksgiving that here was something he could battle with and be a man again.

On top of the world the storms work all their fury. Only there come mist and wind and rain, thunder and lightning and hail together—the pitiless terrible hail: there, where the hare hiding in the grass may know it is the highest thing in all God's world, and nearest to the storm—the one clear mark to draw the lightning—and, knowing, scurries to the sheltered slopes.

But the Boy pressed on—the little path a racing stream to guide him. Then in the one group of ghostly, mist-blurred rocks he stopped to drink; and, as he bent—for all the blackness of the storm— his face leaped out at him reflected for one instant in the shallow pool; the blue-white flame of lightning, blinding his aching eyes, hissed down; the sickening smell of brimstone spread about; and crashing thunder close above his head left him dazed and breathless.

Heedless of the rain, blinking the blackness from his eyes, he sat still for head to clear, and limbs to feel their life again; and, as he waited, slowly there came upon a colder stiller air that other roar, so far, so dull, so uniform; so weird and terrifying—the voice of the coming hail.

Huddled beneath the shelving rock he watched the storm sweep by with awful battering din that swamped

10

and silenced every other sound—the tearing, smashing hail that seemed to strip the mountain to its very bone.

Oh! the wanton fury of the hail; the wild, destructive charge of hordes of savage cavalry; the stamping, smashing sweep along the narrow strip where all the fury concentrates; the long black trail of death and desolation! The birds and beasts, the things that creep and fly, all know the portents, and all flee before it, or aside. But in the darkness—in the night or mist—the slow, the weak, the helpless, and the mothers with their young—for them is little hope.

The dense packed column swept along, ruthless, raging, and unheeding, overwhelming all. . . . A sudden failing of its strength, a little straggling tail, and then—the silence!

The sun came out; the wind died down; light veils of mist came slowly by—bits of floating gossamer —and melted in the clear, pure air.

The Boy stepped out once more. Miles away the black column of the falling hail sped its appointed course. Under his feet, where all had been so green and beautiful, was battered turf, for the time transformed into a mass of dazzling brilliants, where jagged ice-stones caught the sunlight on their countless facets, and threw it back in one fierce flashing glare, blinding in its brilliance.

On the glittering surface many things stood out.

In the narrow pathway near the spring, a snake lay on its back, crushed and broken; beyond it, a tortoise, not yet dead, but bruised and battered

11

through its shell; then a partridge—poor unprotected thing—the wet feathers lying all around, stripped as though a hawk had stricken it, and close behind it all the little brood; and further afield lay something reddish-brown—a buck—the large eyes glazed, an ooze of blood upon its lips and nose. He stooped to touch it, but drew back: the dainty little thing was pulp.

All striving for the sheltering rocks; all caught and stricken by the ruthless storm; and he, going on to face it, while others fled before—he, blindly fighting on —was spared. Was it luck? Or was there something subtle, more? He held to this, that more than chance had swayed the guiding hand of fate—that fortune holds some gifts in store for those who try; and faith resurgent moved him to a mute Te Deum, of which no more reached the conscious brain than: "It is good to be alive! But . . . better *so* than in the cage."

Once more, a little of the fortune that he had come to seek!

At sunset, passing down the long rough gorge, he came upon one battling with the flood to save his all—the white man struggling with the frightened beasts; the kaffir swept from off his feet; the mad bewildered oxen yielding to the stream and heading downwards towards the falls—and in their utmost need the Boy swam in and helped!

And there the long slow ebb was stayed: the Boy was worth his food.

But how recall the life when those who made it set so little store by all that passed, and took its ventures for their daily lot; when those who knew it had no gift or thought to fix the colours of the fading past: the fire of youth; the hopes; the toil; the bright illusions gone! And now, the Story of a Dog to conjure up a face, a name, a voice, or the grip of a friendly hand! And the half-dreamed sound of the tramping feet is all that is left of the live procession long since passed: the young recruits; the laggards and the faint; the few who saw it through; the older men—grave-eyed, thoughtful, unafraid—who judged the future by the battered past, and who knew none more nor less than man—unconscious equals of the best and least; the grey-hued years; the thinning ranks; the summons answered, as they had lived—alone. The tale untold; and, of all who knew it, none left to picture now the life, none left to play a grateful comrade's part, and place their record on a country's scroll—the kindly, constant, nameless Pioneers!

INTO
THE·BUSHVELD

"Distant hills are always green," and the best gold further on. That is a law of nature—human nature—which is quite superior to facts; and thus the world moves on.

So from the Lydenburg Goldfields prospectors 'humping their swags' or driving their small pack-donkeys spread afield, and transport-riders with their long spans and rumbling waggons followed, cutting a wider track where traders with winding strings of carriers had already ventured on. But the hunters had gone first. There were great hunters whose names are known; and others as great who missed the accident of fame; and after them hunters who traded, and traders who hunted. And so too with prospectors, diggers, transport-riders and all.

Between the goldfields and the nearest port lay the Bushveld, and game enough for all to live on. Thus, all were hunters of a sort, but the great hunters—the hunters of big game—were apart; we were the smaller fry, there to admire and to imitate.

Trophies, carried back with pride or by force of habit, lay scattered

14

about, neglected and forgotten, round the outspans, the tents of lone prospectors, the cabins of the diggers, and the grass wayside shanties of the traders. How many a 'record' head must have gone then, when none had thought of time or means to save them! Horns and skins lay in jumbled heaps in the yards or sheds of the big trading stores. The splendid horns of the Koodoo and Sable, and a score of others only less beautiful, could be seen nailed up in crude adornment of the roughest walls; nailed up, and then unnoticed and forgotten! And yet not quite! (or although to the older hands they were of no further interest, to the newcomer they spoke of something yet to see, and something to be done; and the sight set him dreaming of the time when he too would go a-hunting and bring his trophies home.

Perched on the edge of the Berg, we overlooked the wonder-world of the Bushveld, where the big game roamed in thousands and the "wildest tales were true." Living on the fringe of a hunter's paradise, most of us were drawn into it from time to time, for shorter or longer spells, as opportunity and our circumstances allowed; and little by little one got to know the names, appearances, and habits of the many kinds of game below. Long talks in the quiet nights up there under waggons, in grass shelters in the woods, or in the wattle-and-daub shanties of the diggers, where men passed to and fro and swapped lies, as the polite phrase went, were our 'nights' entertainments,' when younger hands might learn much that was useful and true, and more that was neither.

It was a school of grown-up schoolboys; no doubt a hard one, but it had its playground side, and it was the habit of the school to 'drop on to' any breach of the unwritten laws, to 'rub in' with remorseless good humour the mistakes that were made, and to play upon credulity with a shamelessness and nerve quite paralysing to the judgment of the inexperienced. Yet, with it all, there was a kindliness and quick instinct of 'fair do's' which tempered the wind and, in the main, gave no one more than was good for him.

There the new boy had to run the gauntlet, and, if without a watchful instinct or a friendly hint, there was nothing to warn him of it. When Faulkner—dragged to the piano—protested that he remembered nothing but a mere 'morceau,' he was not conscious of transgression, but a delighted audience caught up the word, and thenceforth he was known only as 'Ankore'—Harry the Sailor having explained that 'more so' was a recognised variant.

"Johnny-come-lately's got to learn" was held to be adequate reason for letting many a beginner buy his experience, while those who had been through it all watched him stumble into the well-known pitfalls. It would no doubt have been a much more comfortable arrangement all round had there been a polite ignoring of each other's blunders and absurdities. But that is not the way of schools where the spirit of fun plays its useful part; and, after all, the lesson well 'rubbed in' is well remembered.

The new assayer, primed by us with tales of Sable Antelope round Macmac Camp, shot old Jim Hill's

16

only goat, and had to leave the carcass with a note of explanation—Jim being out when he called. What he heard from us when he returned, all prickly with remorse and shame, was a liberal education; but what he remembers best is Jim's note addressed that evening to our camp:

"Boys! Jim Hill requests your company to dinner to-morrow, Sunday!"

"Mutton!"

As the summer spent itself, and whispers spread around of new strikes further on, a spirit of restlessness —a touch of trek fever—came upon us, and each cast about which way to try his luck. Our camp was the summer headquarters of two transport-riders, and when many months of hard work, timber-cutting on the Berg, contracting for the Companies, pole-slipping in the bush, and other things, gave us at last a 'rise,' it seemed the natural thing to put it all into waggons and oxen, and go transport-riding too.

The charm of a life of freedom and complete independence—a life in which a man goes as and where he lists, and carries his home with him—is great indeed; but great too was the fact that hunting would go with it.

How the little things that mark a new departure stamp themselves indelibly on the memory! A flower in the hedgerow where the roads divide will mark the spot in one's mind for ever; and yet a million more, before and after, and all as beautiful, are passed unseen. In memory, it is all as fresh, bright and glorious as ever: only the years have gone. The

17   C

start, the trek along the plateau, the crystal streams, the ferns and trees, the cool pure air; and, through and over all, the quite intoxicating sense of freedom! Then came the long slow climb to Spitzkop where the Berg is highest and where our descent began. For there, with Africa's contrariness, the highest parts banked up and buttressed by gigantic spurs are most accessible from below, while the lower edges of the plateau are cut off sheer like the walls of some great fortress. There, near Spitzkop, we looked down upon the promised land; there, stood upon the outmost edge, as a diver on his board, and paused and looked and breathed before we took the plunge.

It is well to pitch one's expectations low, and so stave off disappointments. But counsels of perfection are wasted on the young, and when accident combines with the hopefulness of youth to lay the colours on in all their gorgeousness, what chance has Wisdom?

"See here, young feller!" said Wisdom, "don't go fill yourself up with tomfool notions 'bout lions and tigers waitin' behind every bush. You won't see one in a twelvemonth! Most like you won't see a buck for a week! You don't know what to do, what to wear, how to walk, how to look, or what to look for; and you'll make as much noise as a traction engine. This ain't open country: it's bush; they can see and hear, and you can't. An' as for big game, you won't see any for a long while yet, so don't go fool yourself!"

Excellent! But fortune in a sportive mood ordained that the very first thing we saw as we out-

18

spanned at Saunderson's on the very first day in the Bushveld was the fresh skin of a lion stretched out to dry. What would the counsels of Solomon himself have weighed against that wet skin?

Wisdom scratched its head and stared: "Well, I am com—pletely sugared!"

Of course it was a fluke. No lions had been seen in the locality for several years; but the beginner, filled with all the wildest expectations, took no heed of that. If the wish be father to the thought, then surely fact may well beget conviction. It was so in this case, at any rate, and thus not all the cold assurances of Wisdom could banish visions of big game as plentiful as partridges.

A party had set out upon a tiger hunt to clear out one of those marauders who used to haunt the kloofs of the Berg and make descents upon the Kaffir herds of goats and sheep; but there was a special interest in this particular tiger, for he had killed one of the white hunters in the last attempt to get at him a few weeks before. Starting from the store, the party of men and boys worked their way towards the kloof, and the possibility of coming across a lion never entered their heads. No notice was taken of smaller game put up from time to time as they moved carelessly along; a rustle on the left of the line was ignored, and Bill Saunderson was as surprised as Bill ever could be to see a lion facing him at something like six or seven yards. The lion, with head laid level and tail flicking ominously, half crouched for its spring. Bill's

19

bullet glanced along the skull, peeling off the skin. "It was a bad shot," he said afterwards, in answer to the beginner's breathless questions. "He wasn't hurt: just sank a little like a pointer when you check him; but before he steadied up again I took for the nose and got him. You see," he added thoughtfully, "a lion's got no forehead: it is all hair."

That was about all he had to say; but, little store as he may have set on it, the tip was never forgotten and proved of much value to at least one of our party years afterwards. To this day the picture of a lion brings up that scene—the crouching beast, faced by a man with a long brown beard, solemn face, and clear unfaltering eyes; the swift yet quiet action of reloading; and the second shot an inch or so lower, because "a lion's got no forehead: it's all hair."

The shooting of a lion, fair and square, and face to face, was the Blue Riband of the Bush, and no detail would have seemed superfluous; but Bill, whose eye nothing could escape, had, like many great hunters, a laggard tongue. Only now and then a look of grave amusement lighted up his face to show he recognised the hungry enthusiasm and his own inability to satisfy it. The skin with the grazed stripe along the nose, and the broken skull, were handled and looked at many times, and the story was pumped from every Kaffir—all voluble and eager, but none eye-witnesses. Bob, the sociable and more communicative, who had been nearest his brother, was asked a hundred questions, but all he had to say was that the grass was too long for him to see what

20

happened: he reckoned that it was "a pretty near thing after the first shot; but Bill's all right!"

To me it was an absurd and tiresome affectation to show interest in any other topic, and when, during that evening, conversation strayed to other subjects, it seemed waste of time and priceless opportunity. Bob responded good-naturedly to many crude attempts to head them back to the entrancing theme, but the professional interest in rates, loads, rivers, roads, disease, drought, and 'fly' was strong in the older transport-riders, as it should have been, but, for the time at least, was not, in me. If diplomacy failed, however, luck was not all out; for when all the pet subjects of the road had been thrashed out, and it was about time to turn in, a stray question brought the reward of patience.

"Have you heard if Jim reached Durban all right?"

"Yes! Safely shipped."

"You got some one to take him right through?"

"No! A Dutchman took him to Lydenburg, and I got Tom Hardy, going back empty, to take him along from there."

"What about feeding?"

"I sent some goats," said Bob, smiling for a moment at some passing thought, and then went on: "Tom said he had an old span that wouldn't mind it. We loaded him up at Parker's, and I cleared out before he got the cattle up. But they tell me there was a gay jamboree when it came to inspanning; and as soon as they got up to the other waggons and the young bullocks winded Jim, they started

21

off with their tails up—a regular stampede, voorloopers and drivers yelling like mad, all the loose things shaking out of the waggons, and Tom nearly in a fit from running, shouting and swearing."

Judging by the laughter, there was only one person present who did not understand the joke, and I had to ask—with some misgiving—who was this Jim who needed so much care and feeding, and caused such a scare.

There was another burst of laughter as they guessed my thoughts, and it was Bob who answered me: "Only a lion, lad—not a wild man or a lunatic! Only a young lion! Sold him to the Zoo, and had to deliver him in Durban."

"Well, you fairly took me in with the name!"

"Oh! Jim? Well that's his pet name. His real name is Dabulamanzi. Jim, my hunting boy, caught him, so we call him Jim out of compliment," he added with a grin. "But Jim called him Dabulamanzi also out of compliment, and I think that was pretty good for a nigger."

"You see," said Bob, for the benefit of those who were not up in local history, "Dabulamanzi, the big fighting General in the Zulu War, was Jim's own chief and leader; and the name means 'The one who conquers the waters.'"

Then one of the others exclaimed: "Oh! Of course, that's how you got him, isn't it: caught him in a river? Tell us what did happen, Bob. What's the truth of it? It seemed a bit steep as I heard it."

22

"Well, it's really simple enough. We came right on to the lioness waiting for us, and I got her; and then there were shouts from the boys, and I saw a couple of cubs, pretty well grown, making off in the grass. This boy Jim legged it after one of them, a cub about as big as a Newfoundland dog—not so high, but longer. I followed as fast as I could, but he was a big Zulu and went like a buck, yelling like mad all the time. We were in the bend of one of the long pools down near the Komati, and when I got through the reeds the cub was at the water's edge facing Jim, and Jim was dancing around heading it off with only one light stick. As soon as it saw us coming on, the cub took to the water, and Jim after it. It was as good as a play. Jim swam up behind, and putting his hand on its head ducked it right under: the cub turned as it came up and struck out at him viciously, but he was back out of reach: when it turned again to go Jim ducked it again, and it went on like that six or eight times, till the thing was half drowned and had no more fight in it. Then Jim got hold of it by the tail and swam back to us, still shouting and quite mad with excitement.

"Of course," added Bob with a wag of his head, "you can say it was only a cub; but it takes a good man to go up naked and tackle a thing like that, with teeth and claws to cut you into ribbons."

"Was Jim here to-day?" I asked, as soon as there was an opening. Bob shook his head with a kindly regretful smile. "No, Sonny, not here; you'd 'a' heard him. Jim's gone. I had to sack him. A real

23

fine nigger, but a terror to drink, and always in trouble. He fairly wore me right out."

We were generally a party of half a dozen—the owners of the four waggons, a couple of friends trading with Delagoa, a man from Swaziland, and—just then—an old Yankee hunter-prospector. It was our holiday time, before the hard work with loads would commence, and we dawdled along feeding up the cattle and taking it easy ourselves.

It was too early for loads in the Bay, so we moved slowly and hunted on the way, sometimes camping for several days in places where the grass and water were good; and that lion skin was the cause of many disappointments to me. Never a bush or ant-heap, never a donga or a patch of reeds, did I pass for many days after that without the conviction that something was lurking there. Game there was in plenty, no doubt, but it did not come my way. Days went by with, once or twice, the sight of some small buck just as it disappeared, and many times the noise of something in the bush or the sound of galloping feet. Others brought their contributions to the pot daily, and there seemed to be no reason in the world why I alone should fail—no reason except sheer bad luck! It is difficult to believe you have made mistakes when you do not know enough to recognise them, and have no idea of the extent of your own ignorance; and then bad luck is such an easy and such a flattering explanation! If I did not go so far on the easy road of excuse-making as to put all the failures down to bad luck, perhaps some one else deserves the credit.

One evening as we were lounging round the camp fire, Robbie, failing to find a soft spot for his head on a thorn log, got up reluctantly to fetch his blankets, exclaiming with a mock tragic air:

> "The time is out of joint; O cursed spite,
> That ever I was born to set it right."

We knew Robbie's way. There were times when he would spout heroics, suggested by some passing trifle, his own face a marvel of solemnity the whole time, and only the amused expression in his spectacled grey eyes to show he was poking fun at himself. An indulgent smile, a chuckle, and the genial comment "Silly ass!" came from different quarters; for Robbie was a favourite. Only Old Rocky maintained his usual gravity.

As Robbie settled down again in comfort, the old man remarked in level thoughtful tones: "I reckon the feller as said that was a waster, he chucked it!" There was a short pause in which I, in my ignorance, began to wonder if it was possible that Rocky did not know the source; or did he take the quotation seriously? Then Robbie answered in mild protest: "It was a gentleman of the name of Hamlet who said it."

"Well, you can bet he was no good, anyhow," Rocky drawled out. " 'Jus' my luck!' is the waster's motto!"

"They do say he was mad," Robbie replied, as his face twitched with a pull-your-leg expression,

25

"but he got off a lot of first-class things all the same —some of the best things ever said."

"I da' say; they mostly can. But a man as sets down and blames his luck is no good anyhow. He's got no sand, and got no sense, and got no honesty! It ain't the time's wrong: it's the man! It ain't the job's too big: it's the man's too little!"

"You don't believe in luck at all, Rocky?" I ventured to put in.

"I don't say thar's no such thing as luck—good and bad; but it ain't the explanation o' success an' failure—not by a long way. No, sirree, luck's just the thing any man'd like ter believe is the reason for his failure and another feller's success. But it ain't so. When another man pulls off what you don't, the first thing you got ter believe is it's your own fault; and the last, it's his luck. And you jus' got ter wade in an' find out whar you went wrong, an' put it right, 'thout any excuses an' explanations."

"But, Rocky, explanations aren't always excuses, and sometimes you really have to give them!"

"Sonny, you kin reckon it dead sure thar's something wrong 'bout a thing that don't explain itself; an' one explanation's as bad as two mistakes—it don't fool anybody worth speaking of, 'cept yerself. You find the remedy; you can leave other folks put up the excuses."

I was beaten. It was no use going on, for I knew he was right. I suppose the other fellows also knew whom he was getting at, but they said nothing; and the subject seemed to have dropped, when Rocky,

26

harking back to Robbie's quotation, said, with a ghost of a smile: "I reckon ef that sharp o' your'n hed ter keep the camp in meat we'd go pretty nigh hungry."

But it seemed a good deal to give up all at once—the bad luck, the excuses and explanations, and the comfort they afforded; and I could not help thinking of that wretched wrong-headed stembuck that had actually allowed me to pass it, and then cantered away behind me.

Rocky, known, liked, and respected by all, yet intimate with none, was 'going North'—even to the Zambesi, it was whispered—but no one knew where or why. He was going off alone, with two pack-donkeys and not even a boy for company, on a trip of many hundreds of miles and indefinite duration. No doubt he had an idea to work out; perhaps a report of some trader or hunter or even native was his pole-star: most certainly he had a plan, but what it was no living soul would know. That was the way of his kind. With them there was no limit in time or distance, no hint of purpose or direction, no home, no address, no 'people'; perhaps a partner somewhere or a chum, as silent as themselves, who would hear some day—if there was anything to tell.

Rocky had worked near our camp on the Berg. I had known him to nod to, and when we met again at one of the early outspans in the Bush and offered a lift for him and his packs he accepted and joined us, it being still a bit early to attempt crossing the rivers with pack-donkeys. It may be that the 'lift' saved his donkeys something on the roughest roads and in

the early stages; or it may be that we served as a useful screen for his movements, making it difficult for any one else to follow his line and watch him. Anyway, he joined us in the way of those days: that is, we travelled together and as a rule we grubbed together; yet each cooked for himself and used his own stores, and in principle we maintained our separate establishments. The bag alone was common; each man brought what game he got and threw it into the common stock.

The secret of agreement in the veld is—complete independence! Points of contact are points of friction—nowhere more so; and the safest plan is, each man his own outfit and each free to feed or sleep or trek as and when he chooses. I have known partners and friends who would from time to time move a trek apart, or a day apart, and always camp apart when they rejoined; and so remain friends.

Rocky—in full, Rocky Mountain Jack—had another name, but it was known to few besides the Mining Commissioner's clerk who registered his licences from time to time. "In the Rockies whar I was raised" is about the only remark having deliberate reference to his personal history which he was known to have made; but it was enough on which to found the name by which we knew him.

What struck me first about him was the long Colt's revolver, carried on his hip; and for two days this 'gun,' as he called it, conjured up visions of Poker Flat and Roaring Camp, Jack Hamlin and Yuba

28

Bill of cherished memory; and then the inevitable 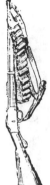 question got itself asked:

"Did you ever shoot a man, Rocky?"

"No, Sonny," he drawled gently, "never hed ter use it yet!"

"It looks very old. Have you had it long?"

"Jus' 'bout thirty years, I reckon!"

"Oh! Seems a long time to carry a thing without using it!"

"Waal," he answered half absently, "thet's so. It's a thing you don't want orfen—but when you do, you want it derned bad!"

Rocky seemed to me to have stepped into our life out of the pages of Bret Harte. For me the glamour of romance was cast by the Master's spell over all that world, and no doubt helped to make old Rocky something of a hero in the eyes of youth; but such help was of small account, for the cardinal fact was Rocky himself. He was a man.

There did not seem to be any known region of the earth where prospectors roam that he had not sampled, and yet whilst gleaning something from every land, his native flavour clung to him unchanged. He was silent by habit and impossible to draw; not helpful to those who looked for short cuts, yet kindly and patient with those who meant to try; he was not to be exploited, and had an illuminating instinct for what was not genuine. He had 'no use for short weight'—and showed it!

I used to watch him in the circle round the fire at nights, his face grave, weather-stained and

29

wrinkled, with clear grey eyes and long brown beard, slightly grizzled then—watch and wonder why Rocky, experienced, wise and steadfast, should—at sixty—be seeking still. Were the prizes so few in the prospector's life? or was there something wanting in him too? Why had he not achieved success?

It was not so clear then that ideals differ. Rocky's ideal was the life—not the escape from it. There was something—sentiment, imagination, poetry, call it what you will—that could make common success seem to him common indeed and cheap! To follow in a new rush, to reap where another had sown, had no charm for him. It may be that an inborn pride disliked it; but it seems more likely that it simply did not attract him. And if—as in the end I thought—Rocky had taken the world as it is and backed himself against it—living up to his ideal, playing a 'lone hand' and playing it fair in all conditions, treading the unbeaten tracks, finding his triumph in his work, always moving on and contented so to end: the crown, "He was a man!"—then surely Rocky's had achieved success!

That is Rocky, as remembered now! A bit idealised? Perhaps so: but who can say! In truth he had his sides and the defects of his qualities, like every one else; and it was not every one who made a hero of him. Many left him respectfully alone; and something of their feeling came to me the first time I was with him, when a stupid chatterer talked and asked too much. He was not surly or taciturn, but I felt frozen through by a calm deadly unrespon-

30

siveness which anything with blood and brain should have shrunk under. The dull monotone, the ominous drawl, the steady something in his clear calm eyes which I cannot define, gave an almost corrosive effect to innocent words and a voice of lazy gentleness.

"What's the best thing to do following up a wounded buffalo?" was the question. The questions sprung briskly, as only a 'yapper' puts them; and the answers came like reluctant drops from a filter.

"Git out!"

"Yes, but if there isn't time?"

"Say yer prayers!"

"No—seriously—what is the best way of tackling one?"

"Ef yer wawnt to know, thar's only one way: Keep cool and shoot straight!"

"Oh, of course—*if you can!*"

"An' ef you can't," he added in fool-killer tones, "best stay right home!"

Rocky had no fancy notions: he hunted for meat and got it as soon as possible; he was seldom out long, and rarely indeed came back empty-handed. I had already learnt not to be too ready with questions. It was better, so Rocky put it, "to keep yer eyes open and yer mouth shut"; but the results at first hardly seemed to justify the process. At the end of a week of failures and disappointments all I knew was that I knew nothing—a very notable advance it is true, but one quite difficult to appreciate! Thus it came to me in the light of a distinction when one evening after a rueful confession of blundering made to the

31

party in general, Rocky passed a brief but not un-friendly glance over me and said, "On'y the born fools stays fools. You'll git ter learn bymbye; you ain't always yappin'!"

It was not an extravagant compliment; but failure and helplessness act on conceit like water on a starched collar: mine was limp by that time, and I was grateful for little things—most grateful when next morning, as we were discussing our several ways, he turned to me and asked gently, "Comin' along, Boy?"

Surprise and gratitude must have produced a touch of effusiveness which jarred on him; for, to the eager exclamation and thanks, he made no answer—just moved on, leaving me to follow. In his scheme of life there was 'no call to slop over.'

There was a quiet unhesitating sureness and a definiteness of purpose about old Rocky's movements which immediately inspired confidence. We had not been gone many minutes before I began to have visions of exciting chases and glorious endings, and as we walked silently along they took possession of me so completely that I failed to notice the difference between his methods and mine. Presently, brimful of excite-ment and hope, I asked cheerily what he thought we would get. The old man stopped and with a gentle graveness of look and a voice from which all trace of tartness or sarcasm was banished, said, "See, Sonny! If you been useter goin' round like a dawg with a tin it ain't any wonder you seen nothin'. You got ter walk soft an' keep yer head shut!"

In reply to my apology he said that there was "no

bell an' curtain in this yere play; you got ter be thar waitin'."

Rocky knew better than I did the extent of his good nature; he knew that in all probability it meant a wasted day; for, with the best will in the world, the beginner is almost certain to spoil sport. It looks so simple and easy when you have only read about it or heard others talk; but there are pitfalls at every step. When, in what seemed to me perfectly still air, Rocky took a pinch of dust and let it drop, and afterwards wet one finger and held it up to feel which side cooled, it was not difficult to know that he was trying the wind; but when he changed direction suddenly for no apparent reason, or when he stopped and, after a glance at the ground, slackened his frame, lost all interest in sport, wind and surroundings, and addressed a remark to me in ordinary tones, I was hopelessly at sea. His manner showed that some possibility was disposed of and some idea abandoned. Once he said "Rietbuck! Heard us I reckon," and then turned off at a right-angle; but a little later on he pointed to other spoor and, indifferently dropping the one word 'Koodoo,' continued straight on. To me the two spoors seemed equally fresh; he saw hours'—perhaps a whole day's— difference between them. That the rietbuck, scared by us, had gone ahead and was keenly on the watch for us and therefore not worth following, and that the koodoo was on the move and had simply struck across our line and was therefore not to be overtaken, were conclusions he drew without hesitation. I only saw

33   D

spoor and began to palpitate with thoughts of bagging a koodoo bull.

We had been out perhaps an hour, and by unceasing watchfulness I had learnt many things: they were about as well learnt and as useful as a sentence in a foreign tongue got off by heart; but to me they seemed the essentials and the fundamentals of hunting. I was feeling very pleased with myself and confident of the result; the stumbling over stones and stumps had ceased; and there was no more catching in thorns, crunching on bare gritty places, clinking on rocks, or crackling of dry twigs; and as we moved on in silence the visions of koodoo and other big game became very real. There was nothing to hinder them: to do as Rocky did had become mechanically easy; a glance in his direction every now and then was enough; there was time and temptation to look about and still perhaps to be the first to spot the game.

It was after taking one such casual glance around that I suddenly missed Rocky: a moment later I saw him moving forward, fast but silently, under cover of an ant-heap—stooping low and signing to me with one hand behind his back. With a horrible feeling of having failed him I made a hurried step sideways to get into line behind him and the ant-heap, and I stepped right on to a pile of dry crackly sticks. Rocky stood up quietly and waited, while I wished the earth would open and swallow me. When I got up abreast he half-turned and looked me over with eyes slightly narrowed and a faint but ominous smile on one side of his mouth, and drawled out gently:

34

"You'd oughter brought some fire crackers!"
If only he had sworn at me it would have been
endurable.

We moved on again and this time I had eyes for
nothing but Rocky's back, and where to put my foot
next. It was not very long before he checked in
midstride and I stood rigid as a pointer. Peering
intently over his shoulder in the direction in which
he looked I could see nothing. The bush was very
open, and yet, even with his raised rifle to guide me,
I could not for the life of me see what he was aiming
at. Then the shot rang out, and a duiker toppled over
kicking in the grass not a hundred yards away.

The remembrance of certain things still makes me
feel uncomfortable; the yell of delight I let out as
the buck fell; the wild dash forward, which died
away to a dead stop as I realised that Rocky himself
had not moved; the sight of him, as I looked back,
calmly reloading; and the silence. To me it was
an event: to him, his work. But these things were
forgotten then—lost behind the everlasting puzzle,
How was it possible I had not seen the buck until it
fell? Rocky must have known what was worrying
me, for, after we had picked up the buck, he remarked
without any preliminary, "It ain't easy in this bush ter
pick up what don't move; an' it ain't hardly possible
ter find what ye don't know!"

"Game you mean?" I asked, somewhat puzzled.

"This one was feeding," he answered, after a nod
in reply. "I saw his head go up ter listen; but when
they don't move, an' you don't jus' know what

35

they look like, you kin 'most walk atop o' them. You got ter kind o' shape 'em in yer eye, an' when you got that fixed you kin pick 'em up 'most anywhere!"

It cost Rocky an effort to volunteer anything. There were others always ready to talk and advise; but they were no help. It was Rocky himself who once said that "the man who's allus offerin' his advice fer nothin' 's askin' 'bout 's much 's it's worth," He seemed to run dry of words—like an overdrawn well. For several days he took no further notice of me, apparently having forgotten my existence or repented his good nature. Once, when in reply to a question, I was owning up to the hopes and chances and failures of the day, I caught his attentive look turned on me and was conscious of it—and a little apprehensive—for the rest of the evening; but nothing happened.

The following evening however it came out. I had felt that that look meant something, and that sooner or later I would catch it. It was characteristic of him that he could always wait, and I never felt quite safe with him—never comfortably sure that something was not being saved up for me for some mistake perhaps days old. He was not to be hurried, nor was he to be put off, and nobody ever interrupted him or headed him off. His quiet voice was never raised, and the lazy gentleness never disturbed; he seemed to know exactly what he wanted to say, and to have opening and attention waiting for him. I suppose it was partly because he spoke so seldom: but there was something else too—the something that

36

was just Rocky himself. Although the talk appeared the result of accident, an instinct told me from the start that it was not really so: it was Rocky's slow and considered way.

The only dog with us was licking a cut on her shoulder—the result of an unauthorised rush at a wounded buck—and after an examination of her wound we had wandered over the account of how she had got it, and so on to discussing the dog herself. Rocky sat in silence, smoking and looking into the fire, and the little discussion was closed by some one saying, "She's no good for a hunting dog—too plucky!" It was then I saw Rocky's eyes turned slowly on the last speaker: he looked at him thoughtfully for a good minute, and then remarked quietly:

"'Thar ain't no sich thing as too plucky!" And with that he stopped, almost as if inviting contradiction. Whether he wanted a reply or not one cannot say; anyway, he got none. No one took Rocky on unnecessarily; and at his leisure he resumed:

"Thar's brave men; an' thar's fools; an' you kin get some that's both. But thar's a whole heap that ain't! An' it's jus' the same with dawgs. She's no fool, but she ain't been taught: that's what's the matter with her. Men ha' got ter larn: dawgs too! Men ain't born equal: no more's dawgs! One's born better 'n another—more brains, more heart; but I ain't yet heard o' the man born with knowledge or experience; that's what they got ter learn—men an' dawgs! The born fool's got to do fool's work all the time: but the others larn; and

the brave man with brains 's got a big pull. He don't get shook up—jus' keeps on thinkin' out his job right along, while the other feller's worryin' about his hide! An' dawgs is the same "

Rocky's eyes—for ever grave and thoughtful—rested on the fire; and the remarks that came from the other men passed unnoticed, but they served to keep the subject alive. Presently he went on again—opening with an observation that caused me to move uneasily before there was time to think why!

"Boys is like pups—you got ter help 'em some; but not too much, an' not too soon. They got ter larn themselves. I reckon ef a man's never made a mistake he's never had a good lesson. Ef you don't pay for a thing you don't know what it's worth; and mistakes is part o' the price o' knowledge—the other part is work! But mistakes is the part you don't like payin': thet's why you remember it. You save a boy from makin' mistakes and ef he's got good stuff in him, most like you spoil it. He don't know anything properly, 'cause he don't think; and he don't think, 'cause you saved him the trouble an' he never learned how! He don't know the meanin' o' consequences and risks, 'cause you kep' 'em off him! an' bymbye he gets ter believe it's born in him ter go right, an' knows everything, an' can't go wrong; an' ef things don't pan out in the end he reckons it's jus' bad luck! No! Sirree! Ef he's gotter swim you let him know right there that the water's deep an' thar ain't no one to hol' him up, an' ef he don't wade in an' larn, it's goin' ter be his funeral!"

38

My eyes were all for Rocky, but he was not looking
my way, and when the next remark came, and my
heart jumped and my hands and feet moved of their
own accord, his face was turned quite away from
me towards the man on his left.

"An' it's jus' the same 'ith huntin'! It looks so
blamed easy he reckons it don't need any teachin'.
Well, let him try! Leave him run on his own till his
boots is walked off an' he's like to set down and cry,
ef he wasn't 'shamed to; let him know every pur-
tickler sort o' blamed fool he can make of himself;
an' then he's fit ter teach, 'cause he'll listen, an'
watch, an' learn—*an'* say thank ye fer it! Mostly you
got ter make a fool o' yourself once or twice ter
know what it feels like an' how t' avoid it: best do
it young—it teaches a boy; but it kind o' breaks a
man up!"

I kept my eyes on Rocky, avoiding the others,
fearing that a look or word might tempt some one
to rub it in; and it was a relief when the old man
naturally and easily picked up his original point, and
turning another look on Jess, said:

"You got ter begin on the pup. It ain't her
fault; it's yours. She's full up o' the right stuff,
but she got no show to larn! Dawgs is all
different, good an' bad—just like men: some larns
quick; some'll never larn. But thar ain't any too
plucky!"

He tossed a chip of green wood into the heart of
the fire and watched it spurtle and smoke, and
after quite a long pause, added:

39

"Thar's times when a dawg's got to see it through an' be killed. It's his dooty—same as a man's. I seen it done!"

The last words were added with a narrowing of his eyes and a curious softening of voice—as of personal affection or regret. Others noticed it too; and in reply to a question as to how it had happened Rocky explained in a few words that a wounded buffalo had waylaid and tossed the man over its back, and as it turned again to gore him the dog rushed in between, fighting it off for a time and eventually fastening on to the nose when the buffalo still pushed on. The check enabled the man to reach his gun and shoot the buffalo; but the dog was trampled to death.

"Were you . . . ?" some one began—and then at the look in Rocky's face, hesitated. Rocky, staring into the fire, answered:

"It was my dawg!"

Long after the other men were asleep I lay in my blankets watching the tricks of light and shadow played by the fire, as fitfully it flamed or died away. It showed the long prostrate figures of the others as they slept full stretch on their backs, wrapped in dark blankets; the waggons, touched with unwonted colours by the flames, and softened to ghostly shadows when they died; the oxen, sleeping contentedly at their yokes; Rocky's two donkeys, black and grey, tethered under a thorn tree—now and then a long ear moving slowly to some distant sound and dropping back again satisfied. I could not sleep; but Rocky

40

"IT WAS MY DAWG"

was sleeping like a babe. He, gaunt and spare—
6 ft. 2 he must have stood—weather-beaten and old,
with the long solitary trip before him and sixty-odd
years of life behind, he slept when he laid his head
down, and was wide awake and rested when he raised
it. He, who had been through it all, slept; but I,
who had only listened, was haunted, bewitched,
possessed by racing thoughts; and all on account
of four words, and the way he said them: "It was
my dawg."

It was still dark, with a faint promise of saffron in
the east, when I felt a hand on my shoulder and heard
Rocky's voice saying, "Comin' along, Sonny?"

One of the drivers raised his head to look at us as
we passed, and then called to his voorlooper to turn
the cattle loose to graze, and dropped back to sleep.
We left them so and sallied out into the pure clear
morning while all the world was still, while the air,
cold and subtly stimulating, put a spring into the
step and an extra beat or two into the pulse, fairly
rinsing lungs and eyes and brain.

What is there to tell of that day? Why! nothing,
really nothing, except that it was a happy day—a day
of little things that all went well, and so it came to
look like the birthday of the hunting. What did it
matter to me that we were soaked through in ten
minutes? for the dew weighed down the heavy-
topped grass with clusters of crystal drops that looked
like diamond sprays. It was all too beautiful for
words: and so it should be in the spring-time of
youth.

41

Rocky was different that day. He showed me things: reading the open book of nature that I could not understand. He pointed out the spoors going to and from the drinking-place, and named the various animals; showed me one more deeply indented than the rest and, murmuring "Scared I guess," pointed to where it had dashed off out of the regular track; picked out the big splayed pad of the hyena sneaking round under cover; stopped quietly in his stride to point where a hare was sitting up cleaning itself, not ten yards off; stopped again at the sound of a clear, almost metallic 'clink' and pointed to a little sandy gully in front of us down which presently came thirty or forty guinea-fowl in single file, moving swiftly, running and walking, and all in absolute silence except for that one 'clink.' How did he know they were there, and which way they would go, and know it all so promptly, were questions I asked myself.

We walked with the sun—that is towards the west —so that the light would show up the game and be in their eyes, making it more difficult for them to see us. We watched a little red stembuck get up from his form, shake the dew from his coat, stretch himself, and then pick his way daintily through the wet grass, nibbling here and there as he went. Rocky did not fire; he wanted something better.

After the sun had risen, flooding the whole country with golden light, and, while the dew lasted, making it glisten like a bespangled transformation scene, we came on a patch of old long grass and, parted by some twenty yards, walked through it abreast. There was a

42

wild rush from under my feet, a yellowish body dashed
through the grass, and I got out in time to see a rietbuck ram cantering away. Then Rocky, beside me,
gave a shrill whistle; the buck stopped, side on, looked
back at us, and Rocky dropped it where it stood.
Instantly following the shot there was another rush on
our left, and before the second rietbuck had gone thirty
yards Rocky toppled it over in its tracks. From the
whistle to the second shot it was all done in about ten
seconds. To me it looked like magic. I could only gasp.

We cleaned the bucks, and hid them in a bush.
There was meat enough for the camp then, and I
thought we would return at once for boys to carry it;
but Rocky, after a moment's glance round, shouldered
his rifle and moved on again. I followed, asking no
questions. We had been gone only a few minutes
when to my great astonishment he stopped and pointing straight in front asked:

"What 'ud you put up for that stump?"

I looked hard, and answered confidently, "Two
hundred!"

"Step it!" was his reply. I paced the distance; it
was eighty-two yards.

It was very bewildering; but he helped me out a
bit with "Bush telescopes, Sonny!"

"You mean it magnifies them?" I asked in surprise.

"No! Magnifies the distance, like lookin' down an
avenue! Gun barr'l looks a mile long when you put
yer eye to it! Open flats brings 'em closer; and 'cross
water or a gully seems like you kin put yer hand on
'em!'

43

"I would have missed—by feet—that time, Rocky!"

"You kin take it fer a start. Halve the distance and aim low!"

"Aim low, as well?"

"Thar's allus somethin' low: legs, an' ground to show what you done! But thar's no 'outers' marked on the sky!"

Once, as we walked along, he paused to look at some freshly overturned ground, and dropped the one word, 'Pig.' We turned then to the right and presently came upon some vlei ground densely covered with tall green reeds. He slowed down as we approached; I tiptoed in sympathy; and when only a few yards off he stopped and beckoned me on, and as I came abreast he raised his hand in warning and pointed into the reeds. There was a curious subdued sort of murmur of many deep voices. It conveys no idea of of the fact to say they were grunts. They were softened out of all recognition: there is only one word for it, they sounded 'confidential.' Then as we listened I could make out the soft silky rustling of the rich undergrowth, and presently could follow, by the quivering and waving of odd reeds, the movements of the animals themselves. They were only a few yards from us—the nearest four or five; they were busy and contented; and it was obvious they were utterly unconscious of our presence. As we peered down to the reeds from our greater height it seemed that we could see the ground and that not so much as a rat could have passed unnoticed. Yet we saw nothing!

44

And then, without the slightest sign, cause or warning that I could detect, in one instant every sound ceased. I watched the reeds like a cat on the pounce: never a stir or sign or sound: they had vanished. I turned to Rocky: he was standing at ease, and there was the faintest look of amusement in his eyes.

"They must be there; they can't have got away!" It was a sort of indignant protest against his evident 'chucking it'; but it was full of doubt all the same.

"Try!" he said, and I jumped into the reeds straight away. The under-foliage, it is true, was thicker and deeper than it had looked; but for all that it was like a conjuring trick—they were not there! I waded through a hundred yards or more of the narrow belt—it was not more than twenty yards wide anywhere—but the place was deserted. It struck me then that if they could dodge us at five to ten yards while we were watching from the bank and they did not know it—well, I 'chucked it' too. Rocky was standing in the same place with the same faint look of friendly amusement when I got back, wet and muddy.

"Pigs is like that," he said, "same as elephants—jus' disappears!"

We went on again, and a quarter of an hour later, it may be, Rocky stopped, subsided to a sitting position, beckoned to me, and pointed with his levelled rifle in front. It was a couple of minutes before he could get me to see the stembuck standing in the shade of a thorn tree. I would never have seen it but for his

45

whisper to look for something moving: that gave it to me; I saw the movement of the head as it cropped.

"High: right!" was Rocky's comment, as the bullet ripped the bark off a tree and the startled stembuck raced away. In the excitement I had forgotten his advice already!

But there was no time to feel sick and disgusted; the buck, puzzled by the report on one side and the smash on the tree on the other, half-circled us and stopped to look back. Rocky laid his hand on my shoulder:

"Take your time, Sonny!" he said, "Aim low; an' *don't pull! Squeeze!*" And at last I got it.

We had our breakfast there—the liver roasted on the coals, and a couple of 'dough-boys,' with the unexpected addition of a bottle of cold tea, weak and unsweetened, produced from Rocky's knapsack! We stayed there a couple of hours, and that is the only time he really opened out. I understood then—at last —that of his deliberate kindliness he had come out that morning meaning to make a happy day of it for a youngster; and he did it.

He had the knack of getting at the heart of things, and putting it all in the fewest words. He spoke in the same slow grave way, with habitual economy of breath and words; and yet the pictures were living and real, and each incident complete. I seemed to get from him that morning all there was to know of the hunting in two great continents—Grizzlies and other 'bar,' Moose and Wapiti, hunted in the snows of the North West; Elephant, Buffalo, Rhino,

46

Lions, and scores more, in the sweltering heat of Africa!

That was a happy day!

When I woke up next morning Rocky was fitting the packs on his donkeys. I was a little puzzled, wondering at first if he was testing the saddles, for he had said nothing about moving on; but when he joined us at breakfast the donkeys stood packed ready to start. Then Robbie asked:

"Going to make a move, Rocky?"

"Yes! Reckon I'll git!" he answered quietly.

I ate in silence, thinking of what he was to face: many hundreds of miles—perhaps a thousand or two; many, many months—maybe a year or two; wild country, wild tribes, and wild beasts; floods and fever; accident, hunger, and disease; and alone!

When we had finished breakfast he rinsed out his beaker and hung it on one of the packs, slung his rifle over his shoulder, and picking up his long assegai-wood walking-stick tapped the donkeys lightly to turn them into the kaffir footpath that led away north. They jogged on into place in single file.

Rocky paused a second before following, turned one brief grave glance on us, and said:

"Well. So long!"

He never came back!

Good dogs were not easy to get; I had tried hard enough for one before starting, but without success. Even unborn puppies had jealous prospective owners waiting to claim them.

There is always plenty of room at the top of the tree, and good hunting dogs were as rare as good men, good horses, and good front-oxen. A lot of qualities are needed in the make-up of a good hunting dog: size, strength, quickness, scent, sense and speed —and plenty of courage. They are very very difficult to get; but even small dogs are useful, and many a fine feat stands to the credit of little terriers in guarding camps at night and in standing off wounded animals that meant mischief.

Dennison was saved from a wounded lioness by his two fox terriers. He had gone out to shoot bush-pheasants, and came unexpectedly on a lioness playing with her cubs: the cubs hid in the grass, but she stood up at bay to protect them, and he, forgetting that he

48

had taken the big 'looper' cartridges from his gun and reloaded with No. 6, fired. The shot only maddened her, and she charged; but the two dogs dashed at her, one at each side, barking, snapping and yelling, rushing in and jumping back so fast and furiously that they flustered her. Leaving the man for the moment, she turned on them, dabbing viciously with her huge paws, first at one, then at the other; quick as lightning she struck right and left as a kitten will at a twirled string; but they kept out of reach. It only lasted seconds, but that was long enough for the man to reload and shoot the lioness through the heart.

There was only the one dog in our camp; and she was not an attractive one. She was a bull terrier with a dull brindled coat—black and grey in shadowy stripes. She had small cross-looking eyes and uncertain always-moving ears; she was bad-tempered and most unsociable; but she was as faithful and as brave a dog as ever lived. She never barked; never howled when beaten for biting strangers or kaffirs or going for the cattle; she was very silent, very savage, and very quick. She belonged to my friend Ted, and never left his side day or night. Her name was Jess.

Jess was not a favourite, but everybody respected her, partly because you knew she would not stand any nonsense—no pushing, patting or punishment, and very little talking to—and partly because she was so faithful and plucky. She was not a hunting dog, but on several

occasions had helped to pull down wounded game; she had no knowledge or skill, and was only fierce and brave, and there was always the risk that she would be killed. She would listen to Ted, but to no one else; one of us might have shouted his lungs out, but it would not have stopped her from giving chase the moment she saw anything and keeping on till she was too dead beat to move any further.

The first time I saw Jess we were having dinner, and I gave her a bone—putting it down close to her and saying, "Here! good dog!" As she did not even look at it, I moved it right under her nose. She gave a low growl, and her little eyes turned on me for just one look as she got up and walked away.

There was a snigger of laughter from some of the others, but nobody said anything, and it seemed wiser to ask no questions just then. Afterwards, when we were alone, one of them told me Ted had trained her not to feed from any one else, adding, "You must not feed another man's dog; a dog has only one master!"

We respected Jess greatly; but no one knew quite how much we respected her until the memorable day near Ship Mountain.

We had rested through the heat of the day under a big tree on the bank of a little stream; it was the tree under which Soltké prayed and died. About sundown, just before we were ready to start, some other waggons passed, and Ted, knowing the owner, went on with him, intending to rejoin us at the next outspan. As he jumped on to the passing waggon

50

he called to Jess, and she ran out of a patch of soft
grass under one of the big trees behind our waggons.
She answered his call instantly, but when she saw
him moving off on the other waggon she sat down
in the road and watched him anxiously for some
seconds, then ran on a few steps in her curious quick
silent way and again stopped, giving swift glances
alternately towards Ted and towards us. Ted remarked laughingly that she evidently thought he had
made a mistake by getting on to the wrong waggon,
and that she would follow presently.

After he had disappeared she ran back to her patch
of grass and lay down, but in a few minutes she was
back again squatting in the road looking with that
same anxious worried expression after her master.
Thus she went to and fro for the quarter of an hour
it took us to inspan, and each time she passed we could
hear a faint anxious little whine.

The oxen were inspanned and the last odd things
were being put up when one of the boys came to say
that he could not get the guns and water-barrel
because Jess would not let him near them. There was
something the matter with the dog, he said; he
thought she was mad.

Knowing how Jess hated kaffirs we laughed at the
notion, and went for the things ourselves. As we
came within five yards of the tree where we had left
the guns there was a rustle in the grass, and Jess came
out with her swift silent run, appearing as unexpectedly
as a snake does, and with some odd suggestion of a
snake in her look and attitude. Her head, body and

tail were in a dead line, and she was crouching slightly as for a spring; her ears were laid flat back, her lips twitching constantly, showing the strong white teeth, and her cross wicked eyes had such a look of remorse-less cruelty in them that we stopped as if we had been turned to stone. She never moved a muscle or made a sound, but kept those eyes steadily fixed on us. We moved back a pace or two and began to coax and wheedle her; but it was no good; she never moved or made a sound, and the unblinking look remained. For a minute we stood our ground, and then the hair on her back and shoulders began very slowly to stand up. That was enough: we cleared off. It was a mighty uncanny appearance.

Then another tried his hand; but it was just the same. No one could do anything with her; no one could get near the guns or the water-barrel; as soon as we returned for a fresh attempt she reappeared in the same place and in the same way.

The position was too ridiculous, and we were at our wits' end, for Jess held the camp. The kaffirs declared the dog was mad, and we began to have very un-comfortable suspicions that they were right; but we decided to make a last attempt, and surrounding the place approached from all sides. But the suddenness with which she appeared before we got into position so demoralised the kaffirs that they bolted, and we gave it up, owning ourselves beaten. We turned to watch her as she ran back for the last time, and as she disappeared in the grass we heard distinctly the cry of a very young puppy. Then the secret of Jess's madness was out.

We had to send for Ted, and when he returned a couple of hours later Jess met him out on the road in the dark where she had been watching half the time ever since he left. She jumped up at his chest giving a long tremulous whimper of welcome, and then ran ahead straight to the nest in the grass.

He took a lantern and we followed, but not too close. When he knelt down to look at the puppies she stood over them and pushed herself in between him and them; when he put out a hand to touch them she pushed it away with her nose, whining softly in protest and trembling with excitement—you could see she would not bite, but she hated him to touch her puppies. Finally, when he picked one up she gave a low cry and caught his wrist gently, but held it.

That was Jess, the mother of Jock!

THE PICK OF THE PUPPIES

THERE were six puppies, and as the waggons were empty we fixed up a roomy nest in one of them for Jess and her family. There was no trouble with Jess; nobody interfered with her, and she interfered with nobody. The boys kept clear of her; but we used to take a look at her and the puppies as we walked along with the waggons; so by degrees she got to know that we would not harm them, and she no longer wanted to eat us alive if we went near and talked to her.

Five of the puppies were fat strong yellow little chaps with dark muzzles—just like their father, as Ted said; and their father was an imported dog, and was always spoken of as the best dog of the breed that had ever been in the country. I never saw him, so I do not really know what he was like—perhaps he was not a yellow dog at all; but, whatever he was, he had at that time a great reputation because he was 'imported,' and there were not half a dozen imported dogs in the whole of the Transvaal then. Many

people used to ask what breed the puppies were—I suppose it was because poor cross faithful old Jess was not much to look at, and because no one had a very high opinion of yellow dogs in general, and nobody seemed to remember any famous yellow bull-terriers. They used to smile in a queer way when they asked the question, as if they were going to get off a joke; but when we answered "Just like their father— Buchanan's *imported* dog," the smile disappeared, and they would give a whistle of surprise and say "By Jove!" and immediately begin to examine the five yellow puppies, remark upon their ears and noses and legs, and praise them up until we were all as proud as if they had belonged to us.

Jess looked after her puppies and knew nothing about the remarks that were made, so they did not worry her, but I often looked at the faithful old thing with her dark brindled face, cross-looking eyes and always-moving ears, and thought it jolly hard lines that nobody had a good word for her; it seemed rough on her that every one should be glad there was only one puppy at all like the mother—the sixth one, a poor miserable little rat of a thing about half the size of the others. He was not yellow like them, nor dark brindled like Jess, but a sort of dirty pale half-and-half colour with some dark faint wavy lines all over him, as if he had tried to be brindled and failed; and he had a dark sharp wizened little muzzle that looked shrivelled up with age.

Most of the fellows said it would be a good thing to drown the odd one because he spoilt the litter and made

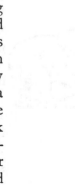

them look as though they were not really thoroughbred, and because he was such a miserable little rat
that he was not worth saving anyhow; but in the end
he was allowed to live. I believe no one fancied the
job of taking one of Jess's puppies away from her;
moreover, as any dog was better than none, I had
offered to take him rather than let him be drowned.
Ted had old friends to whom he had already promised
the pick of the puppies, so when I came along it was
too late, and all he could promise me was that if there
should be one over I might have it.

As they grew older and were able to crawl about
they were taken off the waggons when we outspanned
and put on the ground. Jess got to understand this
at once, and she used to watch us quite quietly as we
took them in our hands to put them down or lift
them back again. When they were two or three
weeks old a man came to the waggons who talked a
great deal about dogs, and appeared to know what
had to be done. He said that the puppies' tails ought
to be docked, and that a bull-terrier would be no
class at all with a long tail, but you should on no
account clip his ears. I thought he was speaking of
fox-terriers, and that with bull-terriers the position
was the other way round, at that time; but as he
said it was 'the thing' in England, and nobody
contradicted him, I shut up. We found out afterwards that he had made a mistake; but it was too
late then, and Jess's puppies started life as bull-terriers
up to date, with long ears and short tails.

I felt sure from the beginning that all

56

the yellow puppies would be claimed and that I should have to take the odd one, or none at all; so I began to look upon him as mine already, and to take an interest in him and look after him. A long time ago somebody wrote that "the sense of possession turns sand into gold," and it is one of the truest things ever said. Until it seemed that this queer-looking odd puppy was going to be mine I used to think and say very much what the others did—but with this difference, that I always felt sorry for him, and sorry for Jess too, because he was like her and not like the father. I used to think that perhaps if he were given a chance he might grow up like poor old Jess herself, ugly, cross and unpopular, but brave and faithful. I felt sorry for him, too, because he was small and weak, and the other five big puppies used to push him away from his food and trample on him; and when they were old enough to play they used to pull him about by his ears and pack on to him—three or four to one—and bully him horribly. Many a time I rescued him, and many a time gave him a little preserved milk and water with bread soaked in it when the others had shouldered him out and eaten everything.

After a little while, when my chance of getting one of the good puppies seemed hopeless and I got used to the idea that I would have to take the odd one I began to notice little things about him that no one else noticed, and got to be quite fond of the little beggar—in a kind of way. Perhaps I was turning my sand into gold, and my geese into swans; perhaps I grew fond of him simply because, finding him lonely

57

and with no one else to depend on, I befriended him; and perhaps it was because he was always cheerful and plucky and it seemed as if there might be some good stuff in him after all. Those were the things I used to think of sometimes when feeding the little outcast. The other puppies would tumble him over and take his food from him; they would bump into him when he was stooping over the dish of milk and porridge, and his head was so big and his legs so weak that he would tip up and go heels over head into the dish. We were always picking him out of the food and scraping it off him: half the time he was wet and sticky, and the other half covered with porridge and sand baked hard by the sun.

One day just after the waggons had started, as I took a final look round the outspan place to see if anything had been forgotten, I found the little chap —who was only about four inches high—struggling to walk through the long grass. He was not big enough or strong enough to push his way—even the stems of the down-trodden grass tripped him—and he stumbled and floundered at every step, but he got up again each time with his little tail standing straight up, his head erect, and his ears cocked. He looked such a ridiculous sight that his little tragedy of "lost in the veld" was forgotten—one could only laugh.

What he thought he was doing, goodness only knows; he looked as proud and important as if he owned the whole world and knew that every one in it was watching him. The poor little chap could not see a yard in that grass; and in any case he was not

old enough to see much, or understand anything, for his eyes still had that bluish blind look that all very young puppies have, but he was marching along as full of confidence as a general at the head of his army. How he fell out of the waggon no one knew; perhaps the big puppies tumbled him out, or he may have tried to follow Jess, or have climbed over the tail-board to see what was the other side, for he was always going off exploring by himself. His little world was small, it may be—only the bedplank of the waggon and the few square yards of the ground on which they were dumped at the outspans—but he took it as seriously as any explorer who ever tackled a continent.

The others were a bit more softened towards the odd puppy when I caught up to the waggons and told them of his valiant struggle to follow; and the man who had docked the puppies' tails allowed, "I believe the rat's got pluck, whatever else is the matter with him, for he was the only one that didn't howl when I snipped them. The little cuss just gave a grunt and turned round as if he wanted to eat me. I think he'd 'a' been terrible angry if he hadn't been so s'prised. Pity he's such an awful-looking mongrel."

But no one else said a good word for him: he was really beneath notice, and if ever they had to speak about him they called him "The Rat." There is no doubt about it he was extremely ugly, and instead of improving as he grew older, he became worse; yet I could not help liking him and looking after him, sometimes feeling sorry for him, sometimes being

tremendously amused, and sometimes—wonderful to relate—really admiring him. He was extraordinarily silent; while the others barked at nothing, howled when lonely, and yelled when frightened or hurt, the odd puppy did none of these things; in fact, he began to show many of Jess's peculiarities; he hardly ever barked, and when he did it was not a wild excited string of barks but little suppressed muffled noises, half bark and half growl, and just one or two at a time; and he did not appear to be afraid of anything, so one could not tell what he would do if he was.

One day we had an amusing instance of his nerve: one of the oxen, sniffing about the outspan, caught sight of him all alone, and filled with curiosity came up to examine him, as a hulking silly old tame ox will do. It moved towards him slowly and heavily with its ears spread wide and its head down, giving great big sniffs at this new object, trying to make out what it was. "The Rat" stood quite still with his stumpy tail cocked up and his head a little on one side, and when the huge ox's nose was about a foot from him he gave one of those funny abrupt little barks. It was as if the object had suddenly 'gone off' like a cracker, and the ox nearly tumbled over with fright; but even when the great mountain of a thing gave a clumsy plunge round and trotted off, "The Rat" was not the least frightened; he was startled, and his tail and ears flickered for a second, but stiffened up again instantly, and with another of those little barks he took a couple of steps forward and cocked his head on the other side. That was his way.

60

He was not a bit like the other puppies; if any one fired off a gun or cracked one of the big whips the whole five would yell at the top of their voices, and wherever they were, would start running, scrambling and floundering as fast as they could towards the waggon without once looking back to see what they were running away from. The odd puppy would drop his bone with a start or would jump round; his ears and tail would flicker up and down for a second; then he would slowly bristle up all over, and with his head cocked first on one side and then on the other, stare hard with his half-blind bluish puppy eyes in the direction of the noise; but he never ran away.

And so, little by little, I got to like him in spite of his awful ugliness. And it really was awful! The other puppies grew big all over, but the odd one at that time seemed to grow only in one part—his tummy! The poor little chap was born small and weak; he had always been bullied and crowded out by the others, and the truth is he was half-starved. The natural consequence of this was that as soon as he could walk about and pick up things for himself he made up for lost time, and filled up his middle piece to an alarming size before the other parts of his body had time to grow; at that time he looked more like a big tock-tockie beetle than a dog.

Besides the balloon-like tummy he had stick-out bandy legs, very like a beetle's too, and a neck so thin that it made the head look enormous, and you wondered how the neck ever held it up. But what made him so supremely ridiculous was that he evidently did

61

not know he was ugly; he walked about as if he was always thinking of his dignity, and he had that puffed-out and stuck-up air of importance that you only see in small people and bantam cocks who are always trying to appear an inch taller than they really are.

When the puppies were about a month old, and could feed on porridge or bread soaked in soup or gravy, they got to be too much for Jess, and she used to leave them for hours at a time and hide in the grass so as to have a little peace and sleep. Puppies are always hungry, so they soon began to hunt about for themselves, and would find scraps of meat and porridge or old bones; and if they could not get anything else, would try to eat the rawhide nekstrops and reims. Then the fights began. As soon as one puppy saw another busy on anything, he would walk over towards him and, if strong enough, fight him for it. All day long it was nothing but wrangle, snarl, bark and yelp. Sometimes four or five would be at it in one scrum; because as soon as one heard a row going on he would trot up hoping to steal the bone while the others were busy fighting.

It was then that I noticed other things about the odd puppy: no matter how many packed on to him, or how they bit or pulled him, he never once let out a yelp; with four or five on top of him you would see him on his back, snapping right and left with bare white teeth, gripping and worrying them when he got a good hold of anything, and all the time growling and snarling with a fierceness that was really comical.

62

It sounded as a lion fight might sound in a toy phonograph.

Before many days passed, it was clear that some of the other puppies were inclined to leave "The Rat" alone, and that only two of them—the two biggest—seemed anxious to fight him and could take his bones away. The reason soon became apparent: instead of wasting his breath in making a noise, or wasting strength in trying to tumble the others over, "The Rat" simply bit hard and hung on; noses, ears, lips, cheeks, feet and even tails—all came handy to him; anything he could get hold of and hang on to was good enough, and the result generally was that in about half a minute the other puppy would leave everything and clear off yelling, and probably holding up one paw or hanging its head on one side to ease a chewed ear.

When either of the big puppies tackled the little fellow the fight lasted much longer. Even if he were tumbled over at once—as generally happened—and the other one stood over him barking and growling, that did not end the fight: as soon as the other chap got off him he would struggle up and begin again; he would not give in. The other puppies seemed to think there was some sort of rule like the 'count out' in boxing, or that once you were tumbled over you ought to give up the bone; but the odd puppy apparently did not care about rules; as far as I could see, he had just one rule: "Stick to it," so it was not very long before even the two big fellows gave up interfering with him. The bites from his little white

63

teeth—sharp as needles—which punctured noses and feet and tore ears, were most unpleasant. But apart from that, they found there was nothing to be gained by fighting him: they might roll him over time after time, but he came back again and worried them so persistently that it was quite impossible to enjoy the bone—they had to keep on fighting for it.

At first I drew attention to these things, but there was no encouragement from the others; they merely laughed at the attempt to make the best of a bad job. Sometimes owners of other puppies were nettled by having their beauties compared with "The Rat," or were annoyed because he had the cheek to fight for his own and beat them. Once, when I had described how well he had stood up to Billy's pup, Robbie caught up "The Rat," and placing him on the table, said: "Hats off to the Duke of Wellington on the field of Waterloo." That seemed to me the poorest sort of joke to send five grown men into fits of laughter. He stood there on the table with his head on one side, one ear standing up, and his stumpy tail twiggling—an absurd picture of friendliness, pride and confidence; yet he was so ugly and ridiculous that my heart sank, and I whisked him away. They made fun of him, and he did not mind; but it was making fun of me too, and I could not help knowing why; it was only necessary to put the puppies together to see the reason.

After that I stopped talking about him, and made the most of the good points he showed,

64

and tried to discover more. It was the only consolation for having to take the leavings of the litter.

Then there came a day when something happened which might easily have turned out very differently, and there would have been no stories and no Jock to tell about; and the best dog in the world would never have been my friend and companion. The puppies had been behaving very badly, and had stolen several nekstrops and chewed up parts of one or two big whips; the drivers were grumbling about all the damage done and the extra work it gave them; and Ted, exasperated by the worry of it all, announced that the puppies were quite old enough to be taken away, and that those who had picked puppies must take them at once and look after them, or let some one else have them. When I heard him say that my heart gave a little thump from excitement, for I knew the day had come when the great question would be settled once and for all. Here was a glorious and unexpected chance; perhaps one of the others would not or could not take his, and I might get one of the good ones. . . . Of course the two big ones would be snapped up: that was certain; for, even if the men who had picked them could not take them, others who had been promised puppies before me would exchange those they had already chosen for the better ones. Still, there were other chances; and I thought of very little else all day long, wondering if any of the good ones would be left; and if so, which.

In the afternoon Ted came up to where we were

65   F

all lying in the shade, and startled us with the momentous announcement:

"Billy Griffiths can't take his pup!"

Every man of us sat up. Billy's pup was the first pick, the champion of the litter, the biggest and strongest of the lot. Several of the others said at once that they would exchange theirs for this one; but Ted smiled and shook his head.

"No," he said, "you had a good pick in the beginning." Then he turned to me. and added: "You've only had leavings." Some one said "The Rat," and there was a shout of laughter, but Ted went on: "You can have Billy's pup."

It seemed too good to be true; not even in my wildest imaginings had I fancied myself getting the pick of the lot. I hardly waited to thank Ted before going off to look at my champion. I had seen and admired him times out of number, but it seemed as if he must look different now that he belonged to me. He was a fine big fellow, well built and strong, and looked as if he could beat all the rest put together. His legs were straight; his neck sturdy; his muzzle dark and shapely; his ears equal and well carried; and in the sunlight his yellow coat looked quite bright, with occasional glints of gold in it. He was indeed a handsome fellow.

As I put him back again with the others the odd puppy, who had stood up and sniffed at me when I came, licked my hand and twiddled his tail with the friendliest and most independent air, as if he knew me quite well and was glad to see me, and I patted the

66

"AND THERE AT MY HEELS WAS THE
ODD PUPPY"

poor little chap as he waddled up. I had forgotten him in the excitement of getting Billy's pup; but the sight of him made me think of his funny ways, his pluck and independence, and of how he had not a friend in the world except Jess and me; and I felt downright sorry for him. I picked him up and talked to him; and when his wizened little face was close to mine he opened his mouth as if laughing, and shooting out his red tongue dabbed me right on the tip of my nose in pure friendliness. The poor little fellow looked more ludicrous than ever: he had been feeding again and was as tight as a drum; his skin was so tight one could not help thinking that if he walked over a mimosa thorn and got a scratch on the tummy he would burst like a toy balloon.

I put him back with the other puppies and returned to the tree where Ted and the rest were sitting. As I came up there was a shout of laughter, and—turning round to see what had provoked it—I found "The Rat" at my heels. He had followed me and was trotting and stumbling along, tripping every yard or so, but getting up again with head erect, ears cocked and his stumpy tail twiddling away just as pleased and proud as if he thought he had really started in life and was doing what only a 'really and truly' grown-up dog is supposed to do—that is, follow his master wherever he goes.

All the old chaff and jokes were fired off at me again, and I had no peace for quite a time. They all had something to say: "He won't swap you off!" "I'll back 'The Rat'!" "He is going to take care of

67

you!" "He is afraid you'll get lost!" and so on; and they were still chaffing about it when I grabbed "The Rat" and took him back again.

Billy's failure to take his puppy was so entirely unexpected and so important that the subject kept cropping up all the evening. It was very amusing then to see how each of those who had wanted to get him succeeded in finding good reasons for thinking that his own puppy was really better than Billy's. However they differed in their estimates of each other's dogs, they all agreed that the best judge in the world could not be certain of picking out the best dog in a good litter until the puppies were several months old; and they all gave instances in which the best-looking puppy had turned out the worst dog, and others in which the one that no one would look at had grown up to be the champion. Goodness knows how long this would have gone on if Robbie had not mischievously suggested that "perhaps 'The Rat' was going to beat the whole lot." There was such a chorus of guffaws at this that no one told any more stories.

The poor little friendless Rat! It was unfortunate, but the truth is that he was uglier than before; and yet I could not help liking him. I fell asleep that night thinking of the two puppies—the best and the worst in the litter. No sooner had I gone over all the splendid points in Billy's pup and made up my mind that he was certainly the finest I had ever seen, than the friendly wizened little face, the half-cocked ears and head on one side, the cocky little stump of

68

a tail, and the comical dignified plucky look of the odd puppy would all come back to me. The thought of how he had licked my hand and twiddled his tail at me, and how he dabbed me on the nose, and then the manful way in which he had struggled after me through the grass, all made my heart go soft towards him, and I fell asleep not knowing what to do.

When I woke up in the morning, my first thought was of the odd puppy—how he looked to me as his only friend, and what he would feel like if, after looking on me as really belonging to him and as the one person that he was going to take care of all his life, he knew he was to be left behind or given away to any one who would take him. It would never have entered his head that he required some one to look after him; from the way he had followed me the night before it was clear he was looking after me; and the other fellows thought the same thing. His whole manner had plainly said: "Never mind old man! Don't you worry: I am here."

We used to make our first trek at about three o'clock in the morning, so as to be outspanned by sunrise; and walking along during that morning trek I recalled all the stories that the others had told of miserable puppies having grown into wonderful dogs, and of great men who had been very ordinary children; and at breakfast I took the plunge.

"Ted," I said, bracing myself for the laughter, "if you don't mind, I'll stick to 'The Rat.' "

If I had fired off a gun under their noses they would have been much less startled. Robbie made a grab for his plate as it slipped from his knees.

"*Don't* do that sort of thing!" he protested indignantly. "My nerves won't stand it!"

The others stopped eating and drinking, held their beakers of steaming coffee well out of the way to get a better look at me, and when they saw it was seriously meant there was a chorus of:

"Well, I'm hanged."

I took him in hand at once—for now he was really mine—and brought him over for his saucer of soaked bread and milk to where we sat at breakfast. Beside me there was a rough camp table—a luxury sometimes indulged in while camping or trekking with empty waggons—on which we put our tinned milk, treacle, and such things to keep them out of reach of the ants, grasshoppers, Hottentot-gods, beetles and dust. I put the puppy and his saucer in a safe place under the table out of the way of stray feet, and sank the saucer into the sand so that when he trod in it he would not spill the food; for puppies are quite as stupid as they are greedy, and seem to think that they can eat faster by getting further into the dish. He appeared to be more ravenous than usual, and we were all amused by the way the little fellow craned his thin neck out further and further until he tipped up behind and his nose bumping into the saucer see-sawed him back again. He finished it all and looked round briskly at me, licking his lips and twiddling his stumpy tail.

70

Well, I meant to make a dog of him, so I gave him another lot. He was just like a little child—he thought he was very hungry still and could eat any amount more; but it was not possible. The lapping became slower and more laboured, with pauses every now and then to get breath or lick his lips and look about him, until at last he was fairly beaten: he could only look at it, blink and lick his chops; and, knowing that he would keep on trying, I took the saucer away. He was too full to object or to run after it; he was too full to move. He stood where he was, with his legs well spread and his little body blown out like a balloon, and finished licking the drops and crumbs off his face without moving a foot.

There was something so extraordinarily funny in the appearance and attitude of the puppy that **we** watched to see what he would do next. He had been standing very close to the leg of the table, but not quite touching it, when he finished feeding; and even after he had done washing his face and cleaning up generally, he stood there stock still for several minutes, as though it was altogether too much trouble to move. One little bandy hind leg stuck out behind the table-leg, and the bulge of his little tummy stuck out in front of it; so that when at last he decided to make a move the very first little lurch brought his hip up against the table-leg. In an instant the puppy's appearance changed completely: the hair on his back and shoulders bristled; his head went up erect; one ear stood up straight and the other at half cock; and his stumpy tail quivered with rage. He evidently thought that one of the other puppies had come up behind to interfere with him. He was too proud to turn round and appear to be nervous: with head erect he glared hard straight in front of him, and, with all the little breath that he had left after his big feed, he growled ferociously in comical little gasps. He stood like that, not moving an inch, with the front foot still ready to take that step forward; and then, as nothing more happened, the hair on his back gradually went flat again; the fierceness died out of his face; and the growling stopped.

After a minute's pause, he again very slowly and carefully began to step forward; of course exactly the same thing happened again, except that this time he shook all over with rage, and the growling was fiercer and more choky. One could not imagine anything so small being in so great a rage. He took longer to cool down, too, and much longer before he made the third attempt to start. But the third time it was all over in a second. He seemed to think that this was more than any dog could stand, and that he must put a stop to it. The instant his hip touched the leg, he whipped round with a ferocious snarl—his little white teeth bared and gleaming—and bumped his nose against the table-leg.

I cannot say whether it was because of the shout of laughter from us, or because he really understood what had happened, that he looked so foolish, but he just gave one crestfallen look at me and with a feeble wag of his tail waddled off as fast as he could.

Then Ted nodded over at me, and said: "I believe you have got the champion after all!"

And I was too proud to speak.   **72**

"I BELIEVE YOU'VE GOT THE CHAMPION AFTER ALL"

JOCK'S·SCHOOLDAYS

AFTER that day no one spoke of "The Rat" or "The Odd Puppy," or used any of the numberless nicknames that they had given him such as "The Specimen," "The Object," "No. 6," "Bully Beef" (because he got his head stuck in a half-pound tin one day), "The Scrap"; and even "The Duke of Wellington" ceased to be a gibe. They still laughed at his ridiculous dignity; and they loved to tease him to see him stiffen with rage and hear his choky little growls; but they liked his independence and admired his tremendous pluck. So they respected his name when he got one.

And his name was "Jock."

No one bothered about the other puppies' names: they were known as "Billy's pup," "Jimmy's pup," "Old Joe's Darling," "Yellow Jack," and "Bandy-Legged Sue"; but they seemed to think that this little chap had earned his name, fighting his way without anybody's help and with everything against him; so they gave up all the nicknames and spoke of him as "Jock."

Jock got such a good advertisement by his fight with the table-leg that  every one took notice of

73

him now and remarked about what he did; and as he was only a very young puppy, they teased him, fed him, petted him, and did their best to spoil him. He was so young that it did not seem to matter, but I think if he had not been a really good dog at heart he would have been quite spoilt.

He soon began to grow and fill out; and it was then that he taught the other puppies to leave him alone. If they had not interfered with him he might perhaps have left them alone, as it was not his nature to interfere with others; but the trouble was they had bullied him so much while he was weak and helpless that he got used to the idea of fighting for everything. It is probably the best thing that could have happened to Jock that as a puppy he was small and weak, but full of pluck; it compelled him to learn how to fight; it made him clever, cool, and careful, for he could not afford to make mistakes. When he fought he meant business; he went for a good spot, bit hard, and hung on for all he was worth; then, as the enemy began to slacken, he would start vigorously worrying and shaking. I often saw him shake himself off his feet because the thing he was fighting was too heavy for him.

The day Jock fought the two big puppies—one after the other—for his bone, and beat them off, was the day of his independence; we all saw the tussle, and cheered the little chap. And then for one whole day he had peace; but it was like the pause at low water before the tide begins to flow the other way. He was so used to being interfered with that I suppose

he did not immediately understand they would never tackle him again.

It took a whole day for him to realise this; but as soon as he did understand it he seemed to make up his mind that now his turn had come, and he went for the first puppy he saw with a bone. He walked up slowly and carefully, and began to make a circle round him. When he got about half-way round the puppy took up the bone and trotted off; but Jock headed him off at once, and again began to walk towards him very slowly and stiffly. The other puppy stood quite still for a moment, and then Jock's fierce determined look was too much for him: he dropped the bone and bolted.

There was mighty little but smell on those bones, for we gave the puppies very little meat, so when Jock had taken what he could off this one, he started on another hunt. A few yards away Billy's pup was having a glorious time, struggling with a big bone and growling all the while as if he wanted to let the world know that it was as much as any one's life was worth to come near him. None of us thought Jock would tackle him, as Billy's pup was still a long way the biggest and strongest of the puppies, and always ready to bully the others.

Jock was about three or four yards away when he caught sight of Billy's pup, and for about a minute he stood still and quietly watched. At first he seemed surprised, and then interested, and then gradually he stiffened up all over in that funny way of his; and when the hair on his shoulders was all on end and

his ears and tail were properly up, he moved forward very deliberately. In this fashion he made a circle round Billy's pup, keeping about two feet away from him, walking infinitely slowly and glaring steadily at the enemy out of the corners of his eyes; and while he was doing this, the other fellow was tearing away at his bone, growling furiously and glaring sideways at Jock. When the circle was finished they stood once more face to face; and then after a short pause Jock began to move in closer, but more slowly even than before.

Billy's pup did not like this: it was beginning to look serious. He could not keep on eating and at the same time watch Jock; moreover, there was such a very unpleasant wicked look about Jock, and he moved so steadily and silently forward, that any one would feel a bit creepy and nervous; so he put his paw on the bone and let out a string of snarly barks, with his ears flat on his neck and his tail rather low down. But Jock still came on—a little more carefully and slowly perhaps, but just as steadily as ever. When about a foot off the enemy's nose he changed his direction slightly, as if to walk past, and Billy's pup turned his head to watch him, keeping his nose pointed towards Jock's, but when they got side by side he again looked straight in front of him.

Perhaps he did this to make sure the bone was still there, or perhaps to show his contempt when he thought Jock was going off. Whatever the reason was, it was a mistake; for, as he turned his head away, Jock flew at him, got a good mouthful of ear, and in

no time they were rolling and struggling in the dust—
Jock's little grunts barely audible in the noise made
by the other one. Billy's pup was big and strong, and
he was not a coward; but Jock was worrying his
ear vigorously, and he could not find anything to bite
in return. In less than a minute he began to howl,
and was making frantic efforts to get away. Then
Jock let go the ear and tackled the bone.

After that he had no more puppy fights. As soon
as any one of the others saw Jock begin to walk slowly
and carefully towards him he seemed to suddenly get
tired of his bone, and moved off.

Most dogs—like most people—when their hearts
fail them will try to hide the truth from one another
and make some sort of effort or pretence to keep their
dignity or self-respect or the good opinion of others.
You may see it all any day in the street, when dogs
meet and stop to 'size' each other up. As a rule the
perfectly shameless cowards are found in the two
extreme classes—the outcasts, whose spirits are broken
by all the world being against them; and the pam-
pered darlings, who have never had to do anything
for themselves. Many dogs who are clearly anxious
to get out of fighting will make a pretence of bravery
at the time, or at least cover up their cowardice, with
a 'wait-till-I-catch-you-next-time' air, as soon as they
are at a safe distance. Day after day at the outspans
the puppies went through every stage of the business,
to our constant amusement and to my unconcealed
pride; for Jock was thenceforth cock of the walk.
If they saw him some distance off, moving towards

77

them or even staring hard and with his ears and tail up, the retreat would be made with a gloomy and dignified air, sometimes even with growls just loud enough to please themselves without provoking him; if he was fairly close up when spotted they wasted no time in putting on airs, but trotted off promptly; but sometimes they would be too busy to notice anything until a growl or a rustle in the grass close behind gave warning; and it was always followed by a jump and a shameless scuttle, very often accompanied by a strangled sort of yowling yelp, just as if he had already got them by the ear or throat.

Some of them became so nervous that we could not resist playing practical jokes on them—making sudden strange noises, imitating Jock's growls, tossing bits of bark at them or touching them from behind with a stick while they were completely occupied with their bones—for the fun of seeing the stampede and hearing the sudden howls of surprise and fright.

One by one the other puppies were taken away by their new masters, and before Jock was three months old he and Jess were the only dogs with the waggons. Then he went to school, and like all schoolboys learnt some things very quickly—the things that he liked; and some things he learnt very slowly, and hated them just as a boy hates extra work in play-time. When I poked about with a stick in the banks of dongas to turn out mice and field-rats for him, or when I hid a partridge or a hare and made him find it, he was as happy as could be; but when I made him lie down and watch my gun or coat while I pretended to go off and leave him, he did not like it; and as for his lessons in manners! well, he simply hated them.

There are some things which a dog in that sort of life simply must learn or you cannot keep him; and the first of these is, not to steal. Every puppy will help himself until he is taught not to; and your dog lives with you and can get at everything. At the out-spans the grub-box is put on the ground, open for each man to help himself; if you make a stew, or roast the leg of a buck, the big three-legged pot is put down handy and left there; if you are lucky enough to have some tinned butter or condensed milk, the tins are opened and stood on the ground; and if you have a dog thief in the camp, nothing is safe.

There was a dog with us once—a year or two later —who was the worst thief I ever knew. He was a one-eyed pointer with feet like a duck's, and his name was Snarleyow. He looked the most foolish and most innocent dog in the world, and was so timid that if you stumbled as you passed him he would instantly start howling and run for the horizon. The first bad experience I had of Snarley was on one of the little hunting trips which we sometimes made in those days, away from the waggons. We travelled light on those occasions, and, except for some tea and a very little flour and salt, took no food; we lived on what we shot and of course kept 'hunter's pot.'

'Hunter's pot' is a perpetual stew; you make one stew, and keep it going as long as necessary, maintaining a full pot by adding to it as fast as you take any out;

scraps of everything go in; any kind of meat—buck, bird, pig, hare—and if you have such luxuries as onions or potatoes, so much the better; then, to make the soup strong, the big bones are added—the old ones being fished out every day and replaced by a fresh lot. When allowed to cool it sets like brawn, and a hungry hunter wants nothing better.

We had had a good feed the first night of this trip and had then filled the pot up, leaving it to simmer as long as the fire lasted, expecting to have cold pie set in jelly—but without the pie-crust—for early breakfast next morning before going off for the day; but, to our amazement, in the morning the pot was empty. There were some strange kaffirs—camp followers—hanging on to our trail for what they could pick up, and we suspected them. There was a great row, but the boys denied having touched the pot, and we could prove nothing.

That night we made the fire close to our sleeping-place and moved the kaffirs further away, but next morning the pot was again empty—cleaned and polished as if it had been washed out. While we, speechless with astonishment and anger, were wondering who the thief was and what we should do with him, one of the hunting boys came up and pointed to the prints of a dog's feet in the soft white ashes of the dead fire. There was only one word: "Snarleyow." The thief was lying fast asleep comfortably curled up on his master's clothes. There could be no mistake about those big

"THE LAST WE SAW OF OUR BIRTHDAY TREAT"

splayed footprints, and in about two minutes Snarleyow was getting a first-class hammering, with his head tied inside the three-legged pot for a lesson.

After that he was kept tied up at night; but Snarleyow was past curing. We had practically nothing to eat but what we shot, and nothing to drink but bush tea—that is, tea made from a certain wild shrub with a very strong scent; it is not nice, but you drink it when you cannot get anything else. We could not afford luxuries then, but two days before Ted's birthday he sent a runner off to Komati Drift and bought a small tin of ground coffee and a tin of condensed milk for his birthday treat. It was to be a real feast that day, so he cut the top off the tin instead of punching two holes and blowing the milk out, as we usually did in order to economise and keep out the dust and insects. What we could not use in the coffee that day we were going to spread on our 'dough-boys' instead of butter and jam. It was to be a real feast!

The five of us sat down in a circle and began on our hunter's pot, saving the good things for the last. While we were still busy on the stew, there came a pathetic heartbreaking yowl from Snarleyow, and we looked round just in time to see him, his tail tucked between his legs and his head high in the air, bolting off into the bush as hard as he could lay legs to the ground, with the milk tin stuck firmly on to his nose. The greedy thief in trying to get the last scrap out had dug his nose and top jaw too far in, and the jagged edges of the tin had gripped him; and the last we saw

of our birthday treat was the tin flashing in the sunlight on Snarley's nose as he tore away howling into the bush.

Snarleyow came to a bad end: h^r master shot him as he was running off with a ham. He was a full-grown dog when he came to our camp, and too old to learn principles and good manners.

Dogs are like people: what they learn when they are young, whether of good or of evil, is not readily forgotten. I began early with Jock, and—remembering what Rocky had said—tried to help him. It is little use punishing a dog for stealing if you take no trouble about feeding him. That is very rough on the dog; he has to find out slowly and by himself what he may take, and what he may not. Sometimes he leaves what he was meant to take, and goes hungry; and sometimes takes what was not intended for him, and gets a thrashing. That is not fair. You cannot expect to have a good dog, and one that will understand you, if you treat him in that way. Some men teach their dogs not to take food from any one but themselves. One day when we were talking about training dogs, Ted told one of the others to open Jess's mouth and put a piece of meat in it, he undertaking not to say a word and not even to look at her. The meat was put in her mouth and her jaws were shut tight on it; but the instant she was free she dropped it, walked round to the other side of Ted and sat close up to him. He waited for a minute or so and, without so much as a glance at her said quietly "All right." She was back again in a second and with one hungry bite bolted the lump of meat.

82

I taught Jock not to touch food in camp until he was told to 'take it.' The lesson began when he got his saucer of porridge in the morning; and he must have thought it cruel to have that put in front of him, and then to be held back or tapped with a finger on the nose each time he tried to dive into it. At first he struggled and fought to get at it; then he tried to back away and dodge round the other side; then he became dazed, and, thinking it was not for him at all, wanted to walk off and have nothing more to do with it. In a few days, however, I got him to lie still and take it only when I patted him and pushed him towards it; and in a very little time he got on so well that I could put his food down without saying anything and let him wait for permission. He would lie down with his head on his paws and his nose right up against the saucer, so as to lose no time when the order came; but he would not touch it until he heard 'Take it.' He never moved his head, but his little browny dark eyes, full of childlike eagerness, used to be turned up sideways and fixed on mine. I believe he watched my lips; he was so quick to obey the order when it came.

When he grew up and had learned his lessons there was no need for these exercises. He got to understand me so well that if I nodded or moved my hand in a way that meant 'all right,' he would go ahead: by that time too he was dignified and patient; and it was only in his puppyhood that he used to crouch up close to his food and tremble with impatience and excitement.

83

There was one lesson that he hated most of all. I used to balance a piece of meat on his nose and make him keep it there until the word to take it came. Time after time he would close his eyes as if the sight of the meat was more than he could bear, and his mouth would water so from the savoury smell that long streels of dribble would hang down on either side.

It seems unnecessary and even cruel to tantalise a dog in that way; but it was not: it was education; and it was true kindness. It taught him to understand his master, and to be obedient, patient, and observant; it taught him not to steal; it saved him from much sickness, and perhaps death, by teaching him not to feed on anything he could find; it taught him manners and made it possible for him to live with his master and be treated like a friend.

Good feeding, good care, and plenty of exercise soon began to make a great change in Jock. He ceased to look like a beetle—grew bigger everywhere, not only in one part as he had done at first; his neck grew thick and strong, and his legs straightened up and filled out with muscle. The others, seeing him every day, were slow to notice these things, but my sand had been changed into gold long ago, and they always said I could not see anything wrong in Jock.

There was one other change which came more slowly and seemed to me much more wonderful. After his morning feed, if there was nothing to do, he used to go to sleep in some shady place, and I remember well one day watching him as he lay. His bit of shade

84

had moved away and left him in the bright sunshine; and as he breathed and his ribs rose and fell, the tips of the hairs on his side and back caught the sunlight and shone like polished gold, and the wavy dark lines seemed more distinct and darker, but still very soft. In fact, I was astonished to see that in a certain light Jock looked quite handsome. That was the first time I noticed the change in colour; and it made me remember two things. The first was what the other fellows had said the day Billy gave up his pup, "You can't tell how a puppy will turn out: even his colour changes"; and the second was a remark made by an old hunter who had offered to buy Jock—the real meaning of which I did not understand at the time.

"The best dog I ever owned was a golden brindle," said the old man thoughtfully, after I had laughed at the idea of selling my dog. I had got so used to thinking that he was only a faded wishy-washy edition of Jess that the idea of his colour changing did not occur to me then, and I never suspected that the old man could see how he would turn out; but the touch of sunlight opened my eyes that day, and after that whenever I looked at Jock the words "golden brindle" came back to my mind, and I pictured him as he was going to be—and as he really did grow up—having a coat like burnished gold with soft, dark, wavy brindles in it and that snow-white V on his chest.

Jock had many things to learn besides the lessons he got from me—the lessons of experience which nobody could teach him. When he was six months old—just old enough, if he had lived in a town, to

85

chase a cat and make a noise—he knew many things that respectable puppies of twice his age who stay at home never get a chance of learning.

On trek there were always new places to see, new roads to travel, and new things to examine, tackle or avoid. He learnt something fresh almost every day: he learnt, for instance, that, although it was shady and cool under the waggon, it was not good enough to lie in the wheel track, not even for the pleasure of feeling the cool iron tyre against your back or head as you slept; and he knew that, because one day he had done it, and the wheel had gone over his foot; and it might just as easily have been his back or head. Fortunately the sand was soft and his foot was not crushed; but he was very lame for some days, and had to travel on the waggon.

He learned a good deal from Jess: among other things, that it was not necessary to poke his nose up against a snake in order to find out what it was. He knew that Jess would fight anything; and when one day he saw her back hair go up and watched her sheer off the footpath wide into the grass, he did the same; and then when we had shot the snake, both he and Jess came up very very cautiously and sniffed at it, with every hair on their bodies standing up.

He found out for himself that it was not a good idea to turn a scorpion over with his paw. The vicious little tail with a thorn in it whipped over the scorpion's back, and Jock had such a foot that he must have thought a scorpion worse than two waggons. He was a very sick dog for some days; but after that

86

whenever he saw a thing that he did not understand, he would watch it very carefully from a little way off and notice what it did and what it looked like, before trying experiments.

So, little by little, Jock got to understand plenty of things that no town dog would ever know, and he got to know—just as some people do—by what we call instinct, whether a thing was dangerous or safe, even though he had never seen anything like it before. That is how he knew that wolves or lions were about —and that they were dangerous—when he heard or scented them; although he had never seen, scented or heard one before to know what sort of animal it might be. You may well wonder how he could tell whether the scent or the cry belonged to a wolf which he must avoid, or to a buck which he might hunt, when he had never seen either a wolf or a buck at the time; but he did know; and he also knew that no dog could safely go outside the ring of the camp fires when wolf or lion was about. I have known many town-bred dogs that could scent them just as well as Jess or Jock could, but having no instinct of danger they went out to see what it was, and of course they never came back.

I used to take Jock with me everywhere so that he could learn everything that a hunting dog ought to know, and above all things to learn that he was my dog, and to understand all that I wanted to tell him. So while he was still a puppy, whenever he stopped to sniff at something new or to look at something strange, I would show him what it was; but if he

87

stayed behind to explore while I moved on, or if he fell asleep and did not hear me get up from where I had sat down to rest, or went off the track on his own account, I used to hide away from him on top of a rock or up a tree and let him hunt about until he found me.

At first he used to be quite excited when he missed me, but after a little time he got to know what to do and would sniff along the ground and canter away after me—always finding me quite easily. Even if I climbed a tree to hide from him he would follow my track to the foot of the tree, sniff up the trunk as far as he could reach standing up against it, and then peer up into the branches. If he could not see me from one place, he would try another—always with his head tilted a bit on one side. He never barked at these times; but as soon as he saw me, his ears would drop, his mouth open wide with the red tongue lolling out, and the stump of a tail would twiggle away to show how pleased he was. Sometimes he would give a few little whimpery grunts: he hardly ever barked; when he did I knew there was something worth looking at.

Jock was not a quarrelsome dog, and he was quick to learn and very obedient, but in one connection I had great difficulty with him for quite a little time. He had a sort of private war with the fowls; and it was due to the same cause as his war with the other puppies: they interfered with him. Now, every one knows what a fowl is like: it is impudent, inquisitive, selfish, always looking for something to eat, and has no principles.

88

A friend of mine once told me a story about a dog of his and the trouble he had with fowls. Several of us had been discussing the characters of dogs, and the different emotions they feel and manage to express, and the kind of things they seem to think about. Every one knows that a dog can feel angry, frightened, pleased, and disappointed. Any one who knows dogs will tell you that they can also feel anxious, hopeful, nervous, inquisitive, surprised, ashamed, interested, sad, loving, jealous, and contented—just like human beings.

We had told many stories illustrating this, when my friend asked the question: "Have dogs a sense of humour?" Now I know that Jock looked very foolish the day he fought the table-leg—and a silly old hen made him look just as foolish another day—but that is not quite what my friend meant. On both occasions Jock clearly felt that he had made himself look ridiculous; but he was very far from looking amused. The question was: Is a dog capable of sufficient thinking to appreciate a simple joke, and is it possible for a dog to feel amused? If Jess had seen Jock bursting to fight the table-leg would she have seen the joke? Well, I certainly did not think so; but he said he was quite certain some dogs have a sense of humour; and he had had proof of it.

He told the story very gravely, but I really do not even now know whether he—Well, here it is: He had once owned a savage old watch-dog, whose box stood in the back-yard where he was kept chained up all day; he used to be fed once a day—in the

89

mornings—and the great plague of his life was the fowls. They ran loose in the yard and picked up food all day, besides getting a really good feed of grain morning and evening; possibly the knowledge of this made the old dog particularly angry when they would come round by ones or twos or dozens trying to steal part of his one meal. Anyhow, he hated them, and whenever he got a chance killed them. The old fowls learned to keep out of his way, and never ventured within his reach unless they were quite sure that he was asleep or lying in his kennel where he could not see them; but there were always new fowls coming, or young ones growing up; and so the war went on.

One Sunday morning my friend was enjoying a smoke on his back stoep when feeding time came round. The cook took the old dog's food to him in a high three-legged pot, and my friend, seeing the fowls begin to gather round and wishing to let the old dog have his meal in peace, told the cook to give the fowls a good feed in another part of the yard to draw them off. So the old fellow polished off his food and licked the pot clean, leaving not a drop or a speck behind.

But fowls are very greedy; they were soon back again wandering about, with their active-looking eyes searching everything. The old dog, feeling pretty satisfied with life, picked out a sandy spot in the sunshine, threw himself down full stretch on his side, and promptly went to sleep—at peace with all the world. Immediately he did this, out stepped a

90

long-legged athletic-looking young cockerel and began to advance against the enemy. As he got nearer he slowed down, and looked first with one eye and then with the other so as to make sure that all was safe, and several times he paused with one foot poised high before deciding to take the next step. My friend was greatly amused to see all the trouble that the fowl was taking to get up to the empty pot, and, for the fun of giving the conceited young cockerel a fright, threw a pebble at him. He was so nervous that when the pebble dropped near him, he gave one great bound and tore off flapping and screaming down the yard as if he thought the old dog was after him. The old fellow himself was startled out of his sleep, and raised his head to see what the row was about; but, as nothing more happened, he lay down again, and the cockerel, finding also that it was a false alarm, turned back not a bit ashamed for another try.

The cockerel had not seen the old dog lift his head; my friend had, and when he looked again he saw that, although the underneath eye—half buried in the sand —was shut, the top eye was open and was steadily watching the cockerel as he came nearer and nearer to the pot. My friend sat dead still, expecting a rush and another fluttering scramble. At last the cockerel took the final step, craned his neck to its utmost and peered down into the empty pot. The old dog gave two gentle pats with his tail in the sand, and closing his eye went to sleep again.

Jock had the same sort of trouble. The fowls tried

to steal his food; and he would not stand it. His way of dealing with them was not good for their health: before I could teach him not to kill, and before the fowls would learn not to steal, he had finished half a dozen of them one after another with just one bite and a shake. He would growl very low as they came up and, without lifting his head from the plate, watch them with his little eyes turning from soft brown to shiny black; and when they came too near and tried to snatch just one mouthful—well, one jump, one shake, and it was all over.

In the end he learned to tumble them over and scare their wits out without hurting them; and they learned to give him a very wide berth.

I used always to keep some fowls with the waggons, partly to have fresh meat if we ran out of game, but mainly to have fresh eggs, which were a very great treat; and as a rule it was only when a hen turned obstinate and would not lay that we ate her. I used to have one old rooster, whose name was Pezulu, and six or eight hens. The hens changed from time to time—as we ate them—but Pezulu remained.

The fowl-coop was carried on top of everything else, and it was always left open so that the fowls could go in and out as they liked. In the very beginning of all, of course, the fowls were shut in and fed in the coop for a day or two to teach them where their home was; but it is surprising how quickly a fowl will learn and how it observes things. For instance, the moving of the coop from one waggon to another is not a thing one would expect the fowls

92

to notice, all the waggons being so much alike and having no regular order at the outspans; but they did notice it, and at once. They would first get on to the waggon on which the coop had been, and look about in a puzzled lost kind of way; then walk all over the load apparently searching for it, with heads cocked this way and that, as if a great big coop was a thing that might have been mislaid somewhere; then one after another would jerk out short cackles of protest, indignation and astonishment, and generally make no end of a fuss. It was only when old Pezulu led the way and perched on the coop itself and crowed and called to them that they would get up on to the other waggon.

Pezulu got his name by accident—in fact, by a misunderstanding. It is a Zulu word meaning 'up' or 'on top,' and when the fowls first joined the waggons and were allowed to wander about at the outspan places, the boys would drive them up when it was time to trek again by cracking their big whips and shouting "Pezulu." In a few days no driving or whip-cracking was necessary; one of the boys would shout "Pezulu" three or four times, and they would all come in and one by one fly and scramble up to the coop. One day, after we had got a new lot of hens, a stranger happened to witness the perform-ance. Old Pezulu was the only one who knew what was meant, and being a terribly fussy nervous old gentleman, came tearing out of the bush making a lot of noise, and scrambled hastily on to the waggon. The stranger, hearing the boys call "Pezulu" and seeing

him hurry up so promptly, remarked: "How well he knows his name!" So we called him Pezulu after that.

Whenever we got new fowls Pezulu became as distracted as a nervous man with a large family trying to find seats in an excursion train. As soon as he saw the oxen being brought up, and before any one had called for the fowls, he would begin fussing and fuming—trying all sorts of dodges to get the hens up to the waggons. He would crow and cluck-cluck or kip-kip; he would go a few yards towards the waggons and scratch in the ground, pretending to have found something good, and invite them to come and share it; he would get on the disselboom and crow and flap his wings loudly; and finally he would mount on top of the coop and make all sorts of signals to the hens, who took not the least notice of him. As the inspanning went on he would get more and more excited; down he would come again—not flying off, but hopping from ledge to ledge to show them the easy way; and once more on the ground he would scrape and pick and cluck to attract them, and the whole game would be played over again and again. So even with new fowls we had very little trouble, as old Pezulu did most of the teaching.

But sometimes Pezulu himself was caught napping —to the high delight of the boys. He was so nervous and so fussy that they thought it great fun to play tricks on him and pretend to go off and leave him behind. It was not easy to do this because, as I say, he did not wait to be called, but got ready the minute

he saw the oxen coming up. He was like those fussy people who drive every one else crazy and waste a lot of time by always being half an hour early, and then annoy you by boasting that they have never missed a train in their lives.

But there was one way in which Pezulu used to get caught. Just as he knew that inspanning meant starting, so, too, he knew that outspanning meant stopping; and whenever the waggons stopped—even for a few minutes—out would pop his head, just like the fussy red-faced father of the big family looking out to see if it was their station or an accident on the line. Right and left he would look, giving excited inquisitive clucks from time to time, and if they did not start in another minute or two, he would get right out and walk anxiously to the edge of the load and have another good look around—as the nervous old gentleman gets half out, and then right out, to look for the guard, but will not let go the handle of the door for fear of being left. Unless he saw the boys outspanning he would not get off, and if one of the hens ventured out he would rush back at her in a great state and try to bustle her back into the coop. But often it happens while trekking that something goes wrong with the gear—a yokeskey or a nekstrop breaks, or an ox will not pull kindly or pulls too hard where he is, and you want to change his place; and in that way it comes about that sometimes you have to outspan one or two or even more oxen in the middle of a trek.

That is how Pezulu used to get caught: the minute

he saw outspanning begin, he would nip off with all the hens following him and wander about looking for food, chasing locusts or grasshoppers, and making darts at beetles and all sorts of dainties—very much interested in his job and wandering further from the waggons at every step. The boys would watch him, and as soon as they were fixed up again, would start off without a word of warning to Pezulu. Then there was a scene. At the first sound of the waggon-wheels moving he would look up from where he was or walk briskly into the open or get on to an ant-heap to see what was up, and when to his horror he saw the waggon actually going without him, he simply screamed open-mouthed and tore along with wings outstretched—the old gentleman shouting "Stop the train, stop the train," with his family straggling along behind him. It never took him long to catch up and scramble on, but even then he was not a bit less excited: he was perfectly hysterical, and his big red comb seemed to get quite purple as if he might be going to have apoplexy, and he twitched and jerked about so that it flapped first over one eye and then over the other. This was the boys' practical joke which they played on him whenever they could.

That was old Pezulu—Pezulu the First. He was thick in the body, all chest and tail, short in the legs, and had enormous spurs; and his big comb made him look so red in the face that one could not help thinking he was too fond of his dinner. In some old Christmas number we came across a coloured carica-ture of a militia colonel in full uniform, and for quite

96

a long time it remained tacked on to the coop with "Pezulu" written on it.

Pezulu the Great—who was Pezulu the Second—was not like that: he was a game cock, all muscle and no frills, with a very resolute manner and a real love of his profession; he was a bit like Jock in some things; and that is why I fancy perhaps Jock and he were friends in a kind of way. But Jock could not get on with the others: they were constantly changing; new ones who had to be taught manners were always coming; so he just lumped them together, and hated fowls. He taught them manners, but they taught him something too—at any rate, one of them did; and one of the biggest surprises and best lessons Jock ever had was given him by a hen while he was still a growing-up puppy.

He was beginning to fancy that he knew a good deal, and like most young dogs was very inquisitive and wanted to know everything and at once. At that time he was very keen on hunting mice, rats and bush squirrels, and had even fought and killed a meerkat after the plucky little rikkitikki had bitten him rather badly through the lip; and he was still much inclined to poke his nose in or rush on to things instead of sniffing round about first.

However, he learned to be careful, and an old hen helped to teach him. The hens usually laid their eggs in the coop because it was their home, but sometimes they would make nests in the bush at the outspan places. One of the hens had done this, and the bush she had chosen was very low and dense. No one saw

97 H

the hen make the nest and no one saw her sitting on it, for the sunshine was so bright everywhere else, and the shade of the bush so dark that it was impossible to see anything there; but while we were at breakfast Jock, who was bustling about everywhere as a puppy will, must have scented the hen or have seen this brown thing in the dark shady hole.

The hen was sitting with her head sunk right down into her chest, so that he could not see any head, eyes or beak—just a sort of brown lump. Suddenly we saw Jock stand stock-still, cock up one ear, put his head down and his nose out, hump up his shoulders a bit and begin to walk very slowly forward in a crouching attitude. He lifted his feet so slowly and so softly that you could count five between each step. We were all greatly amused and thought he was pointing a mouse or a locust, and we watched him.

He crept up like a boy 'showing off' until he was only six inches from the object, giving occasional cautious glances back at us to attract attention. Just as he got to the hole the hen let out a vicious peck on the top of his nose and at the same time flapped over his head, screaming and cackling for dear life. It was all so sudden and so surprising that she was gone before he could think of making a grab at her; and when he heard our shouts of laughter he looked as foolish as if he understood all about it.

THE·FIRST·HUNT

Jock's first experience in hunting was on
the Crocodile River not far from the spot where long
afterwards we had the great fight with the Old Crocodile. In the summer when the heavy rains flood the
country the river runs 'bank high,' hiding everything
—reeds, rocks, islands and stunted trees—in some
places silent and oily like a huge gorged snake, in
others foaming and turbulent as an angry monster. In
the rainless winter when the water is low and clear the
scene is not so grand, but is quiet, peaceful, and much
more beautiful. There is an infinite variety in it
then—the river sometimes winding along in one deep
channel, but more often forking out into two or three
streams in the broad bed. The loops and lacings of
the divided water carve out islands and spaces of all
shapes and sizes, banks of clean white sand or of firm
damp mud swirled up by the floods, on which tall
green reeds with yellow tasselled tops shoot up like
crops of kaffir corn. Looked down upon from the
flood banks the silver streaks of water gleam brightly
in the sun, and the graceful reeds, bowing and swaying
99

slowly with the gentlest breeze and alternately showing their leaf-sheathed stems and crested tops, give the
appearance of an ever-changing sea of green and gold.
Here and there a big rock, black and polished, stands
boldly out, and the sea of reeds laps round it like the
waters of a lake on a bright still day. When there is
no breeze the rustle of the reeds is hushed, and the
only constant sound is the ever-varying voice of the
water, lapping, gurgling, chattering, murmuring, as
it works its way along the rocky channels; sometimes
near and loud, sometimes faint and distant; and sometimes, over long sandy reaches, there is no sound at all.

Get up on some vantage point upon the high bank
and look down there one day in the winter of the
tropics as the heat and hush of noon approach, and
it will seem indeed a scene of peace and beauty—a
place to rest and dream, where there is neither stir nor
sound. Then, as you sit silently watching and thinking, where all the world is so infinitely still, you
will notice that one reed down among all those
countless thousands is moving. It bows slowly and
gracefully a certain distance, and then with a quivering
shuddering motion straightens itself still more slowly
and with evident difficulty, until at last it stands upright again like the rest but still all a-quiver while
they do not move a leaf. Just as you are beginning to
wonder what the reason is, the reed bows slowly
again, and again struggles back; and so it goes on as
regularly as the swing of a pendulum. Then you
know that, down at the roots where you cannot see
it, the water is flowing silently, and that something

attached to this reed is dragging in the stream and pulling it over, and swinging back to do it again each time the reed lifts it free—a perpetual see-saw.

You are glad to find the reason, because it looked a little uncanny; but the behaviour of that one reed has stopped your dreaming and made you look about more carefully. Then you find that, although the reeds appear as still as the rocks, there is hardly a spot where, if you watch for a few minutes, you will not see something moving. A tiny field-mouse climbing one reed will sway it over; a river rat gnawing at the roots will make it shiver and rustle; little birds hopping from one to another will puzzle you; and a lagavaan turning in his sunbath will make half a dozen sway outwards.

All feeling that it is a home of peace, a place to rest and dream, leaves you; you are wondering what goes on down below the green and gold where you can see nothing; and when your eye catches a bigger, slower, continuous movement in another place, and for twenty yards from the bank to the stream you see the tops of the reeds silently and gently parting and closing again as something down below works its way along without the faintest sound, the place seems too quiet, too uncanny and mysterious, too silent, stealthy and treacherous for you to sit still in comfort: you must get up and do something.

There is always good shooting along the rivers in a country where water is scarce. Partridges, bush-pheasants and stembuck were plentiful along the banks and among the thorns, but the reeds themselves

101

were the home of thousands of guinea-fowl, and you could also count on duiker and rietbuck as almost a certainty there. If this were all, it would be like shooting in a well-stocked cover, but it is not only man that is on the watch for game at the drinking-places. The beasts of prey—lions, tigers, hyenas, wild dogs and jackals, and lastly pythons and crocodiles—know that the game must come to water, and they lie in wait near the tracks or the drinking-places. That is what makes the mystery and charm of the reeds; you never know what you will put up. The lions and tigers had deserted the country near the main drifts and followed the big game into more peaceful parts; but the reeds were still the favourite shelter and resting-place of the crocodiles; and there were any number of them left.

There is nothing that one comes across in hunting more horrible and loathsome than the crocodile: nothing that rouses the feeling of horror and hatred as it does: nothing that so surely and quickly gives the sensation of 'creeps in the back' as the noiseless apparition of one in the water just where you least expected anything, or the discovery of one silently and intently watching you with its head resting flat on a sand-spit— the thing you had seen half a dozen times before and mistaken for a small rock. Many things are hunted in the Bushveld; but only the crocodile is hated. There is always the feeling of horror that this hideous, cowardly cruel thing—the enemy of man and beast alike—with its look of a cunning smile in the greeny glassy eyes and great wide mouth, will mercilessly drag you down

102

—down—down to the bottom of some deep still pool, and hold you there till you drown. Utterly helpless yourself to escape or fight, you cannot even call, and if you could, no one could help you there. It is all done in silence: a few bubbles come up where a man went down; and that is the end of it.

We all knew about the crocodiles and were prepared for them, but the sport was good, and when you are fresh at the game and get interested in a hunt it is not very easy to remember all the things you have been warned about and the precautions you were told to take. It was on the first day at the river that one of our party, who was not a very old hand at hunting, came in wet and muddy and told us how a crocodile had scared the wits out of him. He had gone out after guinea-fowl, he said, but as he had no dog to send in and flush them, the birds simply played with him: they would not rise but kept running in the reeds a little way in front of him, just out of sight. He could hear them quite distinctly, and thinking to steal a march on them took off his boots and got on to the rocks. Stepping bare-footed from rock to rock where the reeds were thin, he made no noise at all and got so close up that he could hear the little whispered chink-chink-chink that they give when near danger. The only chance of getting a shot at them was to mount one of the big rocks from which he could see down into the reeds; and he worked his way along a mud-bank towards one. A couple more steps from the mud-bank on to a low black rock would take him to the big one. Without taking his eyes off

103

the reeds where the guinea-fowl were he stepped cautiously on to the low black rock, and in an instant was swept off his feet, tossed and tumbled over and over, into the mud and reeds, and there was a noise of furious rushing and crashing as if a troop of elephants were stampeding through the reeds. He had stepped on the back of a sleeping crocodile; no doubt it was every bit as frightened as he was. There was much laughter over this and the breathless earnestness with which he told the story; but there was also a good deal of chaff, for it seems to be generally accepted that you are not bound to believe all hunting stories; and Jim and his circus crocodile became the joke of the camp.

We were spending a couple of days on the river bank to make the most of the good water and grazing, and all through the day some one or other would be out pottering about among the reeds, gun in hand, to keep the pot full and have some fun, and although we laughed and chaffed about Jim's experience, I fancy we were all very much on the look-out for rocks that looked like crocs and crocs that looked like rocks.

One of the most difficult lessons that a beginner has to learn is to keep cool. The keener you are the more likely you are to get excited and the more bitterly you feel the disappointments; and once you lose your head, there is no mistake too stupid for you to make, and the result is another good chance spoilt. The great silent bush is so lonely; the strain of being on the look-out all the time is so great; the un-certainty as to what may start up—anything from

JIM'S CIRCUS CROCODILE

a partridge to a lion—is so trying that the beginner is wound up like an alarum clock and goes off at the first touch. He is not fit to hit a haystack at twenty yards; will fire without looking or aiming at all; jerk the rifle as he fires; forget to change the sight after the last shot; forget to cock his gun or move the safety catch; forget to load; forget to fire at all: nothing is impossible—nothing too silly.

On a later trip we had with us a man who was out for the first time, and when we came upon a troop of koodoo he started yelling, war-whooping and swearing at them, chasing them on foot and waving his rifle over his head. When we asked him why he, who was nearest to them, had not fired a shot, all he could say was that he never remembered his rifle or anything else until they were gone.

These experiences had been mine, some of them many times, in spite of Rocky's example and advice; and they were always followed by a fresh stock of good resolutions.

I had started out this day with the same old determination to keep cool, but, once into the reeds, Jim's account of how he had stepped on the crocodile put all other thoughts out of my mind, and most of my attention was given to examining suspicious-looking rocks as we stole silently and quietly along.

Jock was with me, as usual; I always took him out even then—not for hunting, because he was too young, but in order to train him. He was still only a puppy, about six months old, as well as I remember, and had never tackled or even followed a wounded buck, so

105

that it was impossible to say what he would do; he had seen me shoot a couple and had wanted to worry them as they fell; but that was all. He was quite obedient and kept his place behind me; and, although he trembled with excitement when he saw or heard anything, he never rushed in or moved ahead of me without permission. The guinea-fowl tormented him that day; he could scent and hear them, and was constantly making little runs forward, half-crouching and with his nose back and tail dead level and his one ear full-cocked and the other half-up.

For about half an hour we went on in this way. There was plenty of fresh duiker spoor to show us that we were in a likely place, one spoor in particular being so fresh in the mud that it seemed only a few minutes old. We were following this one very eagerly but very cautiously, and evidently Jock agreed with me that the duiker must be near, for he took no more notice of the guinea-fowl; and I for my part forgot all about crocodiles and suspicious-looking rocks; there was at that moment only one thing in the world for me, and that was the duiker. We crept along noiselessly in and out of the reeds, round rocks and mudholes, across small stretches of firm mud or soft sand, so silently that nothing could have heard us, and finally we came to a very big rock, with the duiker spoor fresher than ever going close round it down stream. The rock was a long sloping one, polished smooth by the floods and very slippery to walk on. I climbed it in dead silence, peering down into the reeds and expecting every moment to see the duiker.

The slope up which we crept was long and easy, but that on the down-stream side was much steeper. I crawled up to the top on hands and knees, and raising myself slowly, looked carefully about, but no duiker could be seen; yet Jock was sniffing and trembling more than ever, and it was quite clear that he thought we were very close up. Seeing nothing in front or on either side, I stood right up and turned to look back the way we had come and examine the reeds on that side. In doing so a few grains of grit crunched under my foot, and instantly there was a rush in the reeds behind me; I jumped round to face it, believing that a crocodile was grabbing at me from behind, and on the polished surface of the rock my feet slipped and shot from under me, both bare elbows bumped hard on the rock, jerking the rifle out of my hands; and I was launched like a torpedo right into the mass of swaying reeds.

When you think you are tumbling on to a crocodile there is only one thing you want to do—get out as soon as possible. How long it took to reach the top of the rock again, goodness only knows! It seemed like a life-time; but the fact is I was out of those reeds and up that rock in time to see the duiker as it broke out of the reeds, raced up the bank, and disappeared into the bush with Jock tearing after it as hard as ever he could go.

One call stopped him, and he came back to me looking very crestfallen and guilty, no doubt thinking that he had behaved badly and disgraced himself. But he was not to blame at all;

he had known all along that the duiker was there—having had no distracting fancies about crocodiles—and when he saw it dash off and his master instantly jump in after it, he must have thought that the hunt had at last begun and that he was expected to help.

After all that row and excitement there was not much use in trying for anything more in the reeds—and indeed I had had quite enough of them for one afternoon; so we wandered along the upper banks in the hope of finding something where there were no crocodiles, and it was not long before we were interested in something else and able to forget all about the duiker.

Before we had been walking many minutes, Jock raised his head and ears and then lowered himself into a half-crouching attitude and made a little run forward. I looked promptly in the direction he was pointing and about two hundred yards away saw a stembuck standing in the shade of a mimosa bush feeding briskly on the buffalo grass. It was so small and in such bad light that the shot was too difficult for me at that distance, and I crawled along behind bushes, ant-heaps and trees until we were close enough for anything. The ground was soft and sandy, and we could get along easily enough without making any noise; but all the time, whilst thinking how lucky it was to be on ground so soft for the hands and knees, and so easy to move on without being heard, something else was happening. With eyes fixed on the buck I did not notice that in crawling along on all-fours,

the muzzle of the rifle dipped regularly into the sand, picking up a little in the barrel each time. There was not enough to burst the rifle, but the effect was surprising. Following on a painfully careful aim, there was a deafening report that made my head reel and buzz; the kick of the rifle on the shoulder and cheek left me blue for days; and when my eyes were clear enough to see anything the stembuck had disappeared.

I was too disgusted to move, and sat in the sand rubbing my shoulder and thanking my stars that the rifle had not burst. There was plenty to think about, to be sure, and no hurry to do anything else, for the noise of the shot must have startled every living thing for a mile round.

It is not always easy to tell the direction from which a report comes when you are near a river or in broken country or patchy bush; and it is not an uncommon thing to find that a shot which has frightened one animal away from you has startled another and driven it towards you; and that is what happened in this case. As I sat in the shade of the thorns with the loaded rifle across my knees there was the faint sound of a buck cantering along in the sand; I looked up; and only about twenty yards from me a duiker came to a stop, half-fronting me. There it stood looking back over its shoulder, and listening intently, evidently thinking that the danger lay behind it. It was hardly possible to miss that; and as the duiker rolled over, I dropped my rifle and ran to make sure of it.

Of course, it was dead against the rules to leave the rifle behind; but it was simply a case of excitement

again: when the buck rolled over everything else was forgotten! I knew the rule perfectly well—Reload at once and never part with your gun. It was one of Rocky's lessons, and only a few weeks before this, when out for an afternoon's shooting with an old hunter, the lesson had been repeated. The old man shot a rietbuck ram, and as it had been facing us and dropped without a kick we both thought that it was shot through the brain. There was no mark on the head, however, and although we examined it carefully, we failed to find the bullet-mark or a trace of blood; so we put our rifles down to settle the question by skinning the buck. After sawing at the neck for half a minute, however, the old man found his knife too blunt to make an opening, and we both hunted about for a stone to sharpen it on, and while we were fossicking about in the grass there was a noise behind, and looking sharply round we saw the buck scramble to its feet and scamper off before we had time to move. The bullet must have touched one of its horns and stunned it. My companion was too old a hunter to get excited, and while I ran for the rifles and wanted to chase the buck on foot, he stood quite still, gently rubbing the knife on the stone he had picked up. Looking at me under bushy eyebrows and smiling philosophically, he said:

"That's something for you to remember, Boy. It's my belief if you lived for ever there'd always be something to learn at this game."

Unfortunately I did not remember when it would have been useful. As I ran forward the duiker stumbled, struggled and rolled over and over, then got up and made a dash, only to dive head foremost into the sand and somersault over; but in a second it was up again and racing off, again to trip and plunge forward on to its chest with its nose outstretched sliding along the soft ground. The bullet had struck it in the shoulder, and the broken leg was tripping it and bringing it down; but, in far less time than it takes to tell it, the little fellow found out what was wrong, and scrambling once more to its feet was off on three legs at a pace that left me far behind. Jock, remembering the mistake in the reeds, kept his place behind me, and I in the excitement of the moment neither saw nor thought of him until the duiker, gaining at every jump, looked like vanishing for ever. Then I remembered and, with a frantic wave of my hand, shouted, "After him, Jock."

He was gone before my hand was down, and faster than I had ever seen him move, leaving me ploughing through the heavy sand far behind. Past the big bush I saw them again, and there the duiker did as wounded game so often do: taking advantage of cover it changed direction and turned away for some dense thorns. But that suited Jock exactly; he took the short cut across to head it off and was close up in a few more strides. He caught up to it, raced up beside it, and made a jump at its throat; but the duiker darted away in a fresh direction, leaving him yards behind. Again he was after it and tried the other side; but the buck was too quick, and again he missed and overshot the mark in his jump. He was in such

deadly earnest he seemed to turn in the air to get back again and once more was close up—so close that the flying heels of the buck seemed to pass each side of his ears; then he made his spring from behind, catching the duiker high up on one hind leg, and the two rolled over together, kicking and struggling in a cloud of dust. Time after time the duiker got on its feet, trying to get at him with its horns or to break away again; but Jock, although swung off his feet and rolled on, did not let go his grip. In grim silence he hung on while the duiker plunged, and, when it fell, tugged and worried as if to shake the life out of it.

What with the hot sun, the heavy sand, and the pace at which we had gone, I was so pumped that I finished the last hundred yards at a walk, and had plenty of time to see what was going on; but even when I got up to them the struggle was so fierce and the movements so quick that for some time it was not possible to get hold of the duiker to finish it off. At last came one particularly bad fall, when the buck rolled over on its back, and then Jock let go his grip and made a dash for its throat; but again the duiker was too quick for him; with one twist it was up and round facing him on its one knee, and dug, thrust, and swept with its black spiky horns so vigorously that it was impossible to get at its neck. As Jock rushed in the head ducked and the horns flashed round so swiftly that it seemed as if nothing could save him from being stabbed through and through, but his quickness and cleverness were a revelation to me.

If he could not catch the duiker, it could not catch him: they were in a way too quick for each other, and they were a long way too quick for me.

Time after time I tried to get in close enough to grab one of the buck's hind legs, but it was not to be caught. While Jock was at it fast and furious in front, I tried to creep up quietly behind—but it was no use: the duiker kept facing Jock with horns down, and whenever I moved it swung round and kept me in front also. Finally I tried a run straight in; and then it made another dash for liberty. On three legs, however, it had no chance, and in another minute Jock had it again, and down they came together, rolling over and over once more. The duiker struggled hard, but he hung on, and each time it got its feet to the ground to rise he would tug sideways and roll it over again, until I got up to them, and catching the buck by the head, held it down with my knee on its neck and my Bushman's Friend in hand to finish it.

There was, however, still another lesson for us both to learn that day; neither of us knew what a buck can do with its hind feet when it is down. The duiker was flat on its side; Jock, thinking the fight was over, had let go; and, before I could move the supple body doubled up, and the feet whizzed viciously at me right over its head. The little pointed cloven feet are as hard and sharp as horns and will tear the flesh like claws. By good luck the kick only grazed my arm, but although the touch was the lightest

113   I

it cut the skin and little beads of blood shot up marking the line like the scratch of a thorn. Missing my arm, the hoof struck full on the handle of the Bushman's Friend and sent it flying yards out of reach. And it was not merely one kick: faster than the eye could follow them the little feet whizzed and the legs seemed to buzz round like the spokes of a wheel. Holding the horns at arm's length in order to dodge the kicks, I tried to pull the duiker towards the knife; but it was too much for me, and with a sudden twist and a wrench it freed itself and was off again.

All the time Jock was moving round and round panting and licking his chops, stepping in and stepping back, giving anxious little whimpers, and longing to be at it again, but not daring to join in without permission. When the duiker broke away, however, he waited for nothing, and was on to it in one spring—again from behind; and this time he let go as it fell, and jumping free of it, had it by the throat before it could rise. I ran to them again, but the picking up of the knife had delayed me and I was not in time to save Jock the same lesson that the duiker had just taught me.

Down on its side, with Jock's jaws locked in its throat once more, the duiker doubled up and used its feet. The first kick went over his head and scraped harmlessly along his back; but the second caught him at the point of the shoulder, and the razor-like toe ripped his side right to the hip. Then the dog showed his pluck and cleverness. His side was cut open as if it had been slashed by a knife, but he never flinched

114

or loosened his grip for a second; he seemed to go at it more furiously than ever, but more cleverly and warily. He swung his body round clear of the whizzing feet, watching them with his little beady eyes fixed sideways and the gleaming whites showing in the corners; he tugged away incessantly and vigorously, keeping the buck's neck stretched out and pulling it round in a circle backwards so that it could not possibly double its body up enough to kick him again; and before I could catch the feet to help him, the kicks grew weaker; the buck slackened out, and Jock had won.

The sun was hot, the sand was deep, and the rifle was hard to find; it was a long way back to the waggons, and the duiker made a heavy load; but the end of that first chase seemed so good that nothing else mattered. The only thing I did mind was the open cut on Jock's side; but he minded nothing: his tail was going like a telegraph needle; he was panting with his mouth open from ear to ear, and his red tongue hanging out and making great slapping licks at his chops from time to time; he was not still for a second, but kept walking in and stepping back in a circle round the duiker, and looking up at me and then down at it, as if he was not at all sure that there might not be some fresh game on, and was consulting me as to whether it would not be a good thing to have another go in and make it all safe.

 He was just as happy as a dog could be, and perhaps he was proud of the wound that left a straight line from his shoulder to his hip and showed up like a cord under the golden brindle as long as he lived—a memento of his first real hunt.

IN THE HEART OF THE BUSH

WHEN the hen pecked Jock on the nose, she gave him a useful lesson in the art of finding out what you want to know without getting into trouble. As he got older, he also learned that there are only certain things which concerned him and which it was necessary for him to know. A young dog begins by thinking that he can do everything, go everywhere, and know everything; and a hunting dog has to learn to mind his own business, as well as to understand it. Some dogs turn sulky or timid or stupid when they are checked, but an intelligent dog with a stout heart will learn little by little to leave other things alone, and grow steadily keener on his own work. There was no mistake about Jock's keenness. When I took down the rifle from the waggon he did not go off into ecstasies of barking, as most sporting dogs will do, but would give a quick look up and with an eager little

117

run towards me give a whimper of joy, make two or three bounds as if wanting to stretch his muscles and loosen his joints, then shake himself vigorously as though he had just come out of the water, and with a soft suppressed "Woo-woo-woo" full of contentment, drop silently into his place at my heels and give his whole attention to his work.

He was the best of companions, and through the years that we hunted together I never tired of watching him. There was always something to learn, something to admire, something to be grateful for, and very often something to laugh at—in the way in which we laugh only at those whom we are fond of. It was the struggle between Jock's intense keenness and his sense of duty that most often raised the laugh. He knew that his place was behind me; but probably he also knew that nine times out of ten he scented or saw the game long before I knew there was anything near, and naturally wanted to be in front or at least abreast of me to show me whatever there was to be seen.

He noticed, just as surely and as quickly as any human being could, any change in my manner: nothing escaped him, for his eyes and ears were on the move the whole time. It was impossible for me to look for more than a few seconds in any one direction, or to stop or even to turn my head to listen, without being caught by him. His bright brown eyes were everlastingly on the watch and on the move: from me to the bush, from the bush back to me. When we were after game, and he could scent or see it, he would keep a foot or two to the side of me so as to have a clear view; and when he knew by my manner that I thought there was game near, he kept so close up that he would often bump against my heels as I walked, or run right into my legs if I stopped suddenly. Often when stalking buck very quietly and cautiously, thinking only of what was in front, I would get quite a start by feeling something bump up against me behind. At these times it was impossible to say anything without risk of scaring the game, and I got into the habit of making signs with my hand which he understood quite as well.

Sometimes after having crawled up I would be in the act of aiming when he would press up against me. Nothing puts one off so much as a touch or the expectation of being jogged when in the act of firing, and I used to get angry with him then, but dared not breathe a word; I would lower my head slowly, turn round, and give him a look. He knew quite well what it meant. Down would go his ears instantly, and he would back away from me a couple of steps, drop his stump of a tail and wag it in a feeble deprecating way, and open his mouth into a sort of foolish laugh. That was his apology! "I beg your pardon: it was an accident! I won't do it again."

It was quite impossible to be angry with him, he was so keen and he meant so well; and when he saw me laughing softly at him, he would come up again close to me, cock his tail a few inches higher and wag it a bit faster.

There is a deal of expression in a dog's tail:

119

it will generally tell you what his feelings are. My friend maintained that that was how he knew his old dog was enjoying the joke against the cockerel; and that is certainly how I knew what Jock was thinking about once when lost in the veld; and it showed me the way back.

It is easy enough to lose oneself in the Bushveld. The Berg stands up some thousands of feet inland on the west, looking as if it had been put there to hold up the Highveld; and between the foothills and the sea lies the Bushveld, stretching for hundreds of miles north and south. From the height and distance of the Berg it looks as flat as the floor, but in many parts it is very much cut up by deep rough dongas, sharp rises and depressions, and numbers of small kopjes. Still, it has a way of looking flat, because the hills are small, and very much alike; and because hill and hollow are covered and hidden mile after mile by small trees of a wonderful sameness, just near enough together to prevent you from seeing more than a few hundred yards at a time. Most people see no differences in sheep: many believe that all Chinamen are exactly alike; and so it is with the Bushveld: you have to know it first.

So far I had never lost my way out hunting. The experiences of other men and the warnings from the old hands had made me very careful. We were always hearing of men being lost through leaving the road and following up the game while they were excited, without noticing which way they went and how long they had been going. There were no beaten tracks and very few landmarks, so that even experienced hunters went astray sometimes for a few hours or a day or two when the mists or heavy rains came on and nothing could be seen beyond fifty or a hundred yards.

Nearly every one who goes hunting in the Bush-veld gets lost some time or other—generally in the beginning before he has learned to notice things. Some have been lost for many days until they blundered on to a track by accident or were found by a search-party; others have been lost and, finding no water or food, have died; others have been killed by lions, and only a boot or a coat—or, as it happened in one case that I know of, a ring found inside a lion—told what had occurred; others have been lost and nothing more ever heard of them. There is no feeling quite like that of being lost—helplessness, terror, and despair! The horror of it is so great that every beginner has it before him; every one has heard of it, thought of it, and dreamed of it, and every one feels it holding him to the beaten track, as the fear of drowning keeps those who cannot swim to shallow water. That is just in the beginning. Presently, when little excursions, each bolder than the previous, have ended without accident, the fear grows less and confidence develops. Then it is, as a rule, that the accident comes and the lesson is learned, if you are lucky enough to pull through.

When the camp is away in the trackless bush, it needs a good man always to find the way home after a

couple of hours' chase with all its twists and turns and doublings; but when camp is made on a known road—a long main road that strikes a fair line between two points of the compass—it seems impossible for any one to be hopelessly lost. If the road runs east and west you, knowing on which side you left it, have only to walk north or south steadily and you must strike it again. The old hands told the beginners this, and we were glad to know that it was only a matter of walking for a few hours, more or less, and that in the end we were bound to find the road and strike some camp. "Yes," said the old hands, "it is simple enough here where you have a road running east and west; there is only one rule to remember: When you have lost your way, don't lose your head." But indeed that is just the one rule that you are quite unable to observe.

Many stories have been told of men being lost: many volumes could be filled with them for the trouble of writing down what any hunter will tell you. But no one who has not seen it can realise how the thing may happen; no one would believe the effect that the terror of being lost, and the demoralisation which it causes, can have on a sane man's senses. If you want to know that a man can persuade himself to believe against the evidence of his senses—even when his very life depends upon his holding to the absolute truth—then you should see a man who is lost in the bush. He knows that he left the road on the north side; he loses his bearings; he does not know how long, how fast, or how far he has walked; yet if he keeps

his head he will make due south and must inevitably
strike the road. After going for half an hour and
seeing nothing familiar, he begins to feel that he is
going in the wrong direction; something pulls at
him to face right about. Only a few minutes more of
this, and he feels sure that he must have crossed the
road without noticing it, and therefore that he ought
to be going north instead of south, if he hopes ever to
strike it again. How, you will ask, can a man imagine
it possible to cross a big dusty road twenty or thirty
feet wide without seeing it? The idea seems absurd;
yet they do really believe it. One of the first illusions
that occurs to men when they lose their heads is that
they have done this, and it is the cause of scores of
cases of 'lost in the bush.' The idea that they may
have done it is absurd enough; but stranger still is
the fact that they actually *do* it.

If you cannot understand a man thinking he had
done such a thing, what can you say of a man actually
doing it? Impossible, quite impossible, you think.
Ah! but it is a fact: many know it for a fact, and I
have witnessed it twice myself, once in Mashonaland
and once on the Delagoa road. I saw men, tired,
haggard and wild-eyed, staring far in front of them,
never looking at the ground, pressing on, on, on, and
actually cross well-worn waggon roads, coming from
hard veld into a sandy wheel-worn track and kicking
up a cloud of dust as they passed, and utterly blind to
the fact that they were walking across the roads they
had been searching for—in one case for ten hours,
and in the other for three days. When we called to

them they had already crossed and were disappearing again into the bush. In both cases the soundof the human voice and the relief of being 'found' made them collapse. The knees seemed to give way: they could not remain standing.

The man who loses his head is really lost. He cannot think, remember, reason, or understand; and the strangest thing of all is that he often cannot even *see* properly—he fails to see the very things that he most wants to see, even when they are as large as life before him. Crossing the road without seeing it is not the only or the most extraordinary example of this sort of thing. We were out hunting once in a mounted party, but to spare a tired horse I went on foot and took up my stand in a game run among some thorn trees on the low spur of a hill, while the others made a big circuit to head off a troop of koodoo. Among our party there was one who was very nervous: he had been lost once for six or eight hours, and being haunted by the dread of being lost again, his nerve was all gone and he would not go fifty yards without a companion. In the excitement of shooting at and galloping after the koodoo probably this dread was forgotten for a moment: he himself could not tell how it happened that he became separated, and no one else had noticed him.

The strip of wood along the hills in which I was waiting was four or five miles long but only from one to three hundred yards wide, a mere fringe enclosing the little range of kopjes; and between the stems of the trees I could see our camp and waggons in the open a quarter of a mile away. Ten or twelve shots faintly

heard in the distance told me that the others were on
to the koodoo, and knowing the preference of those
animals for the bush I took cover behind a big stump
and waited. For over half an hour, however, nothing
came towards me, and believing then that the game
had broken off another way, I was about to return to
camp when I heard the tapping of galloping feet a long
way off. In a few minutes the hard thud and occasional ring on the ground told that it was not the
koodoo; and soon afterwards I saw a man on horseback. He was leaning eagerly forward and thumping
the exhausted horse with his rifle and his heels to keep
up its staggering gallop. I looked about quickly to see
what it was he was chasing that could have slipped
past me unnoticed, but there was nothing; then
thinking there had been an accident and he was coming
for help, I stepped out into the open and waited for
him to come up. I stood quite still, and he galloped
past within ten yards of me—so close that his muttered
"Get on, you brute; get on, get on!" as he thumped
away at his poor tired horse, was perfectly audible.

"What's up, sportsman?" I asked, no louder than
you would say it across a tennis-court; but the words
brought him up, white-faced and terrified, and he
half slid, half tumbled, off the horse, gasping out,
"I was lost, I was lost!" How he had managed to
keep within that strip of bush, without once getting
into the open where he would have seen the line of
kopjes to which I had told him to stick or could have
seen the waggons and the smoke of the big
camp-fire, he could never explain. I turned
125

him round where he stood, and through the trees showed him the white tents of the waggons and the cattle grazing near by, but he was too dazed to understand or explain anything.

There are many kinds of men. That particular kind is not the kind that will ever do for veld life: they are for other things and other work. You will laugh at them at times—when the absurdity is greatest and no harm has been done. But see it! See it—and realise the suspense, the strain, and the terror; and then even the funniest incident has another side to it. See it once; and recall that the worst of endings have had just such beginnings. See it in the most absurd and farcical circumstances ever known; and laugh—laugh your fill; laugh at the victim and laugh with him, when it is over—and safe. But in the end will come the little chilling thought that the strongest, the bravest, and the best have known something of it too; and that even to those whose courage holds to the last breath, there may come a moment when the pulse beats a little faster and the judgment is at fault.

Buggins who was with us in the first season was no hunter, but he was a good shot and not a bad fellow. In his case there was no tragedy; there was much laughter, and—to me—a wonderful revelation. He showed us, as in a play, how you can be lost; how you can walk for ever in one little circle, as though drawn to a centre by magnetic force, and how you can miss seeing things in the bush if they do not move.

We had outspanned in a flat covered with close grass about two feet high and shady flat-topped thorn trees. The waggons, four in number, were drawn up a few yards off the road, two abreast. The grass was sweet and plentiful; the day was hot and still; and as we had had a very long early morning trek there was not much inclination to move. The cattle soon filled themselves and lay down to sleep; the boys did the same; and we, when breakfast was over, got into the shade of the waggons, some to sleep and others to smoke.

Buggins—that was his pet name—was a passenger returning to "England, Home and Beauty"—that is to say, literally, to a comfortable home, admiring sisters and a rich indulgent father—after having sought his fortune unsuccessfully on the gold fields for fully four months. Buggins was good-natured, unselfish, and credulous; but he had one fault—he 'yapped': he talked until our heads buzzed. He used to sleep contentedly in a rumpled tarpaulin all through the night treks and come up fresh as a daisy and full of accumulated chat at the morning outspan, just when we—unless work or sport called for us— were wanting to get some sleep.

We knew well enough what to expect, so after breakfast Jimmy, who understood Buggins well, told him pleasantly that he could "sleep, shoot, or shut up." To shut up was impossible, and to sleep again —without a rest—difficult, even for Buggins; so with a good-natured laugh he took the shot-gun, saying that he "would potter around a bit and give us a treat." Well, he did!

We had outspanned on the edge of an open space

in the thorn bush; there are plenty of them to be found in the Bushveld—spaces a few hundred yards in diameter, like open park land, where not a single tree breaks the expanse of wavy yellow grass. The waggons with their greyish tents and buck sails and dusty woodwork stood in the fringe of the trees where this little arena touched the road, and into it sallied Buggins, gently drawn by the benevolent purpose of giving us a treat. What he hoped to find in the open on that sweltering day he only could tell; we knew that no living thing but lizards would be out of the shade just then, but we wanted to find him employment harmless to him and us.

He had been gone for more than half an hour when we heard a shot, and a few minutes later Jimmy's voice roused us.

"What the dickens is Buggins doing?" he asked in a tone so puzzled and interested that we all turned to watch that sportsman. According to Jimmy, he had been walking about in an erratic way for some time on the far side of the open ground—going from the one end to the other and then back again; then disappearing for a few minutes in the bush and reappearing to again manœuvre in the open in loops and circles, angles and straight lines. Now he was walking about at a smart pace, looking from side to side apparently searching for something. We could see the whole of the arena as clearly as you can see a cricket-field from the railings—for our waggon formed part of the boundary—but we could see nothing to explain Buggins's manœuvres. Next we saw him face the thorns opposite, raise his gun very deliberately, and fire into the top of the trees.

"Green pigeons," said Jimmy firmly, and we all agreed that Buggins was after specimens for stuffing; but either our guess was wrong or his aim was bad, for after standing dead still for a minute he resumed his vigorous walk. By this time Buggins fairly fascinated us; even the kaffirs had roused each other and were watching him. Away he went at once off to our left, and there he repeated the performance, but again made no attempt to pick up anything and showed no further interest in whatever it was he had fired at, but turned right about face and walked across the open ground in our direction until he was only a couple of hundred yards away. There he stopped and began to look about him and making off some few yards in another direction climbed on to a fair-sized ant-heap five or six feet high, and balancing himself cautiously on this he deliberately fired off both barrels in quick succession. Then the same idea struck us all together, and "Buggins is lost" came from several—all choking with laughter.

Jimmy got up and stepping out into the open beside the waggon, called, "Say, Buggins, what in thunder *are* you doing?"

To see Buggins slide off the ant-heap and shuffle shamefacedly back to the waggon before a gallery of four white men and a lot of kaffirs, all cracking and crying with laughter, was a sight never to be forgotten.

I did not want to get lost and be eaten

alive, or even look ridiculous, so I began very carefully: glanced back regularly to see what the track, trees, rocks, or kopjes looked like from the other side; carefully noted which side of the road I had turned off; and always kept my eye on the sun. But day after day and month after month went by without accident or serious difficulty, and then the same old thing happened: familiarity bred contempt, and I got the beginner's complaint, conceit fever, just as others did: thought I was rather a fine fellow, not like other chaps who always have doubts and difficulties in finding their way back, but something exceptional with the real instinct in me which hunters, natives, and many animals are supposed to have; thought, in fact, I could not get lost. So each day I went further and more boldly off the road, and grew more confident and careless.

The very last thing that would have occurred to me on this particular day was that there was any chance of being lost or any need to take note of where we went. For many weeks we had been hunting in exactly the same sort of country, but not of course in the same part; and the truth is I did not give the matter a thought at all, but went ahead as one does with the things that are done every day as matters of habit.

LOST·IN·THE·VELD

WE were outspanned near some deep shaded water-holes, and at about three o'clock I took my rifle and wandered off in the hope of dropping across something for the larder and having some sport during the three hours before the evening trek would begin; and as there was plenty of spoor of many kinds the prospects seemed good enough.

We had been going along slowly, it may be for half an hour, without seeing more than a little stembuck scurrying away in the distance, when I noticed that Jock was rather busy with his nose, sniffing about in a way that looked like business. He was not sure of anything; that was clear, because he kept trying in different directions; not as you see a pointer do, but very seriously, silently and slowly, moving at a cautious walk for a few yards and then taking a look about.

The day was hot and still, as usual at that time of the year, and any noise would be easily heard, so I had stopped to give Jock a chance of ranging about. At the moment we were in rather open ground, and finding that Jock was still very suspicious I moved on towards where the bush was thicker and we were

131

less likely to be seen from a distance. As we got near the better cover there was a rasping, squawky cry in a cockatoo's voice, "Go 'way; go 'way; go 'way!" and one of those ugly big-beaked Go 'way birds came sailing up from behind and flapped on to the trees we were making for. No doubt they have another name, but in the Bushveld they were known as Go 'way birds, because of this cry and because they are supposed to warn the game when an enemy is coming. But they are not like the tick bird and the rhinoceros bird, who stick close to their friends and as soon as they see or hear anything suspicious flutter straight up filling the air with twittering cries of alarm; the Go 'way birds do not feed on ticks and have nothing to do with the game; you find them where there is no game, and it always seemed to me that it is not concern for the game at all, but simply a combination of vulgar curiosity, disagreeableness and bad manners that makes them interfere as they do.

The reason why I do not believe the Go 'way birds care a rap about the game and only want to worry you is that often one of them will make up its mind to stick to you, and you can turn, twist and double as many ways as you like, but as soon as you begin to walk on again the wretched thing will fly over your head and perch twenty yards or so in front of you, screeching out "Go 'way" at the top of its voice. There it will sit ready to fly off again as you come on, its ugly head on one side and big hooked bill like an aggressive nose, watching you mercilessly, as vigilant as a hungry fowl and as cross as a tired nurse in a big

132

family. They seem to know that you cannot shoot them without making more row and doing more harm than they do.

I stood still for a few minutes to give this one a chance to fly away, and when it would not do so, but kept on screeching and craning its neck at me, I threw a stone at it. It ducked violently and gave a choking hysterical squawk of alarm and anger as the stone whizzed close to its head; then flying on to another tree a few yards off, screamed away more noisily than ever. Evidently the best thing to do was to go ahead taking no notice of the creature and trusting that it would tire and leave me alone; so I walked off briskly.

There was a slight rustling in the bush ahead of us as I stepped out, and then the sound of feet. I made a dash for the chance of a running shot, but it was too late, and all we saw was half a dozen beautiful koodoo disappearing among the tree stems.

I turned towards that Go 'way bird. Perhaps he did not like the look on my face or the way I held the rifle; for he gave one more snarling shriek, as if he was emptying himself for ever of his rage and spite, and flapped away.

Jock was standing like a statue, leaning slightly forward, but with head very erect, jaws tightly closed, and eyes looking straight in front, as bright as black diamonds.

It was a bad disappointment; for that was the first time we had fairly and squarely come upon koodoo. However, it was still early and the game had not been scared, but had gone off quietly; so hoping for another chance we started off at a trot along the fresh spoor.

A big koodoo bull stands as high as a bullock, and although they have the small shapely feet of an antelope the spoor is heavy enough to follow at a trot except on stony ground. Perhaps they know this, for they certainly prefer the rough hard ground when they can get it. We went along at a good pace, but with many short breaks to make sure of the spoor in the stony parts; and it was pretty hot work, although clothing was light for hunting. A rough flannel shirt, open at the throat, and moleskin trousers dyed with coffee—for khaki was unknown to us then—was the usual wear; and we carried as little as possible. Generally a water-bottle filled with unsweetened cold tea and a cartridge belt were all we took besides the rifle. This time I had less than usual. Meaning to be out only for a couple of hours at most and to stick close to the road, I had pocketed half a dozen cartridges and left both bandolier and water-bottle behind.

It was not long before we came upon the koodoo again; but they were on the watch. They were standing in the fringe of some thick bush, broadside on but looking back full at us, and as soon as I stopped to aim the whole lot disappeared with the same easy movement, just melting away in the bush.

If I had only known it, it was a hopeless chase for an inexperienced hunter: they were simply playing with me. The very things that seemed so encouraging to me would have warned an old hand that running on the trail was quite useless. When they moved

134

off quietly, it was not because they were foolhardy or did not realise the danger. When they allowed us to catch up to them time after time, it was not because they did not expect us. When they stood on the edge of thick bush where we could see them, it was not stupidity. When they could disappear with an easy bound, it was not accident. It was all part of the game. They were keeping in touch with us so that we could not surprise them, and whenever they stopped it was always where they could see us coming through the thinner bush for a long way and where they themselves could disappear in the thick bush in a couple of strides. Moreover, with each fresh run they changed their direction with the object of making it difficult for us to follow them up, and with the deliberate purpose of eventually reaching some favourite and safe haunt of theirs.

An old hand might have known this; but a beginner goes blindly along the spoor—exactly where they are expecting him. The chase was long and tiring, but there was no feeling of disappointment and no thought of giving it up: each time they came in sight we got keener and more excited, and the end seemed nearer and more certain. I knew what the six animals were— four cows, one young bull, and a magnificent old fellow with a glorious head and great spiral horns. I carried his picture in my eye and could pick him out instantly wherever he stood and however motionless; for, incredibly difficult as it is to pick out still objects in the bush before your eye becomes accustomed to it, it is wonderful what

you can do when your eye is in and you are cool and intent and know what you are looking for. I had the old bull marked down as mine, and knew his every detail—his splendid bearing, strong shaggy neck with mane to the withers and bearded throat, the soft grey dove-colour of the coat with its white stripes, the easy balancing movement in carrying the massive horns as he cantered away, and the trick of throwing them back to glide them through the bush.

The last run was a long and hard one; and the koodoo seemed to have taken matters seriously and made up their minds to put a safe distance between us and them. The spooring was often difficult and the pace hot. I was wet through from the hard work, and so winded that further effort seemed almost impossible; but we plodded away—the picture of the koodoo bull luring me on, and Jock content with any chase. Without him the spoor would have been lost long before; it was in many places too faint and scattered for me to follow, but he would sniff about quietly, and, by his contented looks back at me and brisk wagging of that stumpy tail, show that he was on it again, and off we would go on another tired straggling trot. But at last even his help was not enough: we had come to the end of the chase, and not a spoor, scratch, or sign of any sort was to be seen.

Time had passed unnoticed, and it was only when it became clear that further search would be quite useless that I looked at my watch and found it was nearly five o'clock. That was rather a shock, for it

seemed reasonable to think that, as we had been out for pretty nearly two hours and going fast for most of the time, it would take almost as long to get back again.

I had not once noticed our direction or looked at the sun, yet when it came to making for camp again the idea of losing the way never occurred to me. I had not the slightest doubt about the way we had come, and it seemed the natural thing to go back the same way.

A short distance from where we finally gave up the chase there was a rise crowned by some good-sized rocks and bare of trees; it was not high enough to be fairly called a kopje, but I climbed it on chance of getting a view of the surrounding country—to see, if possible, how far we had come. The rise was not sufficient, however, to give a view; there was nothing to be seen, and I sat down on the highest rock to rest for a few minutes and smoke a cigarette.

It is over twenty years since that day, but that cigarette is not forgotten, and the little rise where we rested is still, to me, Cigarette Kopje. I was so thoroughly wet from the heat and hard work that the matches in the breast pocket of my shirt were all damp, and the heads came off most of them before one was gently coaxed into giving a light. Five minutes' rest was enough. We both wanted a drink, but there was no time then to hunt for water in such a dry part as that, so off we started for camp and jogged along for a good time, perhaps half an hour. Then little by little I began to feel some uncertainty

137

about the way and to look about from side to side for reminders.

The start back had been easy enough: that part of the ground where we had lost the spoor had been gone over very thoroughly and every object was familiar; but further back, where we had followed the spoor at a trot for long stretches and I had hardly raised my eyes from the ground before me, it was a very different matter. I forgot all about those long stretches in which nothing had been noticed except the koodoo spoor, and was unconsciously looking out for things in regular succession which we had passed at quite long intervals. Of course, they were not to be found, but I kept on looking out for them—first feeling annoyed, then puzzled, then worried. Something had gone wrong, and we were not going back on our old tracks. Several times I looked about for the koodoo spoor as a guide; but it might be anywhere over a width of a hundred yards, and it seemed waste of precious time to search the dry grass-grown and leaf-strewn ground for that.

At the first puzzled stop I tried to recall some of the more noticeable things we had passed during the chase. There were two flat-topped mimosas, looking like great rustic tables on a lawn, and we had passed between them; there was a large ant-heap, with a twisty top like a crooked mud chimney, behind which the koodoo bull had calmly stood watching us approach; then a marula tree with a fork like a giant catapult stick; and so on with a score of other things, all coming readily to mind.

That was what put me hopelessly wrong. I began to look for particular objects instead of taking one direction and keeping to it. Whenever a flat-topped thorn, a quaint ant-heap, a patch of tambookie grass, or a forked marula came in sight, I would turn off to see if they were the same we had passed coming out. It was hopeless folly, of course; for in that country there were hundreds and thousands of such things all looking very much alike, and you could walk yourself to death zigzagging about from one to another and never get any nearer home: when it comes to doing that sort of thing your judgment is gone and you have lost your head; and the worst of it is you do not know it and would not believe it if any one could tell you so. I did not know it; but it was nevertheless the fact.

As the sun sank lower I hurried on faster, but never long in one line—always turning this way and that to search for the particular marks I had in mind. At last we came to four trees in a line, and my heart gave a great jump, for these we had certainly passed before. In order to make quite sure I hunted for koodoo spoor; there was none to be seen, but on an old molehill there was the single print of a dog's foot.

"Ha, Jock's!" I exclaimed aloud; and Jock himself at the sound of his name stepped up briskly and sniffed at his own spoor. Close behind it there was the clear mark of a heeled boot, and there were others further on. There was no doubt about it, they were Jock's and mine, and I could have given a whoop of delight; but a chilly feeling came over me when I realised that the footprints were *leading the same way as we were going*, instead of the opposite way. What on earth did it mean?

I laid the rifle down and sat on an old stump to think it out, and after puzzling over it for some minutes came to the conclusion that by some stupid blunder I must have turned round somewhere and followed the line of the koodoo, instead of going back on it. The only thing to be done was to right about face and go faster than ever; but, bad as the disappointment was, it was a certain consolation to know that we were on the track at last. That at any rate was a certainty; for, besides the footprints, the general appearance of the country and many individual features were perfectly familiar, now that I took a good look at them from this point.

At that moment I had not a shadow of doubt about the way—no more, indeed, than if we had been on the road itself: no suspicion of the truth occurred to me; yet the simple fact is we were not then on the koodoo trail at all, but, having made a complete circle, had come on to our own trail at the molehill and were now doing the circle the second time—but the reverse way now.

The map on the opposite page is an attempt to show what happened; the details are of course only guesswork, but the general idea is correct. The koodoo themselves had moved in a rough circle and in the first attempt to return to the waggons I had started back on their trail but must have turned aside somewhere, and after that, by dodging about looking

140

MAP OF "LOST IN THE VELD"

Thick black line shows track of Koodoo.

Thin black line shows first circle beginning Cigarette Kopje & ending at Z, Jocks footprint in Molehill.

Dotted line shows second circle from Z, where I turned back again, to Cigarette Kopje.

Arrows ➤ show the direction in which we went on each trail.

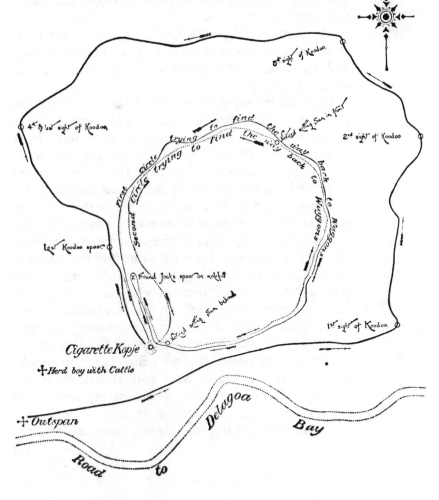

for special landmarks, must have made a complete circle. Thus we eventually came back to the track on which we had started for home, and the things that then looked so convincingly familiar were things seen during the first attempt to return, and not, as I supposed, landmarks on the original koodoo trail. Jock's footprints in the molehill were only a few hundred yards from the Cigarette Kopje and about the same distance from where we had lost the koodoo spoor; and we were, at that moment, actually within a mile of the waggons.

It seems incredible that one could be so near and not see or understand. Why should one walk in circles instead of taking a fairly straight line? How was it possible to pass Cigarette Kopje and not recognise it, for I must have gone within fifty yards or less of it? As for not seeing things, the answer is that the bush does not allow you to see much: the waggons, for instance, might as well have been a hundred miles away. As for Cigarette Kopje—things do not look the same unless seen from the same point; moreover, there are heaps of things easily visible which you will never see at all because you are looking only for something else: you carry a preconceived idea, a sort of picture in your eye, and everything that does not fit in with that is not noticed—not even seen. As for walking in circles, it is my belief that most people, just like most horses, have a natural leaning or tendency towards one side or the other, and unless checked unconsciously indulge it.

When riding in the veld, or any open country, you

will notice that some horses will want to take any turn off to the right, others always go to the left, and only very few keep straight on. When out walking you will find that some people cannot walk on your right hand without coming across your front or working you into the gutter; others 'mule' you from the left. Get them out in open country, walk briskly, and talk; then give way a little each time they bump you. and in a very little while you will have done the circle. If you have this tendency in the Bushveld, where you cannot see any distant object to make for as a goal, any obstacle straight in front of you throws you off to the side you incline to; any openings in the trees which look like avenues or easy ways draw you; and between any two of them you will always choose the one on your favourite side. Finally, a little knowledge is a dangerous thing in the veld, as elsewhere. When you know enough to recognise marks without being able to identify or locate them—that is, when you know you have seen them before but are not sure of the when and the where—goodness only knows what conclusion you will come to or what you will do.

I had passed Cigarette Kopje, it's true; but when coming towards it from a new side it must have looked quite different; and besides that, I had not been expecting it, not looking for it, not even thinking of it—had indeed said good-bye to it for ever. When we turned back at the molehill, beginning to do the circle for the second time, we must have passed quite close to Cigarette Kopje again, but again it was from a different opening in the bush, and this time I had thought of nothing and seen nothing except the things I picked out and recognised as we hurried along. To my half-opened beginner's eyes these things were familiar: we had passed them before; that seemed to be good enough: it must be right; so on we went, simply doing the same circle a second time, but this time the reverse way. The length of my shadow stretching out before me as we started from the molehill was a reminder of the need for haste, and we set off at a smart double. A glance back every few minutes to make sure that we were returning the way we had come was enough, and on we sped, confident for my part that we were securely on the line of the koodoo and going straight for the wagons.

It is very difficult to say how long this lasted before once more a horrible doubt arose. It was when we had done half the circle that I was pulled up as if struck in the face: the setting sun shining into my eyes as we crossed an open space stopped me; for, as the bright gold-dust light of the sunset met me full, I remembered that it was my long shadow *in front* of me as we started from the molehill that had urged me to hurry on. We had started due east: we were going dead west! What on earth was wrong? There were the trees and spaces we had passed, a blackened stump, an ant-bear hole; all familiar. What then was the meaning of it? Was it only a temporary swerve? No! I tested that by pushing on further along the track we were following, and it held steadily to the west. Was it then all imagination about having

144

been there before? No, that was absurd! And yet—
and yet, as I went on, no longer trotting and full of
hope but walking heavily and weighted with doubt,
the feeling of uncertainty grew until I really did not
know whether the familiar-looking objects and scenes
were indeed old acquaintances or merely imagination
playing tricks in a country where every style and
sample was copied a thousand times over.

A few minutes later I again caught sight of the
sunset glow—it was on my direct right: it meant that
the trail had taken another turn, while I could have
sworn we were holding a course straight as an arrow.
It was all a hopeless tangle. I was lost then—and knew
it. It was not the dread of a night out in the bush—
for after many months of roughing it, that had no
great terrors for me—but the helpless feeling of being
lost and the anxiety and uncertainty about finding the
road again, that gnawed at me and made me feel
tucked-up and drawn. I wondered when they would
begin to look for me, if they would light big fires
and fire shots, and if it would be possible to see or hear
the signals. The light would not last much longer; the
dimness, the silence, and the hateful doubts about
the trail made it more and more difficult to recognise
the line; so I thought it was time to fire a signal
shot.

There was no answer. It was silly to hope for one;
for even if it had been heard they would only have
thought that I was shooting at something. Yet the
clinging to hope was so strong that every twenty yards
or so I stopped to listen for a reply; and

145   L

when, after what seemed an eternity, none came, I fired another. When you shoot in the excitement or the chase the noise of the report does not strike you as anything out of the way; but a signal shot when you are alone and lost seems to fill the world with sound and to shake the earth itself. It has a most chilling effect, and the feeling of loneliness becomes acute as the echoes die away and still no answer comes.

Another short spell of tiptoe walking and intent listening, and then it came to me that one shot as a signal was useless; I should have fired more and at regular intervals, like minute-guns at sea. I felt in my pocket: there were only four cartridges there and one in the rifle; there was night before me, with the wolves and the lions; there was the food for to-morrow, and perhaps more than to-morrow! There could be no minute-guns: two shots were all that could be spared, and I looked about for some high and open ground where the sound would travel far and wide. On ahead of us to the right the trees seemed fewer and the light stronger; and there I came upon some rising ground bare of bush. It was not much for my purpose, but it was higher than the rest and quite open, and there were some rocks scattered about the top. The same old feeling of mixed remembrance and doubt came over me as we climbed it: it looked familiar and yet different. Was it memory or imagination?

But there was no time for wonderings. From the biggest rock, which was only waist high, I fired off two

146

of my precious cartridges, and stood like a statue listening for the reply. The silence seemed worse than before: the birds had gone to roost; even the flies had disappeared; there was no sound at all but the beat of my own heart and Jock's panting breath.

There were three cartridges and a few damp matches left. There was no sun to dry them now, but I laid them out carefully on the smooth warm rock, and hoped that one at least would serve to light our camp fire. There was no time to waste: while the light lasted I had to drag up wood for the fire and pick a place for the camp—somewhere where the rocks behind and the fire in front would shelter us from the lions and hyenas, and where I could watch and listen for signals in the night.

There was plenty of wood near by, and thinking anxiously of the damp matches I looked about for dry tindery grass so that any spark would give a start for the fire. As I stooped to look for the grass I came on a patch of bare ground between the scattered tufts, and in the middle of it there lay a half-burnt match; and such a flood of relief and hope surged up that my heart beat up in my throat. Where there were matches there had been men! We were not in the wilds, then, where white men seldom went—not off the beaten track: perhaps not far from the road itself.

You must experience it to know what it meant at that moment. It drew me on to look for more! A yard away I found the burnt end of a cigarette; and before there was time to realise why that should

147

seem queer, I came on eight or ten matches with their heads knocked off.

For a moment things seemed to go round and round. I sat down with my back against the rock and a funny choky feeling in my throat. I knew they were my matches and cigarette, and that we were exactly where we had started from hours before, when we gave up the chase of the koodoo. I began to understand things then: why places and landmarks seemed familiar; why Jock's spoor in the molehill had pointed the wrong way; why my shadow was in front and behind and beside me in turns. We had been going round in a circle. I jumped up and looked about me with a fresh light; and it was all clear as noonday then. Why, this was the fourth time we had been on or close to some part of this same rise that day, each time within fifty yards of the same place; it was the second time I had sat on that very rock. And there was nothing odd or remarkable about that either, for each time I had been looking for the highest point to spy from and had naturally picked the rock-topped rise; and I had not recognised it, only because we came upon it from different sides each time and I was thinking of other things all the while.

All at once it seemed as if my eyes were opened and all was clear at last. I knew what to do: just make the best of it for the night; listen for shots and watch for fires; and if by morning no help came in that way, then strike a line due south for the road and follow it up until we found the waggons. It might take all day or even more, but we were sure of

148

water that way and one could do it. The relief of really understanding was so great that the thought of a night out no longer worried me.

There was enough wood gathered, and I stretched out on the grass to rest as there was nothing else to do. We were both tired out, hot, dusty, and very very thirsty; but it was too late to hunt for water then. I was lying on my side chewing a grass stem, and Jock lay down in front of me a couple of feet away. It was a habit of his: he liked to watch my face, and often when I rolled over to ease one side and lie on the other he would get up when he found my back turned to him and come round deliberately to the other side and sling himself down in front of me again. There he would lie with his hind legs sprawled on one side, his front legs straight out, and his head resting on his paws. He would lie like that without a move, his little dark eyes fixed on mine all the time until the stillness and the rest made him sleepy, and he would blink and blink, like a drowsy child, fighting against sleep until it beat him; and then—one long-drawn breath as he rolled gently over on his side, and Jock was away in Snoozeland.

In the loneliness of that evening I looked into his steadfast resolute face with its darker muzzle and bright faithful eyes that looked so soft and brown when there was nothing to do but got so beady black when it came to fighting. I felt very friendly to the comrade who was little more than a puppy still; and he seemed to feel something too; for as I lay there chewing the straw and looking at him, he stirred

149

his stump of a tail in the dust an inch or so from time to time to let me know that he understood all about it and that it was all right as long as we were together.

But an interruption came. Jock suddenly switched up his head, put it a bit sideways as a man would do, listening over his shoulder with his nose rather up in the air. I watched him, and thinking that it was probably only a buck out to feed in the cool of the evening, I tickled his nose with the long straw, saying, "No good, old chap; only three cartridges left. We must keep them."

No dog likes to have his nose tickled: it makes them sneeze; and many dogs get quite offended, because it hurts their dignity. Jock was not offended, but he got up and, as if to show me that I was frivolous and not attending properly to business, turned away from me and with his ears cocked began to listen again.

He was standing slightly in front of me and I happened to notice his tail: it was not moving; it was drooping slightly and perfectly still, and he kept it like that as he stepped quietly forward on to another sloping rock overlooking a side where we had not yet been. Evidently there was something there, but he did not know what, and he wanted to find out.

I watched him, much amused by his calm business-like manner. He walked to the edge of the rock and looked out: for a few minutes he stood stock-still with his ears cocked and his tail motionless; then his ears dropped and his tail wagged gently from side to side.

150

Something—an instinct or sympathy quickened by the day's experience, that I had never quite known before—taught me to understand, and I jumped up, thinking, "He sees something that he knows: he is pleased." As I walked over to him, he looked back  at me with his mouth open and tongue out, his ears still down and tail wagging—he was smiling all over, in his own way. I looked out over his head, and there, about three hundred yards off, were the oxen peacefully grazing, and the herd-boy in his red coat lounging along behind them.

Shame at losing myself and dread of the others' chaff kept me very quiet, and all they knew for many months was that we had had a long fruitless chase after koodoo and hard work to get back in time.

I had had my lesson, and did not require to have it rubbed in and be roasted as Buggins had been. Only Jock and I knew all about it; but once or twice there were anxious nervous moments when it looked as if we were not the only ones in the secret. The big Zulu driver, Jim Makokel'—always interested in hunting and all that concerned Jock—asked me as we were inspanning what I had fired the last two shots at; and as I pretended not to hear or to notice the question, he went on to say how he had told the other boys that it must have been a klipspringer on a high rock or a monkey or a bird because the bullets had whistled over the waggons. I told him to inspan and not talk so much, and moved round to the other side of the waggon.

That night I slept hard, but woke up once

dreaming that several lions were looking down at me from the top of a big flat rock and Jock was keeping them off.

Jock was in his usual place beside me, lying against my blankets. I gave him an extra pat for the dream, thinking, "Good old boy; we know all about it, you and I, and we're not going to tell. But we've learned some things that we won't forget." And as I dropped off to sleep again I felt a few feeble sleepy pats against my leg, and knew it was Jock's tail wagging "Good night."

THE IMPALA STAMPEDE

Not all our days were spent in excitement—far far from it. For six or seven months the rains were too heavy, the heat too great, the grass too rank, and the fever too bad in the Bushveld for any one to do any good there; so that for more than half of the year we had no hunting to speak of, as there was not much to be done above the Berg. But even during the hunting season there were many off-days and long spells when we never fired a shot. The work with the waggons was hard when we had full loads, the trekking slow and at night, so that there was always something to do in the daytime—repairs to be done, oxen to be doctored, grass and water to be looked for, and so on; and we had to make up sleep when we could. Even when the sport was good and the bag satisfactory there was usually nothing new to tell about it. So Jock and I had many a long spell when there was no hunting, many a bad day when we worked hard but had no sport, and many a good day when we got what we were after, and nothing happened that would interest any one else.

153

Every hunt was exciting and interesting for us, even those in which we got nothing; indeed some of the most interesting were those in which the worst disappointments occurred, when after hard work and long chases the game escaped us. To tell all that happened would be to tell the same old story many times over; but indeed, it would not be possible to tell all, for there were some things—the most interesting of all, perhaps—which only Jock knew.

After the fight with the duiker there was never any doubt as to what he would do if allowed to follow up a wounded animal. It made a deal of difference in the hunting to know that he could be trusted to find it and hold on or bay it until I could get up. The bush was so thick that it was not possible to see more than a very few hundred yards at best, and the country was so dry and rough that if a wounded animal once got out of sight only an expert tracker had any chance of finding it again. Jock soon showed himself to be better than the best of trackers, for besides never losing the trail he would either pull down the buck or, if too big for that, attack and worry even the biggest of them to such an extent that they would have to keep turning on him to protect themselves and thus give me the chance to catch up.

But the first result of my confidence in him was some perfectly hopeless chases. It is natural enough to give oneself the benefit of any doubt; the enthusiastic beginner always does so, and in his case the lack of experience often creates a doubt where none should have existed; and the doubt is often very welcome, helping him out with explanations of the unflattering facts. For the listener it is, at best and worst, only amusing or tiresome; but for the person concerned it is different—for, as Rocky said, "It don't fool any one worth speakin' of 'cept yerself." And "there's the rub." Whenever a bullet struck with a thud, and no dust appeared to show that it had hit the ground, I thought that it must have wounded the buck; and once you get the idea that the buck is hit, all sorts of reasons appear in support of it. There is hardly anything that the buck can do which does not seem to you to prove that it is wounded. It bounds into the air, races off suddenly, or goes away quite slowly; it switches its tail or shakes its head; it stops to look back, or does not stop at all; the spoor looks awkward and scrappy; the rust on the grass looks like dry blood. If you start with a theory instead of weighing the evidence all these things will help to prove that theory: they will, in fact, mean exactly what you want them to mean. You "put up a job on yerself"—to quote Rocky again—and with the sweat of your brow and vexation of spirit you have to work that job out.

Poor old Jock had a few hard chases after animals which I thought were wounded but were not hit at all —not many, however, for he soon got hold of the right idea and was a better judge than his master. He went off the instant he was sent, but if there was nothing wounded—that is, if he could not pick up a 'blood spoor'—he would soon show it by casting across the trail, instead of following hard on it; and I knew then there was nothing in it. Often he would

155

come back of his own accord, and there was something
quite peculiar in his look when he returned from these
wild-goose chases that seemed to say, "No good: you
were quite wrong. You missed the whole lot of them."
He would come up to me with his mouth wide open
and tongue out, a bit blown, and stand still with his
front legs wide apart, looking up at me with that
nothing-in-it sort of look in his eyes and not a movement in his ears or tail and never a turn of his head to
show the least interest in anything else. I got to know
that look quite well; and to me it meant, "Well, that
job was a failure—finished and done for. Now is
there anything else you can think of?"

What always seemed to me so curious and full of
meaning was that he never once looked back in the
direction of the unwounded game, but seemed to
put them out of his mind altogether as of no further
interest. It was very different when he got on to the
trail of a wounded buck and I had to call him off, as
was sometimes necessary when the chase looked hopeless or it was too late to go further. He would obey,
of course—no amount of excitement made him forget
that; but he would follow me in a sort of sideways
trot, looking back over his shoulder all the time, and
whenever there was a stop, turning right round and
staring intently in the direction of the game with
his little tail moving steadily from side to side and his
hind legs crouched as if ready to spring off the instant
he got permission.

Twice I thought he was lost for ever through
following wounded game. The first occasion was also

the first time that we got among the impala and saw them in numbers. There is no more beautiful and fascinating sight than that of a troop of impala or springbuck really on the move and jumping in earnest. The height and distance that they clear is simply incredible. The impala's greater size and its delicate spiral horns give it a special distinction; the spring-buck's brilliant white and red, and the divided crest which fans out along the spine when it is excited, are unique. But who can say which of the many beautiful antelopes is the most beautiful? The oldest hunter will tell you of first one, then another, and then another, as they come to mind, just as he saw them in some supreme unforgettable moment; and each at that moment has seemed quite the most beautiful animal in the world.

It is when they are jumping that the impala are seen at their best. No one knows what they really can do, for there are no fences in their country by which to judge or guess, and as they run in herds it is practically impossible ever to find the take-off or landing place of any single animal. Once when hunting along the Wenhla Mohali River we managed to turn seven of them into an old run ending in a rocky gorge; but suspecting danger they would not face the natural outlet, and turning up the slope cleared a barrier of thick thorn scrub and escaped. When we looked at the place afterwards we found that the bushes were nine feet high. We were not near enough to see whether they touched the tops or cleared them; all we were sure of was that they did not hesitate for

157

a second to face a jump nine feet high at the top of a sharp rise, and that all seven did it in follow-my-leader order with the most perfect ease and grace.

Every hunter has seen a whole troop, old and young, following the example of the leader, clear a road or donga twenty feet wide, apparently in an effortless stride. It is a fine sight, and the steady stream of buck makes an arch of red and white bodies over the road looking like the curve of a great wave. You stand and watch in speechless admiration; and the first gasp at a glorious leap is followed by steady silent wonder at the regularity of the numbers. Then suddenly you see one animal—for no apparent reason: it may be fright or it may be frolic—take off away back behind the others, shoot up, and sail high above the arch of all the rest, and with head erect and feet comfortably gathered, land far beyond them—the difference between ease and effort, and oh! the perfect grace of both! Something is wrung from you—a word, a gasp—and you stand breathless with wonder and admiration until the last one is gone. You have forgotten to shoot; but they have left you something better than a trophy, something which time will only glorify—a picture that in daylight or in dark will fill your mind whenever you hear the name Impala.

Something of this I carried away from my first experience among them. There were a few minutes of complete bewilderment, a scene of the wildest confusion, and flashes of incident that go to make a great picture which it is impossible to forget. But

158

then there followed many hours of keen anxiety when I believed that Jock was gone for ever; and it was long before that day found its place in the gallery of happy memories.

We had gone out after breakfast, striking well away from the main road until we got among the thicker thorns where there was any amount of fresh spoor and we were quite certain to find a troop sooner or later. The day was so still, the ground so dry, and the bush so thick that the chances were the game would hear us before we could get near enough to see them. Several times I heard sounds of rustling bush or feet cantering away: something had heard us and made off unseen; so I dropped down into the sandy bed of a dry donga and used it as a stalking trench. From this it was easy enough to have a good look around every hundred yards or so without risk of being heard or seen. We had been going along cautiously in this way for some time when, peering over the bank, I spied a single impala half hidden by a scraggy bush. It seemed queer that there should be only one, as their habit is to move in troops; but there was nothing else to be seen; indeed it was only the flicker of an ear on this one that had caught my eye. Nothing else in the land moved.

Jock climbed the bank also, following so closely that he bumped against my heels, and when I lay flat actually crawled over my legs to get up beside me and see what was on. Little by little he got into the way of imitating all I did, so that after a while it was hardly necessary to say a word or make a sign to him. He lay down beside me and raised his head to look just as he saw me do. He was all excitement, trembling like a wet spaniel on a cold day, and instead of looking steadily at the impala as I was doing and as he usually did, he was looking here, there and everywhere; it seemed almost as if he was looking at things—not for them. It was my comfortable belief at the moment that he had not yet spotted the buck, but was looking about anxiously to find out what was interesting me. It turned out, as usual, that he had seen a great deal more than his master had.

The stalking looked very easy, as a few yards further up the donga there was excellent cover in some dense thorns, behind which we could walk boldly across open ground to within easy range of the buck and get a clear shot. We reached the cover all right, but I had not taken three steps into the open space beyond before there was a rushing and scrambling on every side of me. The place was a whirlpool of racing and plunging impala; they came from every side and went in every direction as though caught suddenly in an enclosure and, mad with fear and bewilderment, were trying to find a way out. How many there were it was quite impossible to say: the bush was alive with them; and the dust they kicked up, the noise of their feet, their curious sneezy snorts, and their wild confusion completely bewildered me. Not one stood still. Never for a moment could I see any single animal clearly enough or long enough to fire at it; another would cross it; a bush would cover it as I aimed; or it would leap into the air, clearing bushes,

160

"THEY SEEMED TO WHIRL LIKE LEAVES IN A WIND EDDY"

bucks and everything in its way, and disappear again in the moving mass. They seemed to me to whirl like leaves in a wind eddy: my eyes could not follow them and my brain swam as I looked.

It was a hot day; there was no breeze at all; and probably the herd had been resting after their morning feed and drink when we came upon them. By creeping up along the donga we had managed to get unobserved right into the middle of the dozing herd, so they were literally on every side of us. At times it looked as if they were bound to stampede over us and simply trample us down in their numbers; for in their panic they saw nothing, and not one appeared to know what or where the danger was. Time and again, as for part of a second I singled one out and tried to aim, others would come racing straight for us, compelling me to switch round to face them, only to find them swerve with a dart or a mighty bound when within a few paces of me.

What Jock was doing during that time I do not know. It was all such a whirl of excitement and confusion that there are only a few clear impressions left on my mind. One is of a buck coming through the air right at me, jumping over the backs of two others racing across my front. I can see now the sudden wriggle of its body and the look of terror in its eyes when it saw me and realised that it was going to land almost at my feet. I tried to jump aside, but it was not necessary: with one touch on the ground it shot slantingly past me like a ricochet bullet. Another picture that always comes back is that of a splendid ram clearing the first of the dense thorn bushes that were to have been my cover in stalking. He flew over it outlined against the sky in the easiest most graceful and most perfect curve imaginable. It came back to me afterwards that he was eight or ten yards from me, and yet I had to look up into the sky to see his white chest and gracefully gathered feet as he cleared the thorn bush like a soaring bird.

One shot, out of three or four fired in desperation as they were melting away, hit something; the unmistakable thud of the bullet told me so. That time it was the real thing, and when you hear the real thing you cannot mistake it. The wounded animal went off with the rest and I followed, with Jock ahead of me hot on the trail. A hundred yards further on where Jock with his nose to the ground had raced along between some low stones and a marula tree I came to a stop—bush all round me, not a living thing in sight, and all as silent as the grave. On one of the smooth hot stones there was a big drop of blood, and a few yards on I found a couple more. Here and there along the spoor there were smears on the long yellow grass, and it was clear enough, judging by the height of the blood-marks from the ground, that the impala was wounded in the body—probably far back, as there were no frothy bubbles to show a lung shot. I knew that it would be a long chase unless Jock could head the buck off and bay it; but unless he could do this at once, he was so silent in his work that there was little chance of finding him. The trail became more and more difficult to follow; the blood was less

162

frequent, and the hot sun dried it so quickly that it was more than I could do to pick it out from the red streaks on the grass and many coloured leaves. So I gave it up and sat down to smoke and wait.

Half an hour passed, and still no Jock. Then I wandered about whistling and calling for him— calling until the sound of my own voice became quite uncanny, the only sound in an immense silence. Two hours passed in useless calling and listening, searching and waiting, and then I gave it up altogether and made back for the waggons, trying to hope against my real conviction that Jock had struck the road somewhere and had followed it to the outspan, instead of coming back on his own trail through the bush to me.

But there was no Jock at the waggons; and my heart sank, although I was not surprised. It was nearly four hours since he had disappeared, and it was as sure as anything could be that something extraordinary must have happened or he would have come back to me long before this. No one at the waggons had seen him since we started out together; and there was nothing to be done but to wait and see what would happen. It was perfectly useless to look for him: if alive and well, he was better able to find his way than the best tracker that ever lived; if dead or injured and unable to move, there was not one chance in a million of finding him.

There was only one kaffir whom Jock would take any notice of or would allow to touch him—a great big Zulu named Jim Makokel'. Jim was one of the

163

real fighting Zulu breed; and the pride he took in Jock, and the sort of partnership that he claimed in tastes, disposition and exploits, began the day Jock fought the table-leg and grew stronger and stronger to the end. Jim became Jock's devoted champion, and more than once, as will be seen, showed that he would face man or beast to stand by him when he needed help.

This day when I returned to the waggons Jim was sitting with the other drivers in the group round the big pot of porridge. I saw him give one quick look my way and heard him say sharply to the others, "Where is the dog? Where is Jock?" He stood there looking at me with a big wooden spoon full of porridge stopped on the way to his mouth. In a few minutes they all knew what had happened; the other boys took it calmly, saying composedly that the dog would find his way back. But Jim was not calm: it was not his nature. At one moment he would agree with them, swamping them with a flood of reasons why Jock, the best dog in the world, would be sure to come back; and the next—hot with restless excitement—would picture all that the dog might have been doing and all that he might still have to face, and then break off to proclaim loudly that every one ought to go out and hunt for him. Jim was not practical or reasonable—he was too excitable for that; but he was very loyal, and it was his way to show his feelings by doing something—generally and preferably by fighting some one. Knowing only too well how useless it would be to search for Jock, I lay down under the waggon to rest and wait.

After half an hour of this Jim could restrain himself no longer. He came over to where I lay and with a look of severe disapproval and barely controlled indignation, asked me for a gun, saying that he himself meant to go out and look for Jock. It would be nearer the mark to say that he demanded a gun. He was so genuinely anxious and so indignant at what he considered my indifference that it was impossible to be angry; and I let him talk away to me and at me in his exciting bullying way. He would take no answer and listen to no reason; so finally to keep him quiet I gave him the shot-gun, and off he went, muttering his opinions of every one else—a great springy striding picture of fierce resolution.

He came back nearly three hours later, silent, morose, hot and dusty. He put the gun down beside me without a word—just a click of disgust; and as he strode across to his waggon, called roughly to one of the drivers for the drinking water. Lifting the bucket to his mouth he drank like an ox and slammed it down again without a word of thanks; then sat down in the shade of the waggon, filled his pipe, and smoked in silence.

The trekking hour came and passed; but we did not move. The sun went down, and in the quiet of the evening we heard the first jackal's yapping—the first warning of the night. There were still lions and tigers in those parts, and any number of hyenas and wild dogs, and the darker it grew and the more I thought of it, the more hopeless seemed Jock's chance of getting through a night in the bush trying to work his way back to the waggons.

165

It was almost dark when I was startled by a yell from Jim Makokel', and looking round, saw him bound out into the road shouting, "He has come, he has come! What did I tell you?" He ran out to Jock, stooping to pat and talk to him, and then in a lower voice and with growing excitement went on rapidly, "See the blood! See it! He has fought: he has killed! Dog of all dogs! Jock, Jock!" and his savage song of triumph broke off in a burst of rough tenderness, and he called the dog's name five or six times with every note of affection and welcome in his deep voice. Jock took no notice of Jim's dancing out to meet him, nor of his shouts, endearments and antics; slowing his tired trot down to a walk, he came straight on to me, flickered his ears a bit, wagged his tail cordially, and gave my hand a splashy lick as I patted him. Then he turned round in the direction he had just come from, looked steadily out, cocked his ears well up, and moved his tail slowly from side to side. For the next half-hour or so he kept repeating this action every few minutes; but even without that I knew that it had been no wild-goose chase, and that miles away in the bush there was something lying dead which he could show me if I would but follow him back again to see.

What had happened in the eight hours since he had dashed off in pursuit can only be guessed. That he had pulled down the impala and killed it seemed certain—and what a chase and what a fight it must have been to take all that time! The buck could not have been so badly wounded in the body as to be disabled or it would have died in far less time than that: then, what a fight it must have been to kill an animal six or eight times his own weight and armed with such horns and hoofs! But was it only the impala? or had the hyenas and wild dogs followed up the trail, as they so often do, and did Jock have to fight his way through them too?

He was hollow-flanked and empty, parched with thirst, and so blown that his breath still caught in suffocating chokes. He was covered with blood and sand; his beautiful golden coat was dark and stained; his white front had disappeared; and there on his chest and throat, on his jaws and ears, down his front legs even to the toes, the blood was caked on him— mostly black and dried but some still red and sticky. He was a little lame in one fore-leg, but there was no cut or swelling to show the cause. There was only one mark to be seen: over his right eye there was a bluish line where the hair had been shaved off clean, leaving the skin smooth and unbroken. What did it? Was it horn, hoof, tooth, or—what? Only Jock knew.

Hovering round and over me, pacing backwards and forwards between the waggons like a caged animal, Jim, growing more and more excited, filled the air with his talk, his shouts and savage song. Wanting to help, but always in the way, ordering and thrusting the other boys here and there, he worked himself up into a wild frenzy: it was the Zulu fighting blood on fire and he 'saw red' everywhere.

167

I called for water. "Water!" roared Jim, "bring water"; and glaring round he made a spring—stick in hand—at the nearest kaffir. The boy fled in terror, with Jim after him for a few paces, and brought a bucket of water. Jim snatched it from him and with a resounding thump on the ribs sent the unlucky kaffir sprawling on the ground. Jock took the water in great gulpy bites broken by pauses to get his breath again; and Jim paced up and down—talking, talking, talking! Talking to me, to the others, to the kaffirs, to Jock, to the world at large, to the heavens, and to the dead. His eyes glared like a wild beast's and gradually little seams of froth gathered in the corners of his mouth as he poured out his cataract of words, telling of all Jock had done and might have done and would yet do; comparing him with the fighting heroes of his own race, and wandering off into vivid recitals of single episodes and great battles; seizing his sticks, shouting his war cries, and going through all the mimicry of fight with the wild frenzy of one possessed. Time after time I called him, and tried to quiet him; but he was beyond control.

Once before he had broken out like this. I had asked him something about the Zulu war; and that had started a flood of memories and excitement. In the midst of some description I asked why they killed the children; and he turned his glaring eyes on me and said, "Inkos, you are my Inkos; but you are white. If we fight to-morrow, I will kill you. You are good to me, you have

168

saved me; but if our own king says "Kill!" we kill! We see red; we kill all that lives. I must kill you, your wife, your mother, your children, your horses, your oxen, your dog, the fowls that run with the waggons —all that lives I kill. The blood must run." And I believed him; for that was the Zulu fighting spirit. So this time I knew it was useless to order or to talk: he was beyond control, and the fit must run its course.

The night closed in and there was quiet once more. The flames of the camp fires had died down; the big thorn logs had burnt into glowing coals like the pink crisp hearts of giant water-melons; Jock lay sleeping, tired out, but even in his sleep came little spells of panting now and then, like the after-sobs of a child that has cried itself to sleep; we lay rolled in our blankets, and no sound came from where the kaffirs slept. But Jim—only Jim—sat on his rough three-legged stool, elbows on knees and hands clasped together, staring intently into the coals. The fit worked slowly off, and his excitement died gradually away; now and then there was a fresh burst, but always milder and at longer intervals, as you may see it in a dying fire or at the end of a great storm; slowly but surely he subsided until at last there were only occasional mutterings of "Ow, Jock!" followed by the Zulu click, the expressive shake of the head, and that appreciative half grunt, half chuckle by which they pay tribute to what seems truly wonderful. He wanted no sleep that night: he sat on, waiting for the morning trek, staring into the red coals, and thinking

169

of the bygone glories of his race in the days of the mighty Chaka.

That was Jim, when the fit was on him—transported by some trifling and unforeseen incident from the humdrum of the road to the life he once had lived with splendid recklessness.

JOCK'S NIGHT·OUT

JOCK was lost twice: that is to say, he was lost to me, and, as I thought, for ever. It came about both times through his following up wounded animals and leaving me behind, and happened in the days when our hunting was all done on foot; when I could afford a horse and could keep pace with him that difficulty did not trouble us. The experience with the impala had made me very careful not to let him go unless I felt sure that the game was hard hit and that he would be able to pull it down or bay it. But it is not always easy to judge that. A broken leg shows at once; but a body shot is very difficult to place, and animals shot through the lungs, and even through the lower part of the heart, often go away at a cracking pace and are out of sight in no time, perhaps to keep it up for miles, perhaps to drop dead within a few minutes.

After that day with the impala we had many good days together and many hard ones: we had our disappointments, but we had our triumphs; and we were both getting to know our way about by degrees. Buck of many kinds had fallen to us; but so far as I

171

was concerned there was one disappointment that was not to be forgotten. The picture of that koodoo bull as he appeared for the last time looking over the ant-heap the day we were lost was always before me. I could not hear the name or see the spoor of koodoo without a pang of regret and the thought that never again would such a chance occur. Koodoo, like other kinds of game, were not to be found everywhere: they favoured some localities more than others, and when we passed through their known haunts chances of smaller game were often neglected in the hope of coming across the koodoo.

I could not give up whole days to hunting—for we had to keep moving along with the waggons all the time—or it would have been easy enough in many parts to locate the koodoo and make sure of getting a good bag. As it was, on three or four occasions we did come across them, and once I got a running shot, but missed. This was not needed to keep my interest in them alive, but it made me keener than ever. Day by day I went out always hoping to get my chance, and when at last the chance did come it was quite in accordance with the experience of many others that it was not in the least expected.

The great charm of Bushveld hunting is its variety: you never know what will turn up next—the only certainty being that it will not be what you are expecting.

The herd boy came  in one afternoon to say that there was a stembuck feeding among the oxen only a couple of hundred yards away. He had been quite close to it, he said, and it was very tame. Game, so readily alarmed by the sight of white men, will often take no notice of natives, allowing them to approach to very close quarters. They are also easily stalked under cover of cattle or horses, and much more readily approached on horseback than on foot. The presence of other animals seems to give them confidence or to excite mild curiosity without alarm, and thus distract attention from the man. In this case the bonny little red-brown fellow was not a bit scared; he maintained his presence of mind admirably; from time to time he turned his head our way and, with his large but shapely and most sensitive ears thrown forward, examined us frankly while he moved slightly one way or another so as to keep under cover of the oxen and busily continue his browsing.

In and out among some seventy head of cattle we played hide-and-seek for quite a while—I not daring to fire for fear of hitting one of the bullocks—until at last he found himself manœuvred out of the troop; and then without giving me a chance he was off into the bush in a few frisky skips. I followed quietly, knowing that as he was on the feed and not scared he would not go far.

Moving along silently under good cover I reached a thick scrubby bush and peered over the top of it to search the grass under the surrounding thorn trees for the little red-brown form. I was looking about low down in the russety grass—for he was only about

173

twice the size of Jock, and not easy to spot—when a movement on a higher level caught my eye. It was just the flip of a fly-tickled ear; but it was a movement where all else was still, and instantly the form of a koodoo cow appeared before me as a picture is thrown on a screen by a magic-lantern. There it stood within fifty yards, the soft grey-and-white looking still softer in the shadow of the thorns, but as clear to me—and as still—as a figure carved in stone. The stem of a mimosa hid the shoulders, but all the rest was plainly visible as it stood there utterly unconscious of danger. The tree made a dead shot almost impossible, but the risk of trying for another position was too great, and I fired. The thud of the bullet and the tremendous bound of the koodoo straight up in the air told that the shot had gone home; but these things were for a time forgotten in the surprise that followed. At the sound of the shot twenty other koodoo jumped into life and sight before me. The one I had seen and shot was but one of a herd all dozing peacefully in the shade, and strangest of all, it was the one that was furthest from me. To the right and left of this one, at distances from fifteen to thirty yards from me, the magnificent creatures had been standing, and I had not seen them; it was the flicker of this one's ear alone that had caught my eye. My bewilderment was complete when I saw the big bull of the herd start off twenty yards on my right front and pass away like a streak in a few sweeping strides. It was a matter of seconds only, and they were all out of sight—all except the wounded one, which had turned off from the others.

174

For all the flurry and confusion I had not lost sight of her, and noting her tucked-up appearance and shortened strides set Jock on her trail, believing that she would be down in a few minutes.

It is not necessary to go over it all again. it was much the same as the impala chase. I came back tired, disappointed and beaten, and without Jock. It was only after darkness set in that things began to look serious. When it came to midnight, with the camp wrapped in silence and in sleep, and there was still no sign of Jock, things looked very black indeed.

I heard his panting breath before it was possible to see anything. It was past one o'clock when he returned.

* * * * *

As we had missed the night trek to wait for Jock I decided to stay on where we were until the next evening and to have another try for the wounded koodoo, with the chance of coming across the troop again.

By daybreak Jock did not seem much the worse for his night's adventures—whatever they were. There were no marks of blood on him this time; there were some scratches which might have been caused by thorns during the chase, and odd-looking grazes on both hind-quarters near the hip-bones, as though he had been roughly gravelled there. He seemed a little stiff, and flinched when I pressed his sides and muscles, but he was as game as ever when he saw the rifle taken down.

175

The koodoo had been shot through the body, and even without being run to death by Jock must have died in the night, or have lain down and become too cold and stiff to move. If not discovered by wild animals there was a good chance of finding it untouched in the early morning; but after sunrise every minute's delay meant fresh risk from the aasvogels. There is very little which, if left uncovered, will escape their eyes. You may leave your buck for help to bring the meat in, certain from the most careful scrutiny that there is not one of these creatures in sight, and return in half an hour to find nothing but a few bones, the horns and hoofs, a rag of skin, and a group of disgusting gorged vultures squatting on a patch of ground all smeared, torn and feather-strewn from their voracious struggles.

In the winter sky unrelieved by the least fleck of cloud—a dome of spotless polished steel—nothing, you would think, can move unseen. Yet they are there. In the early morning, from their white-splashed eyries on some distant mountain they slide off like a launching ship into their sea of blue, and, striking the currents of the upper air, sweep round and upwards in immense circles, their huge motionless wings carrying them higher and higher until they are lost to human sight. Lie on your back in some dense shade where no side-lights strike in, but where an opening above forms a sort of natural telescope to the sky, and you may see tiny specks where nothing could be seen before. Take your field-glasses: the specks are vultures circling up on high! Look again, and far, far above you will see still other specks; and for

176

aught you know there may be others still beyond. How high are they? And what can they see from there? Who knows? But this is sure, that within a few minutes scores will come swooping down in great spiral rushes where not one was visible before. My own belief is that they watch each other, tier above tier, away into the limitless heavens—watching jealously, as hungry dogs do, for the least suspicious sign—to swoop down and share the spoil.

In the dewy cool of the morning we soon reached the place where Jock had left me behind the evening before; and from there on he led the way. It was much slower work then; as far as I was concerned, there was nothing to guide me, and it was impossible to know what he was after. Did he understand that it was not fresh game but the wounded koodoo that I wanted? And, if so, was he following the scent of the old chase or merely what he might remember of the way he had gone? It seemed impossible that scent could lie in that dry country for twelve hours; yet it was clearly nose more than eyes that guided him. He went ahead soberly and steadily, and once when he stopped completely, to sniff at a particular tuft of grass, I found out what was helping him. The grass was well streaked with blood: quite dry, it is true; still it was blood.

A mile or so on we checked again where the grass was trampled and the ground scored with spoor. The heavy spoor was all in a ring four or five yards in diameter; outside this the grass was also flattened, and there I found a dog's footprints. But it had no further interest for Jock; while I was examining it he

picked up the trail and trotted on. We came upon four or five other rings where they had fought. The last of these was curiously divided by a fallen tree, and it puzzled me to guess how they could have made a circle with a good-sized trunk some two feet high intersecting it. I examined the dead tree and found a big smear of blood and a lot of coarse greyish hair on it. Evidently the koodoo had backed against it whilst facing Jock and had fallen over it, renewing the fight on the other side. There were also some golden hairs sticking on the stumpy end of a broken branch, which may have had something to do with Jock's scraped sides.

Then for a matter of a hundred yards or more it looked as if they had fought and tumbled all the way. Jock was some distance ahead of me, trotting along quietly, when I saw him look up, give that rare growling bark of his—one of suppressed but real fury— lower his head, and charge. Then came heavy flapping and scrambling and the wind of huge wings, as twenty or thirty great lumbering aasvogels flopped along the ground with Jock dashing furiously about among them—taking flying leaps at them as they rose, and his jaws snapping like rat-traps as he missed them.

On a little open flat of hard-baked sand lay the stripped frame of the koodoo: the head and leg-bones were missing: meat-stripped fragments were scattered all about; fifty yards away among some bushes Jock found the head; and still further afield were remains of skin and thigh-bones crushed almost beyond recognition.

"WHAT HAD HAPPENED OUT IN THE SILENT
GHOSTLY BUSH THAT NIGHT?"

No aasvogel had done this: it was hyenas' work. The high-shouldered slinking brute, with jaws like a stone-crusher, alone cracks bones like those and bigger ones which even the lion cannot tackle. I walked back a little way and found the scene of the last stand, all harrowed bare; but there was no spoor of koodoo or of Jock to be seen there—only prints innumerable of wild dogs, hyenas and jackals, and some traces of where the carcass, no doubt already half-eaten, had been dragged by them in the effort to tear it asunder.

Jock had several times shown that he strongly objected to any interference with his quarry; other dogs, kaffirs, and even white men, had suffered or been badly scared for rashly laying hands on what he had pulled down. Without any doubt he had expected to find the koodoo there and had dealt with the aasvogels as trespassers; otherwise he would not have tackled them without word from me. It was also sure that until past midnight he had been there with the koodoo, watching or fighting. Then when had the hyenas and wild dogs come? That was the question I would have given much to have had answered. But only Jock knew that!

I looked at him. The mane on his back and shoulders which had risen at the sight of the vultures was not flat yet; he was sniffing about slowly and carefully on the spoor of the hyenas and wild dogs; and he looked 'fight' all over. But what it all meant was beyond me; I could only guess—just as you will— what had happened out in the silent ghostly bush that night.

THE·KOODOO·BULL

Jock had learned one very clever trick in pulling down wounded animals. It often happens when you come unexpectedly upon game that they are off before you see them, and the only chance you have of getting anything is with a running shot. If they go straight from you the shot is not a very difficult one, although you see nothing but the lifting and falling hind-quarters as they canter away; and a common result of such a shot is the breaking of one of the hind-legs between the hip and the hock. Jock made his discovery while following a rietbuck which I had wounded in this way. He had made several tries at its nose and throat, but the buck was going too strongly and was out of reach; moreover it would not stop or turn when he headed it, but charged straight on, bounding over him. In trying once more for the throat he cannoned against the buck's shoulder and was sent rolling yards away. This seemed to madden him: racing up behind he flew at the dangling leg, caught it at the shin, and thrusting his feet well out, simply dragged until the buck slowed down, and then began furiously tugging sideways. The crossing of the legs brought the wounded animal down immediately and Jock had it by the throat before it could rise again.

Every one who is good at anything has some favourite method or device of his own: that was Jock's. It may have come to him, as it comes to many, by accident; but having once got it, he perfected it and used it whenever it was possible. Only once he made a mistake; and he paid for it—very nearly with his life.

He had already used this device successfully several times, but so far only with the smaller buck. This day he did what I should have thought to be impossible for a dog of three or four times his size. I left the scene of torn carcass and crunched bones, consumed by regrets and disappointment; each fresh detail only added to my feeling of disgust, but Jock did not seem to mind; he jumped out briskly as soon as I started walking in earnest, as though he recognised that we were making a fresh start and he began to look forward immediately.

The little bare flat where the koodoo had fallen for the last time was at the head of one of those depressions which collect the waters of the summer floods and, changing gradually into shallow valleys, are eventually scoured out and become the dongas—dry in winter but full charged with muddy flood in summer—which drain the Bushveld to its rivers. Here and there where an impermeable rock formation crosses these

181

channels there are deep pools which, except in years of drought, last all through the winter; and these are the drinking-places of the game. I followed this one down for a couple of miles without any definite purpose until the sight of some greener and denser wild figs suggested that there might be water, and perhaps a rietbuck or a duiker near by. As we reached the trees Jock showed unmistakable signs of interest in something, and with the utmost caution I moved from tree to tree in the shady grove towards where it seemed the water-hole might be.

There were bushy wild plums flanking the grove, and beyond them the ordinary scattered thorns. As I reached this point, and stopped to look out between the bushes on to the more open ground, a koodoo cow walked quietly up the slope from the water, but before there was time to raise the rifle her easy stride had carried her behind a small mimosa tree. I took one quick step out to follow her up and found myself face to face at less than a dozen yards with a grand koodoo bull. It is impossible to convey in words any real idea of the scene and how things happened. Of course it was only for a fraction of a second that we looked straight into each other's eyes; then, as if by magic, he was round and going from me with the overwhelming rush of speed and strength and weight combined. Yet it is the first sight that remains with me: the proud head, the huge spiral horns, and the wide soft staring eyes—before the wildness of panic had stricken them. The picture seems photographed on eye and brain, never to be forgotten. A whirlwind of

182

dust and leaves marked his course, and through
it I fired, unsteadied by excitement and hardly
able to see. Then the right hind-leg swung out
and the great creature sank for a moment, almost
to the ground; and the sense of triumph, the
longed for and unexpected success, 'went to my
head' like a rush of blood.

There had been no time to aim, and the shot—a
real snap shot—was not at all a bad one. It was
after that that the natural effect of such a meeting
and such a chance began to tell. Thinking it all out
beforehand does not help much, for things never
happen as they are expected to; and even months of
practice among the smaller kinds will not ensure a
steady nerve when you just come face to face with
big game—there seems to be too much at stake.

I fired again as the koodoo recovered himself, but
he was then seventy or eighty yards away and partly
hidden at times by trees and scrub. He struck up the
slope, following the line of the troop through the
scattered thorns, and there, running hard and dropping quickly to my knee for steadier aim, I fired
again and again—but each time a longer shot and
more obscured by the intervening bush; and no tell-
tale thud came back to cheer me on.

Forgetting the last night's experience, forgetting
everything except how we had twice chased and twice
lost them, seeing only another and the grandest prize
slipping away, I sent Jock on and followed as fast as
I could. Once more the koodoo came in sight—just
a chance at four hundred yards as he reached an open

183

space on rising ground. Jock was already closing up, but still unseen, and the noble old fellow turned full broadside to me as he stopped to look back. Once more I knelt, gripping hard and holding my breath to snatch a moment's steadiness, and fired; but I missed again, and as the bullet struck under him he plunged forward and disappeared over the rise at the moment that Jock, dashing out from the scrub, reached his heels.

The old Martini carbine had one bad fault; even I could not deny that; years of rough and careless treatment in all sorts of weather—for it was only a discarded old Mounted Police weapon—had told on it, and both in barrel and breech it was well pitted with rust scars. One result of this was that it was always jamming, and unless the cartridges were kept well greased the empty shells would stick and the ejector fail to work; and this was almost sure to happen when the carbine became hot from quick firing. It jammed now, and fearing to lose sight of the chase I dared not stop a second, but ran on, struggling from time to time to wrench the breach open.

Reaching the place where they had disappeared, I saw with intense relief and excitement Jock and the koodoo having it out less than a hundred yards away. The koodoo's leg was broken right up in the ham, and it was a terrible handicap for an animal so big and heavy, but his nimbleness and quickness were astonishing. Using the sound hind-leg as a pivot he swung round, always facing his enemy; Jock was in and out, here, there and everywhere, as a buzzing fly torments one on a hot day; and

184

indeed, to the koodoo just then he was the fly and nothing more; he could only annoy his big enemy, and was playing with his life to do it. Sometimes he tried to get round; sometimes pretended to charge straight in, stopping himself with all four feet spread—just out of reach; then like a red streak he would fly through the air with a snap for the koodoo's nose. It was a fight for life and a grand sight; for the koodoo, in spite of his wound, easily held his own. No doubt he had fought out many a life and death struggle to win and hold his place as lord of the herd and knew every trick of attack and defence. Maybe too he was blazing with anger and contempt for this persistent little gadfly that worried him so and kept out of reach. Sometimes he snorted and feinted to charge; at other times backed slowly, giving way to draw the enemy on; then with a sudden lunge the great horns swished like a scythe with a tremendous reach out, easily covering the spot where Jock had been a fraction of a second before. There were pauses too in which he watched his tormentor steadily, with occasional impatient shakes of the head, or, raising it to full height, towered up a monument of splendid and contemptuous indifference, looking about with big angry but unfrightened eyes for the herd— his herd—that had deserted him; or with a slight toss of his head he would walk limpingly forward, forcing the ignored Jock before him; then, interrupted and annoyed by a flying snap at his nose, he would spring forward and strike with the sharp cloven fore-foot—zip-zip-zip—at Jock as he landed. Any one of the vicious flashing stabs would have pinned him to the earth and finished him; but Jock was never there.

Keeping what cover there was I came up slowly behind them, struggling and using all the force I dared, short of smashing the lever, to get the empty cartridge out. At last one of the turns in the fight brought me in view, and the koodoo dashed off again. For a little way the pace seemed as great as ever, but it soon died away; the driving power was gone; the strain and weight on the one sound leg and the tripping of the broken one were telling; and from that on I was close enough to see it all. In the first rush the koodoo seemed to dash right over Jock—the swirl of dust and leaves and the bulk of the koodoo hiding him; then I saw him close abreast looking up at it and making furious jumps for its nose, alternately from one side and the other, as they raced along together. The koodoo, holding its nose high and well forward, as they do when on the move, with the horns thrown back almost horizontally, was out of his reach and galloped heavily on completely ignoring his attacks.

There is a suggestion of grace and poise in the movement of the koodoo bull's head as he gallops through the bush which is one of his distinctions above the other antelopes. The same supple balancing movement that one notes in the native girls bearing their calabashes of water upon their heads is seen in the neck of the koodoo, and for the same reason: the movements of the body are softened into mere

186

undulations, and the head with its immense spiral horns seems to sail along in voluntary company— indeed almost as though it were bearing the body below.

At the fourth or fifth attempt by Jock a spurt from the koodoo brought him cannoning against its shoulder, and he was sent rolling unnoticed yards away. He scrambled instantly to his feet, but found himself again behind: it may have been this fact that inspired the next attempt, or perhaps he realised that attack in front was useless; for this time he went determinedly for the broken leg. It swung about in wild eccentric curves, but at the third or fourth attempt he got it and hung on; and with all fours spread he dragged along the ground. The first startled spring of the koodoo jerked him into the air; but there was no let go now, and although dragged along the rough ground and dashed about among the scrub, sometimes swinging in the air, and sometimes sliding on his back, he pulled from side to side in futile attempts to throw the big animal. Ineffectual and even hopeless as it looked at first, Jock's attacks soon began to tell; the koodoo made wild efforts to get at him, but with every turn he turned too, and did it so vigorously that the staggering animal swayed over and had to plunge violently to recover its balance. So they turned this way and that, until a wilder plunge swung Jock off his feet, throwing the broken leg across the other one; then, with feet firmly planted, Jock tugged again, and the koodoo trying to regain its footing was tripped by the crossed legs and came down with a crash.

187

As it fell Jock was round and fastened on the nose; but it was no duiker, impala or rietbuck that he had to deal with this time. The koodoo gave a snort of indignation and shook its head: as a terrier shakes a rat, so it shook Jock, whipping the ground with his swinging body, and with another indignant snort and toss of the head flung him off, sending him skidding along the ground on his back. The koodoo had fallen on the wounded leg and failed to rise with the first effort; Jock while still slithering along the ground on his back was tearing at the air with his feet in his mad haste to get back to the attack, and as he scrambled up, he raced in again with head down and the little eyes black with fury. He was too mad to be wary, and my heart stood still as the long horns went round with a swish; one black point seemed to pierce him through and through, showing a foot out the other side, and a jerky twist of the great head sent him twirling like a tip-cat eight or ten feet up in the air. It had just missed him, passing under his stomach next to the hind-legs; but, until he dropped with a thud and, tearing and scrambling to his feet, he raced in again, I felt certain he had been gored through.

The koodoo was up again then. I had rushed in with rifle clubbed, with the wild idea of stunning it before it could rise, but was met by the lowered horns and unmistakable signs of charging, and beat a retreat quite as speedy as my charge.

It was a running fight from then on: the instant the koodoo turned to go Jock was on to the leg again,

188

and nothing could shake his hold. I had to keep at a respectful distance, for the bull was still good for a furious charge, even with Jock hanging on, and eyed me in the most unpromising fashion whenever I attempted to head it off or even to come close up.

The big eyes were bloodshot then, but there was no look of fear in them—they blazed with baffled rage. Impossible as it seemed to shake Jock off or to get away from us, and in spite of the broken leg and loss of blood, the furious attempts to beat us off did not slacken. It was a desperate running fight, and right bravely he fought it to the end.

Partly barring the way in front were the whitened trunks and branches of several trees struck down by some storm of the year before, and running ahead of the koodoo I made for these, hoping to find a stick straight enough for a ramrod to force the empty cartridge out. As I reached them the koodoo made for me with half a dozen plunges that sent me flying off for other cover; but the broken leg swayed over one of the branches, and Jock with feet planted against the tree hung on; and the koodoo, turning furiously on him, stumbled, floundered, tripped, and came down with a crash amongst the crackling wood. Once more like a flash Jock was over the fallen body and had fastened on the nose—but only to be shaken worse than before. The koodoo literally flogged the ground with him, and for an instant I shut my eyes; it seemed as if the plucky dog would be beaten into pulp. The bull tried to chop him with

189

its fore-feet, but could not raise itself enough, and at each pause, Jock, with his watchful little eyes ever on the alert, dodged his body round to avoid the chopping feet without letting go his hold. Then with a snort of fury the koodoo, half-rising, gave its head a wild upward sweep, and shook. As a springing rod flings a fish, the koodoo flung Jock over its head and on to a low flat-topped thorn tree behind. The dog somer-saulted slowly as he circled in the air, dropped on his back in the thorns some twelve feet from the ground, and came tumbling down through the branches. Surely the tree saved him, for it seemed as if such a throw must break his back. As it was he dropped with a sickening thump; yet even as he fell I saw again the scrambling tearing movement, as if he was trying to race back to the fight even before he reached ground. Without a pause to breathe or even to look, he was in again, and trying once more for the nose.

The koodoo lying partly on its side, with both hind-legs hampered by the mass of dead wood, could not rise, but it swept the clear space in front with the terrible horns, and for some time kept Jock at bay. I tried stick after stick for a ramrod, but without success; at last, in desperation at seeing Jock once more hanging to the koodoo's nose, I hooked the lever on to a branch and setting my foot against the tree wrenched until the empty cartridge flew out, and I went stag-gering backwards.

In the last struggle, while I was busy with

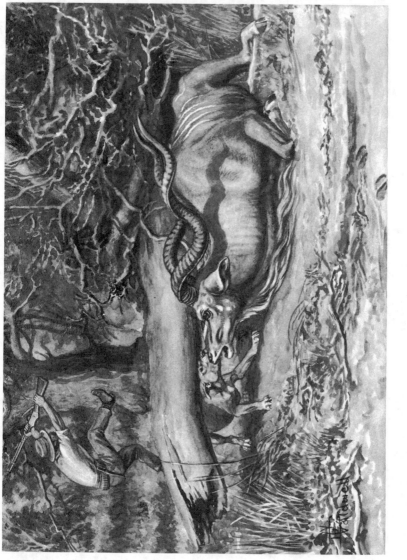

"HIS SHOULDER HUMPED AGAINST THE TREE, HE STOOD THE TUG OF WAR"

the rifle, the koodoo had moved, and it was then lying against one of the fallen trunks. The first swing to get rid of Jock had literally slogged him against the tree; the second swing swept him under it where a bend in the trunk raised it about a foot from the ground, and gaining his foothold there Jock stood fast—there, there, with his feet planted firmly and his shoulder humped against the dead tree, he stood this tug-of-war. The koodoo with its head twisted back, as caught at the end of the swing, could put no weight to the pull; yet the wrenches it gave to free itself drew the nose and upper lip out like tough rubber and seemed to stretch Jock's neck visibly. I had to come round within a few feet of them to avoid risk of hitting Jock, and it seemed impossible for bone and muscle to stand the two or three terrible wrenches that I saw. The shot was the end; and as the splendid head dropped slowly over, Jock let go his hold.

He had not uttered a sound except the grunts that were knocked out of him.

JIM·MAKOKEL·

JIM MAKOKEL' was Jock's ally and champion.
There was a great deal to like and something
to admire in Jim; but, taking him all round,
I am very much afraid that most people would
consider him rather a bad lot. The fact of the matter
is he belonged to another period and other conditions. He was simply a great passionate fighting
savage, and, instead of wearing the cast-off clothing
of the white man and peacefully driving bullock
waggons along a transport road, should have been
decked in his savage finery of leopard skin and black
ostrich feathers, showing off the powerful bronzed
limbs and body all alive with muscle, and sharing in
some wild war-dance; or, equipped with shield and
assegais, leading in some murderous fight. Yes, Jim
was out of date: he should have been one of the great
Chaka's fighting guard—to rise as a leader of men, or
be killed on the way. He had but one argument
and one answer to everything: Fight! It was his
nature, bred and born in him; it ran in his blood
and grew in his bones. He was a survival of a great

192

fighting race—there are still thousands of them in the kraals of Zululand and Swaziland—but it was his fate to belong to one of the expelled families, and to have to live and work among the white men under the Boer Government of the Transvaal.

In a fighting nation Jim's kraal was known as a fighting one, and the turbulent blood that ran in their veins could not settle down into a placid stream merely because the Great White Queen had laid her hand upon his people and said, "There shall be peace!" Chaka, the 'black Napoleon' whose wars had cost South Africa over a million lives, had died—murdered by his brother Dingaan—full of glory, lord and master wherever his impis could reach. "Dogs whom I fed at my kraal!" he gasped, as they stabbed him. Dingaan his successor, as cruel as treacherous, had been crushed by the gallant little band of Boers under Potgieter for his fiendish massacre of Piet Retief and his little band. Panda, the third of the three famous brothers—Panda the peaceful—had come and gone! Ketshwayo, after years of arrogant and unquestioned rule, had loosed his straining impis at the people of the Great White Queen. The awful day of 'Sandhlwana—where the 24th Regiment died almost to a man—and the fight on H'lobani Mountain had blooded the impis to madness; but Rorke's Drift and Kambula had followed those bloody victories—each within a few hours—to tell another tale: and at Ulundi the tides met—the black and the white. And the kingdom and might of the house of Chaka were no more.

193   O

Jim had fought at 'Sandhlwana, and could tell of an umfaan sent out to herd some cattle within sight of the British camp to draw the troops out raiding while the impis crept round by hill and bush and donga behind them; of the fight made by the redcoats as, taken in detail, they were attacked hand to hand with stabbing assegais, ten and twenty to one; of one man in blue—a sailor—who was the last to die, fighting with his back to a waggon wheel against scores before him, and how he fell at last, stabbed in the back through the spokes of the wheel by one who had crept up behind.

Jim had fought at Rorke's Drift! Wild with lust of blood, he had gone on with the maddest of the victory-maddened lot to invade Natal and eat up the little garrison on the way. He could tell how seventy or eighty white men behind a little rampart of biscuit-tins and flour-bags had fought through the long and terrible hours, beating off five thousand of the Zulu best, fresh from a victory without parallel or precedent; how, from the burning hospital, Sergeant Hook, V.C., and others carried sick and wounded through the flames into the laager; how a man in black with a long beard, Father Walsh, moved about with calm face, speaking to some, helping others, carrying wounded back and cartridges forward—Father Walsh, who said "Don't swear, boys: fire low"; how Lieutenants Chard and Bromhead—V.C.s too for that day's work—led and fought, and guided and heartened their heroic little band until the flour-bags and biscuit-tins stood lower than the pile of dead outside, and the Zulu host was beaten and Natal saved that day.

Jim had seen all that—and Ulundi, the Day of Despair! And he knew the power of the Great White Queen and the way that her people fight. But peace was not for him or his kraal: better any fight than no fight. He rallied to Usibepu in the fight for leadership when his King, Ketshwayo, was gone, and Jim's kraal had moved—and moved too soon: they were surrounded one night and massacred; and Jim fought his way out, wounded and alone. Without kith or kin, cattle, king, or country, he fled to the Transvaal—to work for the first time in his life!

Waggon-boys—as the drivers were called—often acquired a certain amount of reputation on the road or in the locality where they worked; but it was, as a rule, only a reputation as good or bad drivers. In Jim's case it was different. He was a character and had an individual reputation, which was exceptional in a kaffir. I had better say at once that not even his best friend would claim that that reputation was a good one. He was known as the best driver, the strongest nigger, the hardest fighter, and the worst drinker on the road.

His real name was Makokela, but in accordance with a common Zulu habit, it was usually abbreviated to Makokel'. Among a certain number of the white men —of the sort who never can get any name right—he was oddly enough known as McCorkindale. I called him

Jim as a rule—Makokel' when relations were strained. The waggon-boys found it safer to use his proper name. When anything had upset him it was not considered wise to take the liberty of shouting "Jim"; the answer sometimes came in the shape of a hammering.

Many men had employed Jim before he came to me, and all had 'sacked' him for fighting, drinking, and the unbearable worry he caused. They told me this, and said that he gave more trouble than his work was worth. It may have been true: he certainly was a living test of patience, purpose, and management; but, for something learnt in that way, I am glad now that Jim never 'got the sack' from me. Why he did not, is not easy to say; perhaps the circumstances under which he came to me and the hard knocks of an unkind fate pleaded for him. But it was not that alone: there was something in Jim himself—something good and fine, something that shone out from time to time through his black skin and battered face as the soul of a real man.

It was in the first season in the Bushveld that we were outspanned one night on the sand-hills overlooking Delagoa Bay among scores of other waggons dotted about in little camps—all loading or waiting for loads to transport to the Transvaal. Delagoa was not a good place to stay in, in those days: liquor was cheap and bad; there was very little in the way of law and order; and every one took care of himself as well as he could. The kaffir kraals were close about the town, and the natives of the place were as rascally a lot of thieves and vagabonds as you could find any-

196

where. The result was everlasting trouble with the waggon-boys and a chronic state of war between them and the natives and the banyans or Arab traders of the place. The boys, with pockets full of wages, haggled and were cheated in the stores, and by the hawkers, and in the canteens; and they often ended up the night with beer-drinking at the kraals or reprisals on their enemies. Every night there were fights and robberies: the natives or Indians would rob and half-kill a waggon-boy; then he in turn would rally his friends, and raid and clear out the kraal or the store. Most of the waggon-boys were Zulus or of Zulu descent, and they were always ready for a fight and would tackle any odds when their blood was up.

It was the third night of our stay, and the usual row was on. Shouts and cries, the beating of tom-toms, and shrill ear-piercing whistles, came from all sides; and through it all the dull hum of hundreds of human voices, all gabbling together. Near to us there was another camp of four waggons drawn up in close order, and as we sat talking and wondering at the strange babel in the beautiful calm moonlight night, one sound was ever recurring, coming away out of all the rest with something in it that fixed our attention. It was the sound of two voices from the next waggons. One voice was a kaffir's—a great, deep, bull-throated voice; it was not raised—it was monotonously steady and low; but it carried far, with the ring and the lingering vibration of a big gong.

"Funa 'nyama, Inkos; funa 'nyama!" ("I want meat, Chief; I want meat!") was what the kaffir's

voice kept repeating at intervals of a minute or two with deadly monotony and persistency.

The white man's voice grew more impatient, louder, and angrier with each refusal; but the boy paid no heed. A few minutes later the same request would be made, supplemented now and then with, "I am hungry, Baas, I can't sleep. Meat! Meat! Meat!"; or, "Porridge and bread are for women and picaninnies. I am a man: I want meat, Baas, meat." From the white man it was, "Go to sleep, I tell you!" "Be quiet, will you?" "Shut up that row!" "Be still, you drunken brute, or I'll tie you up!" and "You'll get twenty-five in a minute!"

It may have lasted half an hour when one of our party said, "That's Bob's old driver, the big Zulu. There'll be a row to-night; he's with a foreigner chap from Natal now. New chums are always roughest on the niggers."

In a flash I remembered Bob Saunderson's story of the boy who had caught the lion alive, and Bob's own words, "a real fine nigger, but a terror to drink, and always in trouble. He fairly wore me right out."

A few minutes later there was a short scuffle, and the boy's voice could be heard protesting in the same deep low tone: they were tying him up to the waggon-wheel for a flogging. Others were helping the white man, but the boy was not resisting.

At the second thin whistling stroke some one said, "That's a sjambok he's using, not a nek-strop!" Sjambok, that will cut a bullock's hide! At about the eighth there was a wrench that made the waggon rattle, and the deep voice was raised in protest, "Ow, Inkos!"

198

It made me choke: it was the first I knew of such things, and the horror of it was unbearable; but the man who had spoken before—a good man too, straight and strong, and trusted by black and white—said, "Sonny, you must not interfere between a man and his boys here; it's hard sometimes, but we'd not live a day if they didn't know who was baas."

I think we counted eighteen, and then everything seemed going to burst.

    *   *   *   *   *

The white man looked about at the faces close to him—and stopped. He began slowly to untie the outstretched arms, and blustered out some threats. But no one said a word!

    *   *   *   *   *

The noises died down as the night wore on, until the stillness was broken only by the desultory barking of a kaffir dog or the crowing of some awakened rooster who had mistaken the bright moonlight for the dawn and thought that all the world had overslept itself. But for me there was one other sound for which I listened into the cool of morning with the quivering sensitiveness of a bruised nerve. Sometimes it was a long catchy sigh, and sometimes it broke into a groan just audible, like the faintest rumble of most distant surf. Twice in the long night there came the same request to one of the boys near him, uttered in a deep clear unshaken voice and in

199

a tone that was civil but firm, and strangely moving from its quiet indifference.

"Landela manzi, Umganaam!" ("Bring water, friend!") was all he said; and each time the request was so quickly answered that I had the guilty feeling of being one in a great conspiracy of silence. The hush was unreal; the stillness alive with racing thoughts; the darkness full of watching eyes.

There is, we believe, in the heart of every being a little germ of justice which men call conscience! If that be so, there must have been in the heart of the white man that night some uneasy movement—the first life-throb of the thought which one who had not yet written has since set down:

> Though I've belted you and flayed you,
> By the living God that made you,
> You're a better man than I am, Gunga Din!

*   *   *   *   *

The following afternoon I received an ultimatum. We had just returned from the town when from a group of boys squatting round the fire there stood up one big fellow—a stranger—who raised his hand high above his head in Zulu fashion and gave their salute in the deep bell-like voice that there was no mistaking, "Inkos! Bayete!"

He stepped forward, looking me all over, and announced with calm and settled conviction, "I have come to work for you!" I said nothing. Then he rapped a chest like a big drum, and nodding his head with a sort of defiant confidence added in quaint

200

English, "My naam Makokela! Jim Makokel'! Yes!
My catchum lion 'live! Makokela, me!"

He had heard that I wanted a driver, had waited
for my return, and annexed me as his future 'baas'
without a moment's doubt or hesitation.

I looked him over. Big, broad-shouldered, loose-
limbed, and as straight as an assegai! A neck and
head like a bull's; a face like a weather-beaten rock,
storm-scarred and furrowed, rugged and ugly, but
steadfast, massive and strong! So it looked then, and
so it turned out: for good and for evil Jim was
strong.

I nodded and said, "You can come."

Once more he raised his head aloft, and, simply and
without a trace of surprise or gratification, said:

"Yes, you are my chief, I will work for you." In
his own mind it had been settled already: it had never
been in doubt.

Jim—when sober—was a splendid worker and the
most willing of servants, and, drunk or sober, he was
always respectful in an independent, upstanding,
hearty kind of way. His manner was as rough and
rugged as his face and character; in his most peaceful
moments it was—to one who did not understand him
—almost fierce and aggressive; but this was only skin
deep; for the childlike simplicity of the African
native was in him to the full, and rude bursts of
titanic laughter came readily—laughter as strong and
unrestrained as his bursts of passion.

To the other boys he was what his nature and
training had made him—not really a bully, but

201

masterful and overriding. He gave his orders with the curtness of a drill sergeant and the rude assurance of a savage chief. Walking, he walked his course, giving way for none of them. At the outspan or on the road or footpath he shouldered them aside as one walks through standing corn, not aggressively but with the superb indifference of right and habit unquestioned. If one, loitering before him, blocked his way unseeing, there was no pause or step aside—just "Suka!" ("Get out") and a push that looked effortless enough but sent the offender staggering; or, if he had his sticks, more likely a smart whack on the stern that was still more surprising; and not even the compliment of a glance back from Jim as he stalked on. He was like the old bull in a herd—he walked his course; none molested and none disputed; the way opened before him.

When sober Jim spoke Zulu; when drunk, he broke into the strangest and most laughable medley of kitchen-Kaffir, bad Dutch, and worse English—the idea being in part to consider our meaner intelligences and in part to show what an accomplished linguist he was. There was no difficulty in knowing when Jim would go wrong: he broke out whenever he got a chance, whether at a kraal, where he could always quicken the reluctant hospitality of any native, at a wayside canteen, or in a town. Money was fatal—he drank it all out; but want of money was no security, for he was known to every one and seemed to have friends everywhere; and if he had not, he made them on the spot—annexed and overwhelmed them.

From time to time you do meet people like that. The world's their oyster, and the gift of a masterful and infinite confidence opens it every time: they walk through life taking of the best as a right, and the world unquestionably submits.

I had many troubles with Jim, but never on account of white men: drunk or sober, there was never trouble there. It may have been Rorke's Drift and Ulundi that did it; but whatever it was, the question of black and white was settled in his mind for ever. He was respectful, yet stood upright with the rough dignity of an unvanquished spirit; but on the one great issue he never raised his hand or voice again. His troubles all came from drink, and the exasperation was at times almost unbearable—so great, indeed, that on many occasions I heartily repented ever having taken him on. Warnings were useless, and punishment—well, the shiny new skin that made patterns in lines and stars and crosses on his back for the rest of his life made answer for always upon that point.

The trials and worries were often great indeed. The trouble began as soon as we reached a town, and he had a hundred excuses for going in, and a hundred more for not coming out: he had some one to see, boots to be mended, clothes to buy, or medicine to get—the only illness I ever knew him have was 'a pain inside,' and the only medicine wanted—grog!

some one owed him money—a stock excuse, and the idea of Jim, always penniless and always in debt, posing as a creditor never failed to raise a laugh, and he would shake his head with a half-fierce half-sad disgust at the general scepticism and his failure to convince me. Then he had relations in every town! Jim, the sole survivor of his fighting kraal, produced 'blulus,' 'babas,' 'sisteles,' and even 'mamas,' in profusion, and they died just before we reached the place, as regularly as the office-boy's aunt dies before Derby Day, and with the same consequence—he had to go to the funeral.

The first precaution was to keep him at the waggons and put the towns and canteens 'out of bounds'; and the last defence, to banish him entirely until he came back sober, and meanwhile set other boys to do his work, paying them his wages in cash in his presence when he returned fit for duty.

"Is it as I told you? Is it just?" I would ask when this was done.

"It is just, Inkos," he would answer with a calm dispassionate simplicity which appealed for forgiveness and confidence with far greater force than any repentance; and it did so because it was genuine; it was natural and unstudied. There was never a trace of feeling to be detected when these affairs were squared off, but I knew how he hated the treatment, and it helped a little from time to time to keep him right.

The banishing of him from the waggons in order that he might go away and have it over was not a device to save myself trouble, and I did it only when it was clear that he could stand the strain no longer. It was simply a choice of evils, and it seemed to me better to let him go, clearly understanding the conditions, than drive him into breaking away with the bad results to him and the bad effects on the others of disobeying orders. It was, as a rule, far indeed from saving me trouble, for after the first bout of drinking he almost invariably found his way back to the waggons: the drink always produced a ravenous craving for meat, and when his money was gone and he had fought his fill and cleared out all opposition, he would come back to the waggons at any hour of the night, perhaps even two or three times between dark and dawn, to beg for meat. Warnings and orders had no effect whatever; he was unconscious of everything except the overmastering craving for meat. He would come to my waggon and begin that deadly monotonous recitation, "Funa 'nyama, Inkos! Wanta meat, Baas!" There was a kind of hopeless determination in the tone conveying complete indifference to all consequences: meat he must have. He was perfectly respectful; every order to be quiet or go away or go to bed was received with the formal raising of the hand aloft, the most respectful of salutations, and the assenting, "Inkos!" but in the very next breath would come the old monotonous request, "Funa 'nyama, Inkos," just as if he was saying it for the first time. The persistency was awful—it was maddening; and there was no remedy, for it was not the result of voluntary or even conscious effort on his part; it was a sort of automatic process, a result of his physical condition. Had he

205

known it would cost him his life, he could no more have resisted it than have resisted breathing.

When the meat was there I gave it, and he would sit by the fire for hours eating incredible quantities—cutting it off in slabs and devouring it when not much more than warmed. But it was not always possible to satisfy him in that way; meat was expensive in the towns and often we had none at all at the waggons. Then the night became one long torment: the spells of rest might extend from a quarter of an hour to an hour; then from the dead sleep of downright weariness I would be roused by the deep, far-reaching voice; "Funa 'nyama, Inkos" wove itself into my dreams, and waking I would find Jim standing beside me remorselessly urging the same request in Zulu, in broken English, and in Dutch—"My wanta meat, Baas," "Wil fleisch krij, Baas," and the old, old, hatefully familiar explanation of the difference between "man's food" and "picanins' food," interspersed with grandiose declarations that he was "Makokela—Jim Makokel'," who "catchum lion 'live." Sometimes he would expand this into comparisons between himself and the other boys, much to their disadvantage; and on these occasions he invariably worked round to his private grievances, and expressed his candid opinions of Sam.

Sam was the boy whom I usually set to do Jim's neglected work. He was a 'mission boy,' that is a Christian kaffir—very proper in his behaviour, but a weakling and not much good at work. Jim would enumerate all Sam's shortcomings; how he got his oxen mixed up on dark nights and could not pick them out of the herd—a quite unpardonable offence; how he stuck in the drifts and had to be 'double-spanned' and pulled out by Jim; how he once lost his way in the bush; and how he upset the waggon coming down the Devil's Shoot.

Jim had once brought down the Berg from Spitzkop a loaded waggon on which there was a cottage piano packed standing upright. The road was an awful one, it is true, and few drivers could have handled so top-heavy a load without capsizing—he had received a bansela for his skill—but to him the feat was one without parallel in the history of waggon driving; and when drunk he usually coupled it with his other great achievement of catching a lion alive. His contempt for Sam's misadventure on the Devil's Shoot was therefore great, and to it was added resentment against Sam's respectability and superior education, which the latter was able to rub in in safety by ostentatiously reading his Bible aloud at nights as they sat round the fire. Jim was a heathen, and openly affirmed his conviction that a Christian kaffir was an impostor, a bastard, and a hypocrite—a thing not to be trusted under any circumstances whatever. The end of his morose outburst was always the same. When his detailed indictment of Sam was completed he would wind up with "My catchum lion 'live. My bling panyanna fon Diskop (I bring piano from Spitzkop). My naam Makokela: Jim Makokel'. Sam no good; Sam leada Bible (Sam reads the Bible). Sam no good!" The intensity of conviction and the gloomy disgust put into the last reference to Sam are not to be expressed in words.

Where warning and punishment availed nothing, threats would have been worse than foolish. Once, when he had broken bounds and left the waggons, I threatened that if he did it again I would tie him up, since he was like a dog that could not be trusted; and I did it. He had no excuse but the old ones; some one, he said, had brought him liquor to the waggons and he had not known what he was doing. The truth was that the craving grew so with the nearer prospect of drink that by hook or by crook he would find some one, a passer-by or a boy from other waggons, to fetch some for him; and after that nothing could hold him.

If Jim ever wavered in his loyalty to me, it must have been the day I tied him up: he must have been very near hating me then. I had caught him as he was leaving the waggons and still sober; brought him back and told him to sit under his own waggon where I would tie him up like a dog. I took a piece of sail twine, tied it to one wrist, and, fastening the other end to the waggon-wheel, left him.

A kaffir's face becomes, when he wishes it, quite inscrutable—as expressionless as a blank wall. But there are exceptions to every rule; and Jim's stoicism was not equal to this occasion. The look of unspeakable disgust and humiliation on his face was more than I could bear with comfort; and after half an hour or so in the pillory I released him. He did not say a word, but, heedless of the hot sun, rolled himself in his blankets and, sleeping or not, never moved for the rest of the day. 208

THE·ALLIES

Jock disliked kaffirs: so did Jim. To Jim there were three big divisions of the human race—white men, Zulus and niggers. Zulu, old or young, was greeted by him as equal, friend and comrade; but the rest were trash, and he cherished a most particular contempt for the Shangaans and Chopis, as a lot who were just about good enough for what they did—that is, work in the mines. They could neither fight nor handle animals; and the sight of them stirred him to contempt and pricked him to hostilities.

It was not long before Jim discovered this bond of sympathy between him and Jock, and I am perfectly sure that the one bad habit which Jock was never cured of was due to deliberate encouragement from Jim on every possible opportunity. It would have been a matter of difficulty and patience in any case to teach Jock not to unnecessarily attack strange kaffirs. It was very important that he should have nothing to do with them, and should treat them with suspicion as possible enemies and keep them off the premises. I was glad that he did it by his own choice and instinct;

but this being so, it needed all the more intelligence and training to get him to understand just where to draw the line. Jim made it worse; he made the already difficult task practically impossible by egging Jock on; and what finally made it quite impossible was the extremely funny turn it took, which caused such general amusement that every one joined in the conspiracy and backed up Jock.

Every one knows how laughable it is to see a person dancing about like a mad dervish, with legs and arms going in all directions, dodging the rushes of a dog, especially if the spectator knows that the dog will not do any real harm and is more intent on scaring his victim, just for the fun of the thing, than on hunting him. Well, that is how it began.

As far as I know the first incident arose out of the intrusion of a strange kaffir at one of the outspans. Jock objected, and he was forcing a scared boy back step by step—doing the same feinting rushes that he practised with game—until the boy tripped over a camp stool and sat plump down on the three-legged pot of porridge cooking at the camp fire. I did not see it; for Jock was, as usual, quite silent—a feature which always had a most terrifying effect on his victims: it was a roar like a lion's from Jim that roused me. Jock was standing off with his feet on the move forwards and backwards, his head on one side and his face full of interest, as if he would dearly love another romp in; and the waggon-boys were reeling and rolling about the grass, helpless with laughter.

A dog is just as quick as a child to find out when he can take liberties; he knows that laughter and serious disapproval do not go together; and Jock with the backing of the boys thoroughly enjoyed himself. That was how it began; and by degrees it developed into the great practical joke. The curious thing to note was the way in which Jock entered into the spirit of the thing, and how he improved and varied his methods. It was never certain what he would do; sometimes it would be a wild romp, as it was that day; at other times he would stalk the intruder in the open, much as a pointer approaches his birds in the last strides, and with eyes fixed steadily and mouth tightly pursed up, he would move straight at him with infinite slowness and deliberation until the boy's nerve failed, and he turned and ran. At other times again he trotted out as if he had seen nothing, and then stopped suddenly. If the boy came on, Jock waited; but if there was any sign of fear or hesitation, he lowered his head, humped up his shoulders—as a stagey boxer does when he wants to appear ferocious—and gave his head a kind of chuck forward, as if in the act of charging: this seldom failed to shake the intruder's nerve, and as soon as he turned or backed, the romp began. Still another trick was to make a round in the bush and come up behind unobserved, and then make a furious dash with rumbly gurgly growls; the startled boy invariably dropped all he had, breaking into a series of fantastic capers and excited yells, to the huge delight of Jim and the others.

211

But these things were considered trifles: the piece that always 'brought the house down' was the Shangaan gang trick, which on one occasion nearly got us all into serious trouble. The natives going to or from the gold-fields travel in gangs of from four or five to forty or fifty; they walk along in Indian file, and even when going across the veld or walking on wide roads they wind along singly in the footsteps of the leader. What prompted the dog to start this new game I cannot imagine: certainly no one could have taught it to him; and as well as one could judge, he did it entirely 'off his own bat,' without anything to lead up to or suggest it.

One day a gang of about thirty of these Shangaans, each carrying his load of blankets, clothing, pots, billies and other valuables on his head, was coming along a footpath beside the road some twenty yards away from the waggons. Jock strolled out and sat himself down in the middle of the path; it was the way he did it and his air, utterly devoid of hostile or even serious purpose, that attracted my attention without rousing any doubts. The leader of the gang, however, was suspicious and shied off wide into the veld; he passed in a semicircle round Jock, a good ten yards away, and came safely back to the path again, and the dog with his nose in the air merely eyed him with a look of humorous interest and mild curiosity. The second kaffir made the loop shorter, and the third shorter still, as they found their alarm and suspicions unjustified; and so on, as each came along, the loop was lessened until they passed in safety

*"WITH HIS NOSE IN THE AIR EYED THEM
WITH MILD CURIOSITY"*

almost brushing against Jock's nose. And still he never budged—never moved—except, as each boy approached, to look up at his face and, slowly turning his head, follow him round with his eyes until he re-entered the path. There was something extremely funny in the mechanical regularity with which his head swung round. It was so funny that not only the boys at the waggons noticed it and laughed; the unsuspecting Shangaans themselves shared the joke. When half a dozen had passed round in safety, comments followed by grunts of agreement or laughter ran along the line, and then, as each fresh boy passed and Jock's calm inspection was repeated, a regular chorus of guffaws and remarks broke out. The long heavy bundles on their heads made turning round a slow process, so that, except for the first half-dozen, they were content to enjoy what they saw in front and to know by the laughter from behind that the joke had been repeated all down the line.

The last one walked calmly by; but as he did so there came one short muffled bark, "Whoop!" from Jock as he sprang out and nipped the unsuspecting Shangaan behind. The boy let out a yell that made the whole gang jump and clutch wildly at their toppling bundles, and Jock raced along the footpath, leaping, gurgling and snapping behind each one he came near, scattering them this way and that, in a romp of wild enjoyment. The shouts of the scared boys, the clatter of the tins as their bundles toppled down, the scrambling and scratching as they clawed the ground pretending to pick up stones or sticks to

213

stop his rushes, and the ridiculous rout of the thirty Shangaans in every direction, abandoning their baggage and fleeing from the little red enemy only just visible in the grass as he hunted and harried them, were too much for my principles and far too much for my gravity. To be quite honest, I weakened badly, and from that day on preferred to look another way when Jock sallied out to inspect a gang of Shangaans. Between them Jim and Jock had beaten me.

But the weakening brought its own punishment and the joke was not far from making a tragedy. Many times while lying some way off in the shade of a tree or under another waggon I heard Jim, all unconscious of my presence, call in a low deep voice, almost a whisper, "Jock; Jock: kaffirs; Shangaans!" Jock's head was up in a moment, and a romp of some sort followed unless I intervened. Afterwards, when Jock was deaf, Jim used to reach out and pull his foot or throw a handful of sand or a bunch of grass to rouse him, and when Jock's head switched up Jim's big black fist pointing to their common enemy was quite enough.

Jim had his faults, but getting others into mischief while keeping out of it himself was not one of them. If he egged Jock on, he was more than ready to stand by him, and on these occasions his first act was to jump for his sticks, which were always pretty handy, and lie in readiness to take a hand if any of the gang should use what he considered unfair means of defence, such as throwing stones and kerries, or using assegais or knives; and Jim—the friend of Jock, the avoided enemy of all Shangaans, aching for an excuse to take a hand in the row himself—was not, I fear, a very impartial judge.

There was a day outside Barberton which I remember well. We were to start that evening, and knowing that if Jim got into the town he might not be back and fit to work for days, I made him stay with the waggons. He lay there flat out under his waggon with his chin resting on his arms, staring steadily at the glistening corrugated iron roofs of the town, as morose and unapproachable as a surly old watch-dog. From the tent of my waggon I saw him raise his head, and following his glance, picked out a row of bundles against the sky-line. Presently a long string of about fifty time-expired mine-boys came in sight. Jim, on his hands and knees, scrambled over to where Jock lay asleep, and shook him; for this incident occurred after Jock had become deaf.

"Shangaans, Jock; Shangaans! Kill them; kill, kill, kill!" said Jim in gusty ferocious whispers. It must have seemed as if Fate had kindly provided an outlet for the rebellious rage and the craving for a fight that were consuming him.

As Jock trotted out to head them off Jim reached up to the buck-rails and pulled down his bundle of sticks and lay down like a tiger on the spring. I had had a lot of trouble with Jim that day, and this annoyed me; but my angry call to stop was unavailing. Jim, pretending not to understand, made no attempt to stop Jock, but contented himself with calling to him to come back; and Jock, stone deaf, trotted evenly

along with his head, neck, back, and tail, all level—an old trick of Jess's which generally meant trouble for some one. Slowing down as he neared the Shangaans he walked quietly on until he headed off the leader, and there he stood across the path. It was just the same as before: the boys, finding that he did nothing, merely stepped aside to avoid bumping against him. They were boys taking back their purchases to their kraals to dazzle the eyes of the ignorant with the wonders of civilisation—gaudy blankets, collections of bright tin billies and mugs, tin plates, three-legged pots, clothing, hats, and even small tin trunks painted brilliant yellow, helped to make up their huge bundles. The last boy was wearing a pair of Royal Artillery trousers, and I have no doubt he regarded it ever afterwards as nothing less than a calamity that they were not safely stowed away in his bundle—for a kaffir would sacrifice his skin rather than his new pants any day. It was from the seat of these too ample bags that Jock took a good mouthful; and it was the boy's frantic jump, rather than Jock's tug, that made the piece come out. The sudden fright and the attempts to face about quickly caused several downfalls; the clatter of these spread the panic; and on top of it all came Jock's charge along the broken line, and the excited shouts of those who thought they were going to be worried to death.

Jim had burst into great bellows of laughter and excited—but quite superfluous—shouts of encouragement to Jock, who could not have heard a trumpet at ten yards.

But there came a very unexpected change. One big Shangaan had drawn from his bundle a brand new side-axe: I saw the bright steel head flash, as he held it menacingly aloft by the short handle and marched towards Jock. There was a scrambling bound from under the waggon and Jim, with face distorted and grey with fury, rushed out. In his right hand he brandished a tough stout fighting stick; in his left I was horrified to see an assegai, and well I knew that, with the fighting fury on him, he would think nothing of using it. The Shangaan saw him coming, and stopped; then, still facing Jim, and with the axe raised and feinting repeatedly to throw it, he began to back away. Jim never paused for a second: he came straight on with wild leaps and blood-curdling yells in Zulu fighting fashion and ended with a bound that seemed to drop him right on top of the other. The stick came down with a whirr and a crash that crimped every nerve in my body; and the Shangaan dropped like a log.

I had shouted myself hoarse at Jim, but he heard or heeded nothing; and seizing a stick from one of the other boys I was already on the way to stop him, but before I got near him he had wrenched the axe from the kicking boy and, without pause, gone head-long for the next Shangaan he saw. Then everything went wrong: the more I shouted and the harder I ran, the worse the row. The Shangaans seemed to think I had joined in and was directing operations against them: Jim seemed to be inspired to wilder madness by my shouts and gesticulations; and Jock—well, Jock, at any rate had not the remotest doubt

as to what he should do. When he saw me and Jim in full chase behind him, his plain duty was to go in for all he was worth; and he did it.

It was half an hour before I got that mad savage back. He was as unmanageable as a runaway horse. He had walloped the majority of the fifty himself; he had broken his own two sticks and used up a number of theirs; on his forehead there was a small cut and a lump like half an orange; and on the back of his head another cut left by the sticks of the enemy when eight or ten had rallied once in a half-hearted attempt to stand against him.

It was strange how Jim, even in that mood, yielded to the touch of one whom he regarded as his 'Inkos.' I could not have forced him back: in that maniac condition it would have needed a powerful combination indeed to bring him back against his will. He yielded to the light grip of my hand on his wrist and walked freely along with me; but a fiery bounding vitality possessed him, and with long springy strides he stepped out—looking excitedly about, turning to right and left or even right about, and stepping sideways or even backwards to keep pace with me—yet always yielding the imprisoned arm so as not to pull me about. And all the time there came from him a torrent of excited gabble in pure Zulu, too fast and too high-flown for me to follow, which was punctuated and paragraphed by bursting allusions to 'dogs of Shangaans,' 'axes,' 'sticks,' and 'Jock.'

Near the waggons we passed over the 'battle-field,' and a huge guffaw of laughter broke from Jim as we came on the abandoned impedimenta of the defeated enemy. Several of the bundles had burst open from the violence of the fall, and the odd collections of the natives were scattered about; others had merely shed the outside luggage of tin billies, beakers, pans, boots and hats. Jim looked on it all as the spoils of war, wanting to stop and gather in his loot there and then, and when I pressed on, he shouted to the other drivers to come out and collect the booty.

But my chief anxiety was to end the wretched escapade as quickly as possible and get the Shangaans on their way again; so I sent Jim back to his place under the waggon, and told the cook-boy to give him the rest of my coffee and half a cup of sugar to provide him with something else to think of and to calm him down.

After a wait of half an hour or so, a head appeared just over the rise, and then another, and another, at irregular intervals and at various points: they were scouting very cautiously before venturing back again. I sat in the tent-waggon out of sight and kept quiet, hoping that in a few minutes they would gain confidence, collect their goods, and go their way again. Jim, lying flat under the waggon, was much lower than I was, and—continuing his gabble to the other boys—saw nothing. Unfortunately he looked round just as a scared face peered cautiously over the top of an ant-heap. The temptation was, I suppose, irresistible: he scrambled to his knees with a pretence of starting afresh and let out one ferocious yell that made my hair stand up; and in that second every head bobbed down and the field was deserted once more.

If this went on there could be but one ending: the police would be appealed to, Jim arrested, and I should spend days hanging about the courts waiting for a trial from which the noble Jim would probably emerge with three months' hard labour; so I sallied out as my own herald of peace. But the position was more difficult than it looked: as soon as the Shangaans saw my head appearing over the rise, they scattered like chaff before the wind, and ran as if they would never stop. They evidently took me for the advance guard in a fresh attack, and from the way they ran seemed to suspect that Jim and Jock might be doing separate flanking movements to cut them off. I stood upon an ant-heap and waved and called, but each shout resulted in a fresh spurt and each movement only made them more suspicious. It seemed a hopeless case, and I gave it up.

On the way back to the waggons, however, I thought of Sam—Sam, with his neatly patched European clothes, with the slouchy heavy-footed walk of a nigger in boots, with his slack lanky figure and serious timid face! Sam would surely be the right envoy; even the routed Shangaans would feel that there was nothing to fear there. But Sam was by no means anxious to earn laurels; he was clearly of the poet's view that "the paths of glory lead but to the grave"; and it was a poor-looking weak-kneed and much dejected scarecrow that dragged its way reluctantly out into the veld to hold parley with the routed enemy that day.

At the first mention of Sam's name Jim had twitched round with a snort, but the humour of the situation tickled him when he saw the too obvious reluctance with which his rival received the honour conferred on him. Between rough gusts of laughter Jim rained on him crude ridicule and rude comments; and Sam slouched off with head bent, relieving his heart with occasional clicks and low murmurs of disgust. How far the new herald would have ventured, if he had not received most unexpected encouragement, is a matter for speculation. Jim's last shout was to advise him not to hide in an ant-bear hole; but, to Sam's relief, the Shangaans seemed to view him merely as a decoy, even more dangerous than I was; for, as no one else appeared, they had now no idea at all from which quarter the expected attack would come. They were widely scattered more than half a mile away when Sam came in sight; a brief pause followed in which they looked anxiously around, and then, after some aimless dashes about like a startled troop of buck, they seemed to find the line of flight and headed off in a long string down the valley towards the river.

Now, no one had ever run away from Sam before, and the exhilarating sight so encouraged him that he marched boldly on after them. Goodness knows when, if ever, they would have stopped, if Sam had not met a couple of other natives whom the Shangaans had passed and induced them to turn back and reassure the fugitives.

221

An hour later Sam came back in mild triumph, at the head of the Shangaan gang; and, 'clothed in a little brief authority,' stood guard and superintended while they collected their scattered goods—all except the axe that caused the trouble. That they failed to find. The owner may have thought it wise to make no claim on me; Sam, if he remembered it, would have seen the Shangaans and all their belongings burned in a pile rather than raise so delicate a question with Jim; I had forgotten all about it—being anxious only to end the trouble and get the Shangaans off; and that villain Jim 'lay low.' At the first outspan from Barberton next day I saw him carving his mark on the handle, unabashed, under my very nose.

The next time Jim got drunk he added something to his opinion of Sam:

"Sam no good: Sam leada Bible! Shangaan, Sam; Shangaan!"

THE BERG

THE last day of each trip in the Bushveld was always a day of trial and hard work for man and beast. The Berg stood up before us like an impassable barrier. Looked at from below, the prospect was despairing—from above, appalling. There was no road that the eye could follow. Here and there a broad furrowed streak of red soil straight down some steep grass-covered spur was visible: it looked like a mountain timberslide or the scour of some tropical storm; and that was all one could see of it from below. For perhaps a week the towering bulwarks of the Highveld were visible as we toiled along—at first only in occasional hazy glimpses, then daily clearer higher and grander, as the great barrier it was.

After many hard treks through the broken foothills, with their rocky sideling slopes and boulderstrewn torrent beds, at last the Berg itself was reached. There, on a flat-topped terrace-like spur where the last outspan was, we took breath, halved our loads, doublespanned, and pulled ourselves together for the last big climb.

From there the scoured red streaks stood out revealed as road tracks—for made road there was none; from there, lines of whitish rock and loose stones and big boulders, that one had taken for the beds of mountain torrents, stood revealed as bits of 'road,' linking up some of the broken sections of the route; but even from there not nearly all the track was visible. The bumpy rumbling and heavy clattering of waggons on the rocky trail, the shouts of drivers and the crack of whips, mixed with confusing echoes from somewhere above, set one puzzling and searching higher still. Then in unexpected places here and there other waggons would be seen against the shadowy mountains, creeping up with infinite labour foot by foot, tacking at all sorts of angles, winding by undetected spur and slope and ridge towards the summit—the long spans of oxen and the bulky loads, dwarfed into miniature by the vast background, looking like snails upon a face of rock.

To those who do not know, there is not much difference between spans of oxen; and the driving of them seems merely a matter of brute strength in arm and lung. One span looks like another; and the weird unearthly yells of the drivers, the cracks—like rifle-shots—of the long lashes, and the hum and thud of the more cruel doubled whip, seem to be all that is needed. But it is not so; heart and training in the cattle, skill and judgment in the driver, are needed there; for the Berg is a searching test of man and beast. Some, double-spanned and relieved of half their

224

three-ton loads, will stick for a whole day where the pull is steepest, the road too narrow to swing the spans, and the curves too sharp to let the fifteen couples of bewildered and despairing oxen get a straight pull; whilst others will pass along slowly but steadily and without check, knowing what each beast will do and stand, when to urge and when to ease it, when and where to stop them for a blow, and how to get them all leaning to the yoke, ready and willing for the 'heave together' that is essential for restarting a heavy load against such a hill. Patience, understanding, judgment, and decision: those are the qualities it calls for, and here again the white man justifies his claim to lead and rule; for, although they are as ten or twenty to one, there is not a native driver who can compare with the best of the white men.

It was on the Berg that I first saw what a really first-class man can do. There were many waggons facing the pass that day; portions of loads, dumped off to ease the pull, dotted the roadside; tangles of disordered maddened spans blocked the way; and fragments of yokes, skeys, strops, and reims, and broken disselbooms, told the tale of trouble.

Old Charlie Roberts came along with his two waggons. He was 'old' with us—being nearly fifty; he was also stout and in poor health. We buried him at Pilgrim's Rest a week later: the cold, clear air on top of the Berg that night, when he brought the last load up, brought out the fever. It was his last trek.

He walked slowly up past us, to "take a squint at things," as he put it, and see if it was possible to get past the stuck waggons; and a little later he started, making three loads of his two and going up with single spans of eighteen oxen each, because the other waggons, stuck in various places on the road, did not give him room to work double spans. To us it seemed madness to attempt with eighteen oxen a harder task than we and others were essaying with thirty; we would have waited until the road ahead was clear.

We were half-way up when we saw old Charlie coming along steadily and without any fuss at all. He had no second driver to help him; he did no shouting; he walked along heavily and with difficulty beside the span, playing the long whip lightly about as he gave the word to go or called quietly to individual oxen by name, but he did not touch them; and when he paused to 'blow' them he leaned heavily on his whip-stick to rest himself. We were stopped by some break in the gear and were completely blocking the road when he caught up. Any one else would have waited: he pulled out into the rough sideling track on the slope below, to pass us. Even a good span with a good driver may well come to grief in trying to pass another that is stuck—for the sight and example are demoralising—but old Charlie did not turn a hair; he went steadily on, giving a brisker call and touching up his oxen here and there with light flicks. They used to say he could kill a fly on a front ox or on the toe of his own boot with the voorslag of his big whip.

"OLD CHARLIE COMING ALONG WITHOUT
ANY FUSS AT ALL"

The track he took was merely the scorings made by skidding waggons coming down the mountain; it was so steep and rough there that a pull of ten yards between the spells for breath was all one could hope for; and many were thankful to have done much less. At the second pause, as they were passing us, one of his oxen turned, leaning inwards against the chain, and looked back. Old Charlie remarked quietly, "I thought he would chuck it; only bought him last week. He's got no heart."

He walked along the span up to the shirking animal, which continued to glare back at him in a frightened way, and touched it behind with the butt of his long whip-stick to bring it up to the yoke. The ox started forward into place with a jerk, but eased back again slightly as Charlie went back to his place near the after oxen. Once more the span went on and the shirker got a smart reminder as Charlie gave the call to start, and he warmed it up well as a lesson while they pulled. At the next stop it lay back worse than before.

Not one driver in a hundred would have done then what he did: they would have tried other courses first. Charlie dropped his whip quietly and out-spanned the ox and its mate, saying to me as I gave him a hand:

"When I strike a rotter, I chuck him out before he spoils the others!" In another ten minutes he and his stalwarts had left us behind.

Old Charlie knew

his oxen—each one of them, their characters, and what they could do. I think he loved them too; at any rate, it was his care for them that day—handling them himself instead of leaving it to his boys—that killed him.

Other men had other methods. Some are by nature brutal; others, only undiscerning or impatient. Most of them sooner or later realise that they are only harming themselves by ill-treating their own cattle; and that is one—but only the meanest—reason why the white man learns to drive better than the native, who seldom owns the span he drives; the better and bigger reasons belong to the qualities of race and the effects of civilisation. But, with all this, experience is as essential as ever; a beginner has no balanced judgment, and that explains something that I heard an old transport-rider say in the earliest days—something which I did not understand then, and heard with resentment and a boy's uppish scorn.

"The Lord help the beginner's boys and bullocks: starts by pettin', and ends by killin'. Too clever to learn; too young to own up; swearin' and sloggin' all the time; and never sets down to *think* until the boys are gone and the bullocks done!"

I felt hot all over, but had learned enough to keep quiet; besides, the hit was not meant for me, although the tip, I believe, was: the hit was at some one else who had just left us—one who had been given a start before he had gained experience and, naturally, was then busy making a mess of things himself and laying

228

down the law for others. It was when the offender
had gone that the old transport-rider took up the
general question and finished his observations with a
proverb which I had not heard before—perhaps he
invented it:

"Yah!" he said, rising and stretching himself,
"there's no rule for a young fool."

I did not quite know what he meant, and it seemed
safer not to inquire.

The driving of bullocks is not an exalted occupation:
it is a very humble calling indeed; yet, if one is able to
learn, there are things worth learning in that useful
school. But it is not good to stay at school all one's
life.

Brains and character tell there as everywhere;
experience only gives them scope; it is not a substitute.
The men themselves would not tell you so; they never
trouble themselves with introspections and analyses,
and if you asked one of them the secret of success, he
might tell you "Commonsense and hard work," or
curtly give you the maxims "Watch it," and "Stick to
it"— which to him express the whole creed, and to
you, I suppose, convey nothing. Among themselves,
when the prime topics of loads, rates, grass, water
and disease have been disposed of, there is as much
interest in talking about their own and each other's
oxen as there is in babies at a mothers' meeting.
Spans are compared; individual oxen discussed in
minute detail; and the reputations of
'front oxen,' in pairs or singly, are
canvassed as earnestly as the import-

ance of the subject warrants—for, "The front oxen are half the span," they say. The simple fact is that they 'talk shop,' and when you hear them discussing the characters and qualities of each individual animal you may be tempted to smile in a superior way, but it will not eventually escape you that they think and observe, and that they study their animals and reason out what to do to make the most of them; and when they preach patience, consistency and purpose, it is the fruit of much experience, and nothing more than what the best of them practise.

Every class has its world; each one's world—however small—is a whole world, and therefore a big world; for the little things are magnified and seem big, which is much the same thing: Crusoe's island was a world to him and he got as much satisfaction out of it as Alexander or Napoleon—probably a great deal more. The little world is less complicated than the big, but the factors do not vary; and so it may be that the simpler the calling, the more clearly apparent are the working of principles and the relations of cause and effect. It was so with us. To you, as a beginner, there surely comes a day when things get out of hand and your span, which was a good one when you bought it, goes wrong: the load is not too heavy; the hill not too steep; the work is not beyond them for they have done it all before; but now no power on earth, it seems, will make them face the pull. Some jib and pull back; some bellow and thrust across; some stand out or swerve under the chain; some turn tail to front, half-choked by the twisted strops, the worn-out front oxen turn and charge downhill; and all are half-frantic with excitement, bewilderment or terror. The constant shouting, the battle with refractory animals, the work with the whip, and the hopeless chaos and failure, have just about done you up; and then some one—who knows—comes along, and, because you block the way where he would pass and he can see what is wrong, offers to give a hand. Dropping his whip he moves the front oxen to where the foothold is best and a straight pull is possible; then walks up and down the team a couple of times talking to the oxen and getting them into place, using his hand to prod them up without frightening them, until he has the sixteen standing as true as soldiers on parade —their excitement calmed, their confidence won, and their attention given to him. Then, one word of encouragement and one clear call to start, and the sixteen lean forward like one, the waggon lifts and heaves, and out it goes with a rattle and rush.

It looks magical in its simplicity; but no lecturer is needed to explain the magic, and if honest with yourself you will turn it over that night, and with a sense of vague discomfort it will all become clear. You may be tempted, under cover of darkness, to find a translation for 'watch it' and 'stick to it!' more befitting your dignity and aspirations: 'observation and reasoning,' 'patience and purpose,' will seem better; but probably you will not say so to any one else, for fear of being laughed at.

And when the new-found knowledge has risen like yeast, and is ready to froth over in advice to others,

certain things will be brought home to you with simple directness: that, sufficient unto the yeast is the loaf it has to make; that, there is only one person who has got to learn from you—yourself; and that, it is better to be still, for if you keep your knowledge to yourself you keep your ignorance from others.

A marked span brands the driver. The scored bullock may be a rogue or may be a sulky obstinate brute; but the chances are he is either badly trained or overworked, and the whip only makes matters worse; the beginner cannot judge, and the oxen suffer. Indeed, the beginner may well fail in the task, for there are many and great differences in the temperaments and characters of oxen, just as there are in other animals or in human beings. Once in Mashonaland, when lions broke into a kraal and killed and ate two donkeys out of a mixed lot, the mules were found next day twenty miles away; some of the oxen ran for several miles, and some stopped within a few hundred yards; two men who had been roused by the uproar saw in the moonlight one old bullock stroll out through the gap in the kraal and stop to scratch his back with his horn; and three others were contentedly dozing within ten yards of the half-eaten donkeys when we went to the kraal in the early morning and found out what had happened.

There are no two alike! You find them nervous and lethargic, timid and bold, independent and sociable, exceptional and ordinary, willing and sulky, restless and content, staunch and faint-hearted—

232

just like human beings. I can remember some of
them now far better than many of the men known
then and since: Achmoed and Bakir, the big
after-oxen who carried the disselboom contentedly
through the trek and were spared all other work
to save them for emergencies; who, at a word,
heaved together—their great backs bent like bows
and their giant strength thrown in to hoist the waggon
from the deepest hole and up the steepest hill; who
were the stand-by in the worst descents, lying back
on their haunches to hold the waggon up when brakes
could do no more; and inseparables always—even when
outspanned the two old comrades walked together.
There was little Zole, contented, sociable and short
of wind, looking like a fat boy on a hot day, always
in distress. There was Bantom, the big red ox with
the white band, lazy and selfish, with an enduring
evil obstinacy that was simply incredible. There was
Rooiland, the light red, with yellow eyeballs and
topped horns, a fierce, wild, unapproachable, unappeas-
able creature, restless and impatient, always straining
to start, always moaning fretfully when delayed,
nervous as a young thoroughbred, aloof and unfriendly
to man and beast, ever ready to stab or kick even those
who handled him daily, wild as a buck, but untouched
by whip and uncalled by name; who would work
with a straining, tearing impatience that there was no
checking, ever ready to outpace the rest, and at the
outspan, standing out alone, hollow flanked and panting, eyes and nostrils wide with fierceness and distress,
yet always ready to start again—a miracle of intense

233

vitality! And then there was old Zwaartland, the coal-black front ox, and the best of all: the sober, steadfast leader of the span, who knew his work by heart and answered with quickened pace to any call of his name; swinging wide at every curve to avoid cutting corners; easing up, yet leading free, at every steep descent, so as neither to rush the incline nor entangle the span; holding his ground, steady as a rock when the big pull came, heedless of how the team swayed and strained—steadfast even when his mate gave in. He stood out from all the rest; the massive horns—like one huge spiral pin passed through his head, eight feet from tip to tip—balancing with easy swing; the clean limbs and small neat feet moving with the quick precision of a buck's tread; and the large grey eyes so soft and clear and deep!

For those who had eyes to see the book lay open: there, as elsewhere; there, as always. Jock, with his courage, fidelity and concentration, held the secrets of success! Jim—dissolute, turbulent and savage—could yield a lesson too; not a warning only, sometimes a crude but clear example! The work itself was full of test and teaching; the hard abstemious life had its daily lessons in patience and resource, driven home by every variety of means and incident on that unkindly road. And the dumb cattle—in their plodding toil, in their sufferings from drought and over-work, and in their strength and weakness—taught and tested too. There is little food for self-content when all that is best and worst comes out; but there is much food for thought.

234

There was a day at Kruger's Post when everything seemed small beside the figure of one black front ox, who held his ground when all others failed. The waggon had sunk to the bed-plank in gluey turf, and, although the whole load had been taken off, three spans linked together failed to move it. For eight hours that day we tried to dig and pull it out, but forty-four oxen on that soft greasy flat toiled in vain. The long string of bullocks, desperate from failure and bewilderment, swayed in the middle from side to side to seek escape from the flying whips; the unyielding waggon held them at one end, and the front oxen, with their straining forefeet scoring the slippery surface as they were dragged backwards, strove to hold them true at the other. Seven times that day we changed, trying to find a mate who would stand with Zwaartland, but he wore them all down. He broke their hearts and stood it out alone! I looked at the ground afterwards: it was grooved in long parallel lines where the swaying spans had pulled him backwards, with his four feet clawing the ground in the effort to hold them true; but he had never once turned or wavered.

And there was a day at Sand River, when we saw a different picture. The waggons were empty, yet as we came up out of the stony drift, Bantom the sulky hung lazily back, dragging on his yoke and throwing the span out of line. Jim curled the big whip round him, without any good effect, and when the span stopped for a breather in the deep narrow road, he lay down and rerused to budge. There was no reason in the world for it except

235

the animal's obstinate sulky temper. When the whip —the giraffe-hide thong, doubled into a heavy loop— produced no effect, the boys took the yoke off to see if freedom would tempt the animal to rise! It did. At the first touch of the whip Bantom jumped up and charged them; and then, seeing that there was nothing at all the matter, the boys inspanned him and made a fresh start—not touching him again for fear of another fit of sulks; but at the first call on the team, down he went again.

Many are the stories of cruelty to oxen, and I had never understood how human beings could be so fiendishly cruel as to do some of the things that one heard of, such as stabbing, smothering and burning cattle; nor under what circumstances or for what reasons such acts of brutality could be perpetrated; but what I saw that day threw some light on these questions, and, more than anything else, it showed the length to which sulkiness and obstinacy will go, and made me wonder whether the explanation was to be sought in endurance of pain through temper or in sheer incapacity to feel pain at all. This is no defence of such things; it is a bare recital of what took place— the only scene I can recall of what would be regarded as wanton cruelty to oxen; and to that extent it is an explanation, and nothing more! Much greater and real cruelty I have seen done by work and punishment; but it was due to ignorance, impatience, or—on rare occasions—uncontrollable temper; it did not look deliberate and wanton.

There were two considerations here which governed the whole case. The first was that as long as the ox

236

lay there it was impossible to move the waggon, and there was no way for the others to pass it; the second, that the ox was free, strong and perfectly well, and all he had to do was to get up and walk.

The drivers from the other waggons came up to lend a hand and clear the way so that they might get on; sometimes three were at it together with their double whips; and, before they could be stopped, sticks and stones were used to hammer the animal on the head and horns, along the spine, on the hocks and shins, and wherever he was supposed to have feeling; then he was tied by the horns to the trek-chain, so that the span would drag him bodily; but not once did he make the smallest effort to rise. The road was merely a gutter scoured out by the floods and it was not possible either to drag the animal up the steep sides or to leave him and go on—the waggon would have had to pass over him. And all this time he was out-spanned and free to go; but would not stir.

Then they did the kaffir trick—doubled the tail and bit it; very few bullocks will stand that, but Bantom never winced. Then they took their clasp knives and used them as spurs—not stabbing to do real injury, but pricking enough to draw blood in the fleshy parts, where it would be most felt: he twitched to the pricks—but nothing more. Then they made a fire close behind him, and as the wood blazed up, the heat seemed unendurable; the smell of singed hair was strong, and the flames, not a foot away, seemed to roast the flesh, and one of the drivers took a brand and pressed the glowing red coal against the inside of the hams; but, beyond a vicious kick at the fire,

there was no result. Then they tried to suffocate him, gripping the mouth and nostrils so that he could not breathe; but, when the limit of endurance was reached and even the spectators tightened up with a sense of suffocation, a savage shake of the head always freed it—the brute was too strong for them. Then they raised the head with reims, and with the nose held high poured water down the nostrils, at the same time keeping the mouth firmly closed; but he blew the water all over them and shook himself free again.

For the better part of an hour the struggle went on, but there was not the least sign of yielding on Bantom's part, and the string of waiting waggons grew longer, and many others, white men and black, gathered round watching, helping or suggesting. At last some one brought a bucket of water, and into this Bantom's muzzle was thrust as far as it would go, and reims passed through the ears of the bucket were slipped round his horns so that he could not shake himself free at will. We stood back and watched the animal's sides for signs of breathing. For an incredible time he held out; but at last with a sudden plunge he was up; a bubbling muffled bellow came from the bucket; the boys let go the reims; and the terrified animal, ridding himself of the bucket after a frantic struggle, stood with legs apart and eyeballs starting from the sockets, shaking like a reed.

But nothing that had happened revealed the vicious ingrained obstinacy of the   animal's nature

so clearly as the last act in the struggle: it stood passive, and apparently beaten, while the boys inspanned it again. But at the first call to the team to start, and without a touch to provoke its temper again, it dropped down once more. Not one of all those looking on would have believed it possible; but there it was! In the most deliberate manner the challenge was again flung down, and the whole fight begun afresh.

We felt really desperate: one could think of nothing but to repeat the bucket trick; for it was the only one that had succeeded at all. The bucket had been flung aside on the stones as the ox freed itself, and one of the boys picked it up to fetch more water. But no more was needed: the rattle of the bucket brought Bantom to his feet with a terrified jump, and flinging his whole weight into the yoke, he gave the waggon a heave that started the whole span, and they went out at a run. The drivers had not even picked up their whips: the only incentive applied was the bucket, which the boy—grasping the position at once—rattled vigorously behind Bantom, doubling his frantic eagerness to get away, amid shouts of encouragement and laughter from the watching group.

The trials and lessons of the work came in various shapes and at every turn; and there were many trials where the lesson was not easy to read. It would have taken a good man to handle Bantom, at any time—even in the beginning; but, full-grown, and confirmed in his evil ways, only the butcher could make anything out of him.

And only the butcher did!

PARADISE · CAMP

THERE is a spot on the edge of the Berg which we made our summer quarters. When September came round and the sun swung higher in the steely blue, blazing down more pitilessly than ever; when the little creeks were running dry and the water-holes became saucers of cracked mud; when the whole country smelt of fine impalpable dust; it was a relief to quit the Bushveld, and even the hunting was given up almost without regret.

On the Berg the air was clear and bracing, as well it might be five to seven thousand feet above the sea. The long green sweeps of undulating country were broken by deep gorges where the mountain streams had cut their way through the up-tilted outer edge of the big plateau and tumbled in countless waterfalls into the Bushveld below; and behind the rolling downs again stood the remnants of the upper formation—the last tough fragments of those rocks which the miners believed originally held the gold —worn and washed away, inch by inch and ounce

240

by ounce ever since the Deluge. These broken parapets stood up like ruins of giant castles with every layer in their formation visible across their rugged time-worn fronts—lines, in places a few yards only and in others a mile or more in length, laid one upon another as true as any spirit level could set them— and a wealth of colouring over all that, day by day, one thought more wonderful in variety and blend. Grey and black and yellow, white and red and brown, were there; yet all harmonising, all shaded by growths of shrub and creeper, by festoons of moss or brilliant lichen, all weather-stained and softened, all toned, as time and nature do it, to make straight lines and many colours blend into the picturesque.

Paradise Camp perched on the very edge of the Berg. Behind us rolled green slopes to the feet of the higher peaks, and in front of us lay the Bushveld. From the broken battlements of the Berg we looked down three thousand feet, and eastward to the sea a hundred and fifty miles away, across the vast panorama. Black densely timbered kloofs broke the edge of the plateau into a long series of projecting turrets, in some places cutting far in, deep crevices into which the bigger waterfalls plunged and were lost. But the top of the Berg itself was bare of trees: the breeze blew cool and fresh for ever there; the waters trickled and splashed in every little break or tumbled with steady roar down the greater gorges; deep pools, fringed with masses of ferns, smooth as mirrors or flecked with dancing sunlight, were set like brilliants in the silver chain of each little stream; and rocks and pebbles, wonderful in their colours, were magnified and glorified into polished gems by the sparkling water.

But Nature has her moods, and it was not always thus at Paradise Camp. When the cold mist-rains, like wet grey fogs, swept over us and for a week blotted out creation, it was neither pleasant nor safe to grope along the edge of the Berg, in search of strayed cattle —wet and cold, unable to see, and checked from time to time by a keener straighter gust that leapt up over the unseen precipice a few yards off.

And there was still another mood when the summer rains set in and the storms burst over us, and the lightning stabbed viciously in all directions, and the crackling crash of the thunder seemed as if the very Berg itself must be split and shattered. Then the rivers rose; the roar of waters was all around us; and Paradise Camp was isolated from the rest by floods which no man would lightly face.

Paradise Camp stood on the edge of the kloof where the nearest timber grew; Tumbling Waters, where stood the thousand grey sandstone sentinels of strange fantastic shapes, was a couple of miles away facing Black Bluff, the highest point of all, and The Camel, The Wolf, The Sitting Hen, and scores more, rough casts in rock by Nature's hand, stood there. Close below us was the Bathing Pool, with its twenty feet of purest water, its three rock-ledge 'springboards,' and its banks of moss and canopies of tree ferns. Further down the stream spread in a thousand pools and rapids over a mile of black bedrock and then poured in one broad sheet over Graskop Falls. And still further down were the Mac Mac Falls, three hundred feet, straight drop into the rock-strewn gorge, where the straight walls were draped with staghorn moss, like countless folds of delicate green lace, bespangled by the spray. We were felling and slipping timber for the goldfields then, and it was in these surroundings that the work was done.

It was a Sunday morning, and I was lying on my back on a sack-stretcher taking it easy, when Jock gave a growl and trotted out. Presently I heard voices in the next hut and wondered who the visitors were—too lazily content to get up and see; then a cold nose was poked against my cheek and I looked round to see Jess's little eyes and flickering ears within a few inches of my face. For the moment she did not look cross, but as if a faint smile of welcome were flitting across a soured face; then she trotted back to the other hut where Ted was patting Jock and trying to trace a likeness to The Rat.

It was a long time since mother and son had been together, and if the difference between them was remarkable, the likeness seemed to me more striking still. Jock had grown up by himself and made himself; he was so different from other dogs that I had forgotten how much he owed to good old Jess; but now that they were once more side by side everything he did and had done recalled the likeness and yet showed the difference between them. Many times as we moved about the camp or worked in the woods they walked or stood together, sometimes sniffing along some spoor and sometimes waiting and watching

243

for us to come up—handsome son and ugly mother. Ugly she might be, with her little fretful hostile eyes and her uncertain ever-moving ears, and silent, sour and cross; but stubborn fidelity and reckless courage were hers too; and all the good Jock had in him came from Jess.

To see them side by side was enough: every line in his golden brindled coat had its counterpart in her dull markings; his jaw was hers, with a difference, every whit as determined but without the savage look; his eyes were hers—brown to black as the moods changed—yet not fretful and cross, but serenely observant, when quiet, and black, hot and angry, like hers, when roused—yet without the look of relentless cruelty; his ears were hers—and yet how different, not shifting, flickering and ever on the move, nor flattened back with the look of most uncertain temper, but sure in their movements and faithful reflectors of more sober moods and more balanced temper, and so often cocked—one full and one half—with a look of genuinely friendly interest which, when he put his head on one side, seemed to change in a curiously comical way into an expression of quiet amusement.

The work kept us close to camp and we gave no thought to shooting; yet Jess and Jock had some good sport together. We gave them courses for breathers after oribi in the open, but these fleetest of little antelopes left them out of sight in very few minutes. Bushbuck too were plentiful enough, but so wily in keeping to the dark woods and deep kloofs that unless we organised

244

a drive the only chance one got was to stalk them in the early morning as they fed on the fringes of the bush. I often wondered how the dogs would have fared with those desperate fighters that have injured and killed more dogs and more men than any other buck, save perhaps the sable.

Once they caught an ant-bear in the open, and there was a rough-and-tumble; we had no weapons—not even sticks—with us, and the dogs had it all to themselves. The clumsy creature could do nothing with them; his powerful digging claws looked dangerous, but the dogs never gave him a chance; he tried hard to reach his hole, but they caught him as he somersaulted to dodge them, and, one in front and one behind, worried the life out of him.

Once they killed a tiger-cat. We heard the rush and the row, and scrambled down through the tangled woods as fast as we could, but they fought on, tumbling and rolling downhill before us, and when we came up to them it was all over and they were tugging and tearing at the lifeless black and white body, Jess at the throat and Jock at the stomach. The cat was as big as either of them and armed with most formidable claws, which it had used to some purpose, for both dogs were torn and bleeding freely in several places. Still they thoroughly enjoyed it and searched the place afresh every time we passed it, as regularly as a boy looks about where he once picked up a sixpence.

Then the dainty little klipspringers led them many a crazy dance along the crags and ledges of the mountain face, jumping from rock to rock with

245

the utmost ease and certainty and looking down with calm curiosity at the clumsy scrambling dogs as they vainly tried to follow. The dassies too—watchful, silent and rubber-footed—played hide-and-seek with them in the cracks and crevices; but the dogs had no chance there.

Often there were races after baboons. There were thousands of them along the Berg, but except when a few were found in the open, we always called the dogs in. Among a troop of baboons the best of dogs would have no show at all. Ugly, savage and treacherous as they are, they have at least one quality which compels admiration—they stand by each other. If one is attacked or wounded the others will often turn back and help, and they will literally tear a dog to pieces. Even against one full-grown male a dog has little or no chance; for they are very powerful, quick as lightning, and fierce fighters. Their enormous jaws and teeth outmatch a dog's, and with four 'hands' to help them the advantage is altogether too great. Their method of fighting is to hold the dog with all four feet and tear pieces out of him with their teeth.

We knew the danger well, for there was a fighting baboon at a wayside place not far from us—a savage brute, owned by a still greater savage. It was kept chained up to a pole with its house on the top of the pole; and what the owner considered to be a good joke was to entice dogs up, either to attack the baboon or at least to come sniffing about within reach of it, and then see them worried to death. The excuse was always the same: "Your dog attacked the baboon. I can't help it." Sometimes the dogs were rescued by their owners; but many were killed. To its native cunning this brute added all the tricks that experience had taught, sometimes hiding up in its box to induce the dog to come sniffing close up; sometimes grubbing in the sand for food, pretending not to see the intruder until he was well within reach; sometimes running back in feigned alarm to draw him on. Once it got a grip the baboon threw itself on its side or back and, with all four feet holding the dog off, tore lumps out of the helpless animal. A plucky dog that would try to make a fight of it had no chance; the only hope was to get away, if possible.

Not every baboon is a fighter like this, but in almost every troop there will be at least one terrible old fellow, and the biggest, strongest, and fiercest always dominate and lead the others; and their hostility and audacity are such that they will loiter behind the retreating troop and face a man on foot or on horseback, slowly and reluctantly giving way, or sometimes moving along abreast, a hostile escort, giving loud roars of defiance and hoarse challenges as though ready on the least provocation or excuse to charge. It is not a pleasant position for an unarmed man, as at the first move or call from the leader the whole troop would come charging down again. It is not actual danger that impresses one, but the uncanny effect of the short defiant roars, the savage half-human look of the repulsive creatures, their still more human methods of facial expression and threatening attitudes, their tactics

247

in encircling their object and using cover to approach and peer out cautiously from behind it, and their evident co-operation and obedience to the leader's directions and example.

One day while at work in the woods there came to us a grizzled worn-looking old kaffir, whose head ring of polished black wax attested his dignity as a kehla. He carried an old musket and was attended by two youngsters armed with throwing-sticks and a hunting assegai each. He appeared to be a 'somebody' in a small way, and we knew at a glance that he had not come for nothing.

There is a certain courtesy and a good deal of formality observed among the natives which is appreciated by but few of the white men who come in contact with them. One reason for this failure in appreciation is that native courtesy is in its method and expression sometimes just the reverse of what we consider proper; and if actions which seem suggestive of disrespect were judged from the native's standpoint, and according to his code, there would be no misunderstanding. The old man, passing and ignoring the group of boys, came towards us as we sat in the shade for the midday rest, and slowly came to a stand a few yards off, leaning on his long flint-lock quietly taking stock of us each in turn, and waiting for us to inspect him. Then, after three or four minutes of this, he proceeded to salute us separately with "Sakubona, Umlungu!" delivered with measured deliberation at intervals of about a quarter of a minute, each salutation being accompanied by the customary upward

248

movement of the head—their respectful equivalent of our nod or bow. When he had done the round, his two attendants took their turns, and when this was over, and another long pause had served to mark his respect, he drew back a few paces to a spot about half-way between us and where the kaffirs sat, and, tucking his loin skins comfortably under him, squatted down. Ten minutes more elapsed before he allowed his eyes to wander absently round towards the boys and finally to settle on them for a repetition of the performance that we had been favoured with. But in this case it was they who led off with the "Sakubona, Umganaam!" which he acknowledged with the raising of the head and a soft murmur of contented recognition, "A-hé."

Once more there was silence for a spell, while he waited to be questioned in the customary manner, and to give an account of himself, before it would be courteous or proper to introduce the subject of his visit. It was Jim's voice that broke the silence—clear and imperative, as usual, but not uncivil. It always was Jim who cut in, as those do who are naturally impatient of delays and formalities.

"Velapi, Umganaam?" (Where do you come from, friend?) he asked, putting the question which is recognised as courteously providing the stranger with an opening to give an account of himself; and he is expected and required to do so to their satisfaction before he in turn can ask all about them, their occupations, homes, destination and master, and his occupation, purpose and possessions.

The talk went round in low exchanges until at last the old man moved closer and joined the circle; and then the other voices dropped out, only to be heard once in a while in some brief question or that briefest of all comments—the kaffir click and "Ow!" It may mean anything, according to the tone, but it was clearly sympathetic on that occasion. The old man's voice went on monotonously in a low-pitched impassive tone; but the boys hung intent on every word to the end. Then one or two questions, briefly answered in the same tone of detached philosophic indifference, brought their talk to a close. The old fellow tapped his carved wood snuff-box with the carefully preserved long yellowish nail of one forefinger, and pouring some snuff into the palm of his hand, drew it into each nostril in turn with long luxurious sniffs; and then, resting his arms on his knees, he relapsed into complete silence.

We called the boys to start work again, and they came away, as is their custom, without a word or look towards the man whose story had held them for the last half-hour. Nor did he speak or stir, but sat on unmoved, a picture of stoical indifference. But who can say if it be indifference or fatalism or the most astute diplomacy? Among white men opinions differ: I put it down as fatalism.

We asked no questions, for we knew it was no accident that had brought the old man our way: he wanted something, and we would learn soon enough what it was. So we waited.

As we gathered round the fallen tree to finish the

cleaning and slip it down to the track Jim remarked irrelevantly that tigers were 'schelms,' and it was his conviction that there were a great many in the kloofs round about. At intervals during the next hour or so he dropped other scraps about tigers and their ways, and how to get at them and what good sport it was, winding up with a short account of how two seasons back an English 'Capitaine' had been killed by one only a few miles away.

Jim was no diplomatist: he had tiger on the brain, and showed it; so when I asked him bluntly what the old man had been talking about, the whole story came out. There was a tiger—it was of course the biggest ever seen—which had been preying on the old chief's kraal for the last six months: dogs, goats and kaffir sheep innumerable had disappeared, even fowls were not despised; and only two days ago the climax had been reached when, in the cool of the afternoon and in defiance of the yelling herdboy, it had slipped into the herd at the drinking-place and carried off a calf—a heifer-calf too! The old man was poor: the tiger had nearly ruined him; and he had come up to see if we, "who were great hunters," would come down and kill the thief, or at least lend him a tiger-trap, as he could not afford to buy one.

In the evening when we returned to camp we found the old fellow there, and heard the story told with the same patient resignation or stoical indifference with which he had told it to the boys; and, if there was something inscrutable in the smoky eyes that might

have hidden a more calculating spirit, it did not trouble us—the tiger was what we wanted; the chance seemed good enough; and we decided to go. Tigers —as they are almost invariably called, but properly, leopards—were plentiful enough and were often to be heard at night in the kloofs below; but they are extremely wary animals and in the inhabited parts rarely move about by day; however, the marauding habits and the audacity of this fellow were full of promise.

The following afternoon we set off with our guns and blankets, a little food for two days, and the tiger-trap; and by nightfall we had reached the foot of the Berg by paths and ways which you might think only a baboon could follow.

It was moonlight, and we moved along through the heavily timbered kloofs in single file behind the shadowy figure of the shrivelled old chief. His years seemed no handicap to him, as with long easy soft-footed strides he went on hour after hour. The air was delightfully cool and sweet with the fresh smells of the woods; the damp carpet of moss and dead leaves dulled the sound of our more blundering steps; now and again through the thick canopy of evergreens we caught glimpses of the moon, and in odd places the light threw stumps or rocks into quaint relief or turned some tall bare trunk into a ghostly sentinel of the forest.

We had crossed the last of the many mountain streams and reached open ground when the old chief stopped, and pointing to the face of a high krans— black and threatening in the shadow, as it seemed

252

to overhang us—said that somewhere up there was a cave which was the tiger's home, and it was from this safe refuge that he raided the countryside.

The kraal was not far off. From the top of the spur we could look round, as from the pit of some vast coliseum, and see the huge wall of the Berg towering up above and half-enclosing us, thewhole arena roofed over by the star-spattered sky. The brilliant moon-light picked out every ridge and hill, deepening the velvet black of the shadowy valleys, and on the rise before us there was the twinkling light of a small fire, and the sound of voices came to us, borne on the still night air, so clearly that words picked out here and there were repeated by our boys with grunting comments and chuckles of amusement.

We started on again down an easy slope passing through some bush, and at the bottom came on level ground thinly covered with big shady trees and scattered undergrowth. As we walked briskly through the flecked and dappled light and shade, we were startled by the sudden and furious rush of Jess and Jock off the path and away into the scrub on the left; and immediately after there was a grunting noise, a crashing and scrambling, and then one sharp clear yelp of pain from one of the dogs. The old chief ran back behind us, shouting "Ingwa, ingwa!" (Tiger, tiger.) We slipped our rifles round and stood facing front, unable to see anything and not knowing what to expect. There were sounds of some sort in the bush—something like a faint scratching, and something like smothered sobbing grunts, but so indistinct

253

as to be more ominous and disquieting than absolute silence.

"He has killed the dogs," the old chief said, in a low voice.

But as he said it there was a rustle in front, and something came out towards us. The guns were up and levelled instantly, but dropped again when we saw it was a dog; and Jess came back limping badly and stopping every few paces to shake her head and rub her mouth against her fore-paws. She was in great pain and breathed out faint barely audible whines from time to time.

We waited for minutes, but Jock did not appear; and as the curious sounds still came from the bush we moved forward in open order, very slowly and with infinite caution. As we got closer, scouting each bush and open space, the sounds grew clearer, and suddenly it came to me that it was the noise of a body being dragged and the grunting breathing of a dog. I called sharply to Jock and the sound stopped; and taking a few paces forward then, I saw him in a moon-lit space turning round and round on the pivot of his hind-legs and swinging or dragging something much bigger than himself.

Jim gave a yell and shot past me, plunging his assegai into the object and shouting "Porcupine, porcupine," at the top of his voice. We were all round it in a couple of seconds, but I think the porcupine was as good as dead even before Jim had stabbed it. Jock was still holding on grimly, tugging with all his might and always with the same movement of

254

"TUGGING WITH ALL HIS MIGHT"

swinging it round him, or of himself circling round it
—perhaps that is the fairer description, for the porcupine was much the heavier. He had it by the throat
where the flesh is bare of quills, and had kept himself
out of reach of the terrible spikes by pulling away
all the time, just as he had done with the duiker and
other buck to avoid their hind-feet.

This encounter with the porcupine gave us a better
chance of getting the tiger than we ever expected—
too good a chance to be neglected; so we cut the
animal up and used the worthless parts to bait the big
tiger-trap, having first dragged them across the veld
for a good distance each way to leave a blood spoor
which would lead the tiger up to the trap. This,
with the quantity of blood spread about in the fight,
lying right in the track of his usual prowling ought
to attract his attention, we thought; and we fastened
the trap to a big tree, making an avenue of bushes up
to the bait so that he would have to walk right over the
trap hidden under the dead leaves, in order to get at
the bait. We hoped that, if it failed to hold, it would
at least wound him badly enough to enable us to
follow him up in the morning.

In the bright light of the fire that night, as Jock
lay beside me having his share of the porcupine steaks,
I noticed something curious about his chest, and on
looking closer found the whole of his white 'shirt
front' speckled with dots of blood; he had been
pricked in dozens of places, and it was clear that it
had been no walk-over for him; he must have had a
pretty rough handling before he got the porcupine

on the swing. He was none the worse, however, and was the picture of contentment as he lay beside me in the ring facing the fire.

But Jess was a puzzle. From the time that she had come hobbling back to us, carrying her one foot in the air and stopping to rub her mouth on her paws, we had been trying to find out what was the matter. The foot trouble was clear enough, for there was a quill fifteen inches long and as stiff and thick as a lead pencil still piercing the ball of her foot, with the needle-like point sticking out between her toes. Fortunately it had not been driven far through and the hole was small, so that once it was drawn and the foot bandaged she got along fairly well. It was not the foot that was troubling her; all through the evening she kept repeating the movement of her head, either rubbing it on her front legs or wiping her muzzle with the paws, much as a cat does when washing its face. She would not touch food and could not lie still for five minutes; and we could do nothing to help her.

THE · TIGER · & · BABOONS

No one had doubted Jess's courage, even when we saw her come back alone: we knew there was something wrong, but in spite of every care and effort we could not find out what it was, and poor old Jess went through the night in suffering, making no sound, but moving from place to place weary and restless, giving long tired quivering sighs, and pawing at her mouth from time to time. In the morning light we again looked her all over carefully, and especially opened her mouth and examined that and her nostrils, but could find nothing to show what was wrong.

The puzzle was solved by accident: Ted was sitting on the ground when she came up to him, looking wistfully into his face again with one of the mute appeals for help.

"What is it, Jess, old girl?" he said, and reaching out, he caught her head in both hands and drew her towards him; but with a sharp exclamation he instantly

257   S

 let go again, pricked by something, and a drop of blood oozed from one finger-tip. Under Jess's right ear there was a hard sharp point just showing through the skin: we all felt it, and when the skin was forced back we saw it was the tip of a porcupine quill. There was no pulling it out or moving it, however, nor could we for a long time find where it had entered. At last Ted noticed what looked like a tiny narrow strip of bark adhering to the outside of her lower lip, and this turned out to be the broken end of the quill, snapped off close to the flesh; not even the end of the quill was visible—only the little strip that had peeled off in the breaking.

Poor old Jess! We had no very grand appliances for surgery, and had to slit her lip down with an ordinary skinning knife. Ted held her between his knees and gripped her head with both hands, while one of us pulled with steel pliers on the broken quill until it came out. The quill had pierced her lower lip, entered the gums beside the front teeth, run all along the jaw and through the flesh behind, coming out just below the ear. It was over seven inches long. She struggled a little under the rough treatment, and there was a protesting whimper when we tugged; but she did not let out one cry under all the pain.

We knew then that Jess had done her share in the fight, and guessed that it was she who in her reckless charge had rolled the porcupine over and given Jock his chance.

The doctoring of Jess had delayed us considerably, and while we were still busy at it the old chief came

up to say that his scouts had returned and reported that there was no tiger to be seen, but that they thought the trap had been sprung. They had not liked to go close up, preferring to observe the spot from a tree some way off.

The first question was what to do with Jess. We had no collar or chain, of course, and nothing would induce her to stay behind once Ted started; she would have bitten through ropes and reims in a few minutes, and no kaffir would have faced the job of watching over and checking her. Finally we put her into one of the reed and mud huts, closing the entrance with some raw hides weighted with heavy stones; and off we went.

We found the trap sprung and the bait untouched. The spoor was a tiger's, right enough, and we saw where it had circled suspiciously all round before finally entering the little fenced approach which we had built to shepherd it on to the trap. There each footprint was clear, and it appeared that instead of cautiously creeping right up to the bait and stepping on the setting-plate, it had made a pounce at the bait from about ten feet away, releasing the trap by knocking the spring or by touching the plate with the barrel of its body. The tiger had evidently been nipped, but the body was too big for the teeth to close on, and no doubt the spring it gave on feeling the grip underneath set it free with nothing worse than a bad scraping and a tremendous fright. There was plenty of hair and some skin on the teeth of the trap, but very little blood there, and none at all to be found round about.

259

That was almost the worst result we could have had: the tiger was not crippled, nor was it wounded enough to enable us to track it, but must have been so thoroughly alarmed that it would certainly be extremely nervous and suspicious of everything now, and would probably avoid the neighbourhood for some time to come.

The trap was clearly of no further use, but after coming so far for the tiger we were not disposed to give up the hunt without another effort. The natives told us it was quite useless to follow it up as it was a real 'schelm,' and by that time would be miles away in some inaccessible krans. We determined however to go on, and if we failed to get a trace of the tiger, to put in the day hunting bushbuck or wild pig, both of which were fairly plentiful.

We had not gone more than a few hundred yards when an exclamation from one of the boys made us look round, and we saw Jess on the opposite slope coming along full speed after us with her nose to the trail. She had scratched and bitten her way through the reed and mud wall of the hut, scared the wits out of a couple of boys who had tried to head her off, and raced away after us with a pack of kaffir mongrels yelping unnoticed at her heels. She really did not seem much the worse for her wounds, and was—for her—quite demonstrative in her delight at finding us again.

In any case there was nothing to be done but to let her come, and we went on once more beating up towards the lair in the black krans with the two dogs in the lead.

The guides led us down into the bed of one of the mountain streams, and following this up we were soon in the woods where the big trees meeting overhead made it dark and cool. It was difficult in that light to see anything clearly at first, and the considerable undergrowth of shrub and creepers and the boulders shed from the Berg added to the difficulty and made progress slow. We moved along as much as possible abreast, five or six yards apart, but were often driven by obstacles into the bed of the stream for short distances in order to make headway at all, and although there did not seem to be much chance of finding the tiger at home, we crept along cautiously and noiselessly, talking—when we had to—only in whispers.

We were bunched together, preparing to crawl along a rock overhanging a little pool, when the boy in front made a sign and pointed with his assegai to the dogs. They had crossed the stream and were walking—very slowly and abreast—near the water's edge. The rawest of beginners would have needed no explanation. The two stood for a few seconds sniffing at a particular spot and then both together looked steadily upstream: there was another pause and they moved very slowly and carefully forward a yard or so and sniffed again with their noses almost touching. As they did this the hair on their backs and shoulders began to rise until, as they reached the head of the pool, they were bristling like hedgehogs and giving little purring growls.

The guide went over to them while we waited, afraid to move lest the noise of our boots on the stones

261

should betray us. After looking round for a bit he pointed to a spot on the bank where he had found the fresh spoor of the tiger, and picking up something there to show to us he came back to our side. It was a little fragment of whitish skin with white hairs on it. There was no doubt about it then: we were on the fresh spoor of the tiger where it had stopped to drink at the pool and probably to lick the scratches made by the trap; and leaving the bed of the stream it had gone through the thick undergrowth up towards the krans.

We were not more than a hundred yards from the krans then, and the track taken by the tiger was not at all an inviting one. It was at first merely a narrow tunnel in the undergrowth up the steep hillside, through which we crept in single file with the two dogs a few yards in front; they moved on in the same silent deliberate way, so intent and strung up that they started slightly and instantly looked up in front at the least sound. As the ascent became steeper and more rocky, the undergrowth thinned, and we were able to spread out into line once more, threading our way through several roughly parallel game tracks or natural openings and stooping low to watch the dogs and take our cue from them.

We were about fifteen yards from the precipitous face of the krans, and had just worked round a huge boulder into a space fairly free of bush but cumbered with many big rocks and loose stones, when the dogs stopped and stood quivering and bristling all over, moving their heads slowly about with noses well

262

raised and sniffing persistently. There was something now that interested them more than the spoor; they winded the tiger itself, but could not tell where. No one stirred: we stood watching the dogs and snatching glances right and left among the boulders and their shady creeper-hidden caves and recesses, and as we stood thus, grouped together in breathless silence, an electrifying snarling roar came from the krans above and the spotted body of the tiger shot like a streak out of the black mouth of a cave and across our front into the bush; there was a series of crashing bounds as though a stone rolled from the mountain were leaping through the jungle; and then absolute silence.

We explored the den; but there was nothing of interest in it—no remains of food, no old bones, or other signs of cubs. It seemed to be the retreat of a male tiger—secluded, quiet and cool. The opening was not visible from any distance, a split-off slab of rock partly hiding it; but when we stood upon the rock platform we found that almost the whole of the horseshoe bay in the Berg into which we had descended was visible, and it was with a "Wow!" of surprise and mortification that the kraal boys found they could see the kraal itself and their goats and cattle grazing on the slopes and in the valley below.

Tigers do not take their kill to their dens unless there are young cubs to be fed; as a rule they feed where they kill, or as near to it as safety permits, and when they have fed their fill they carry off the remainder of the carcass

263

and hide it. Lions, hyenas, and others leave what they cannot eat and return to it for their next feed; but tigers are more provident and more cunning, and—being able to climb trees—they are very much more difficult to follow or waylay by means of their kill. They are not big fellows, rarely exceeding seven feet from nose to tip of tail and 130 lb. in weight; but they are extraordinarily active and strong, and it is difficult to believe until one has seen the proof of it that they are able to climb the bare trunk of a tree carrying a kill much bigger and heavier than themselves, and hang it safely wedged in some hidden fork out of reach of any other animal. I have repeatedly seen the remains of their victims in the forks of trees; once it was part of a pig, but on the other occasions the remains were of horned animals; the pig was balanced in the fork; the others were hooked in by the heads and horns.

A well-known hunter once told me an experience of his illustrating the strength and habits of tigers. He had shot a young giraffe and carried off as much as he could put on his horse, and hid the rest; but when he returned next morning it had disappeared, and the spoor of a full-grown tiger told him why. He followed the drag mark up to the foot of a big tree and found the remains of the carcass, fully 300 lb. in weight, in a fork more than twenty feet from the ground.

He left it there as a bait and returned again the following morning on the chance of a shot; but the meat had once more been removed and on following up the spoor he found what was left hidden in another tree some two hundred yards away.

It would have been waste of time to follow our tiger—he would be on the watch and on the move for hours; so we gave it up at once, and struck across the spurs for another part of the big arena where pig and bushbuck were known to feed in the mornings. It was slow and difficult work, as the bush was very dense and the ground rough. The place was riddled with game tracks, and we saw spoor of koodoo and eland several times, and tracks innumerable of wild pig, rietbuck, bushbuck, and duiker. But there was more than spoor: a dozen times we heard the crash of startled animals through the reeds or bush only a few yards away without being able to see a thing.

We had nearly reached the kloof we were aiming for when we had the good luck to get a bushbuck in a very unexpected way. We had worked our way out of a particularly dense patch of bush and brambles into a corner of the woods and were resting on the mossy ground in the shade of the big trees when the sound of clattering stones a good way off made us start up again and grab our rifles; and presently we saw, outlined against the band of light which marked the edge of the timber, a buck charging down towards us. Three of us fired together, and the buck rolled over within a few yards of where we stood.

We were then in a 'dead end' up against the precipitous face of the Berg where there was no road or path other than game tracks, and where no human being ever went except for the purpose of hunting.

265

We knew there was no one else shooting there, and it puzzled us considerably to think what had scared the bushbuck; for the animal had certainly been startled and perhaps chased; the pace, the noise it made, and the blind recklessness of its dash, all showed that. The only explanation we could think of was that the tiger, in making a circuit along the slopes of the Berg to get away from us, must have put the buck up and driven it down on to us in the woods below, and if that were so, the reports of our rifles must have made him think that he was never going to get rid of us.

We skinned and cut up the buck and pushed on again; but the roughness of the trail and the various stoppages had delayed us greatly, and we failed to get the expected bag. We got one rietbuck and a young boar; the rietbuck was a dead shot; but the pig, from the shooting standpoint, was a most humiliating failure. A troop of twenty or thirty started up from under our feet as we came out of the blazing sunlight into the gloom of the woods, and no one could see well enough to aim. They were led by a grand boar, and the whole lot looked like a troop of charging lions as they raced by with their bristly manes erect and their tufted tails standing straight up.

As we stood there, crestfallen and disgusted, we heard fresh grunting behind, and turning round we saw one pig racing past in the open, having apparently missed the troop while wallowing in a mudhole and known nothing of our intrusion until he heard the shooting. We gave him a regular broadside, and—as is usually the case when you think that quantity

266

will do in place of quality—made an awful mess of it, and before we had time to reload Jess and Jock had cut in, and we could not fire again for fear of hitting them. The boys, wildly delighted by this irregular development which gave them such a chance, joined in the chase and in a few seconds it became a chaotic romp like a rat hunt in a schoolroom. The dogs ranged up on each side and were on to the pig together, Jess hanging on to one ear and Jock at the neck; the boar dug right and left at them, but his tusks were short and blunt, and if he managed to get at them at all they bore no mark of it afterwards. For about twenty yards they dragged and tugged, and then all three came somersaulting over together. In the scramble Jock got his grip on the throat, and Jess—rolled and trampled on—appeared between the pig's hind-legs, sliding on her back with her teeth embedded in one of the hams. For half a minute the boar, grunting and snorting, plunged about madly, trying to get at them or to free himself; and then the boys caught up and riddled him with their assegais.

After the two bombardments of the pigs and the fearful row made by the boys there was not much chance of putting up anything more, and we made for the nearest stream in the woods for a feed and a rest before returning to camp.

We had failed to get the tiger, it is true, and it would be useless giving more time or further thought to him, for in all probability it would be a week or more before he returned to his old hunting-ground and his old marauding tricks, but the porcu-

267

pine and the pig had provided more interest and amusement than much bigger game might have done, and on the whole, although disappointed, we were not dissatisfied: in fact, it would have needed an ungrateful spirit indeed to feel discontented in such surroundings.

Big trees of many kinds and shapes united to make a canopy of leaves overhead through which only occasional shafts of sunlight struck. The cold mountain stream tumbling over ledges, swirling among rocks or rippling over pebble-strewn reaches, gurgled, splashed and bubbled with that wonderful medley of sounds that go to make the lullaby of the brook. The floor of the forest was carpeted with a pile of staghorn moss a foot thick, and maidenhair fern grew everywhere with the luxuriant profusion of weeds in a tropical garden. Traveller's Joy covered whole trees with dense creamy bloom and spread its fragrance everywhere; wild clematis trailed over stumps and fallen branches; quantities of maidenhair overflowed the banks and drooped to the water all along the course of the stream; whilst, marshalled on either side, huddled together on little islands, perched on rocks, and grouped on overhanging ledges, stood the tree-ferns—as though they had come to drink—their wide-reaching delicate fronds like giant green ostrich-feathers waving gently to each breath of air or quivering as the movement of the water shook the trunks.

Long-tailed greeny-grey monkeys with black faces peered down at us, moving lightly on their branch trapezes, and pulled faces or chattered their indignant

protest against intrusion; in the tops of the wild fig
trees bright green pigeons watched us shyly—great big
birds of a wonderful green; gorgeous louries too
flashed their colours and raised their crests—pictures
of extreme and comical surprise; golden cuckoos
there were also and beautiful little green-backed ruby-
throated honey-suckers flitted like butterflies among
the flowers on the sunlit fringe of the woods.

Now and again guinea-fowl and bush-pheasant
craned their necks over some fallen log or stone to
peer curiously at us, then stooping low again darted
along their well-worn runs into the thick bush. The
place was in fact a natural preserve; a 'bay' let into
the wall of the Berg, half-encircled by cliffs which
nothing could climb, a little world where the common
enemy—man—seldom indeed intruded.

We stayed there until the afternoon sun had passed
behind the crest of the Berg above us; and, instead
of going back the way we came, skirted along the other
arm enclosing the bay to have the cool shade of the
mountain with us on our return journey. But the
way was rough; the jungle was dense; we were hot
and torn and tired; and the shadow of the mountain
stretched far out across the foothills by the time the
corner was reached. We sat down to rest at last in
the open on the long spur on which, a couple of miles
away, the slanting sun picked out the red and black
cattle, the white goats, and the brown huts of the
kaffir kraal.

Our route lay along the side of the spur, skirting
the rocky backbone and winding between occasional

boulders, clumps of trees and bush, and we had moved on only a little way when a loud "Waugh" from a baboon on the mountain behind made us stop to look back. The hoarse shout was repeated several times, and each time more loudly and emphatically; it seemed like the warning call of a sentry who had seen us. Moved by curiosity we turned aside on to the ridge itself, and from the top of a big rock scanned the almost precipitous face opposite. The spur on which we stood was divided from the Berg itself only by a deep but narrow kloof or ravine, and every detail of the mountainside stood out in the clear evening air, but against the many-coloured rocks the grey figure of a baboon was not easy to find as long as it remained still, and although from time to time the barking roar was repeated, we were still scanning the opposite hill when one of the boys pointed down the slope immediately below us and called out, "There, there, Baas!"

The troop of baboons had evidently been quite close to us—hidden from us only by the little line of rocks—and on getting warning from their sentry on the mountain had stolen quietly away and were then disappearing into the timbered depth of the ravine. We sat still to watch them come out on the opposite side a few minutes later and clamber up the rocky face, for they are always worth watching; but while we watched, the stillness was broken by an agonised scream—horribly human in its expression of terror—followed by roars, barks, bellows and screams from scores of voices in every key; and the crackle of break-

ing sticks and the rattle of stones added to the medley
of sound as the baboons raced out of the wood and
up the bare rocky slope.

"What is it?" "What's the matter?" "There's
something after them." "Look, look! there they
come!" burst from one and another of us as we
watched the extraordinary scene. The cries from
below seemed to waken the whole mountain; great
booming "waughs" came from different places far
apart and ever so high up the face of the Berg; each
big roar seemed to act like a trumpet-call and bring
forth a multitude of others; and the air rang with
bewildering shouts and echoes volleying round the
kloofs and faces of the Berg. The strange thing was
that the baboons did not continue their terrified
scramble up the mountain, but, once out of the bush,
they turned and rallied. Forming an irregular semicircle they faced down hill, thrusting their heads
forward with sudden jerks as though to launch their
cries with greater vehemence, and feinting to charge;
they showered loose earth, stones and debris of all sorts
down with awkward underhand scrapes of their fore-
paws, and gradually but surely descended to within
a dozen yards of the bush's edge.

"Baas, Baas, the tiger! Look, the tiger! There,
there on the rock below!"

Jim shot the words out in vehement gusts, choky
with excitement; and true enough, there the tiger
was. The long spotted body was crouched on a flat
rock just below the baboons; he was broadside to
us, with his fore-quarters slightly raised and his

271

face turned towards the baboons; with wide-opened mouth he snarled savagely at the advancing line, and with right paw raised made threatening dabs in their direction. His left paw pinned down the body of a baboon.

The voices from the mountain boomed louder and nearer as, clattering and scrambling down the face, came more and more baboons: there must have been hundreds of them; the semicircle grew thicker and blacker, more and more threatening, foot by foot closer. The tiger raised himself a little more and took swift looks from side to side across the advancing front, and then his nerve went, and with one spring he shot from the rock into the bush.

There was an instant forward rush of the half-moon, and the rock was covered with roaring baboons, swarming over their rescued comrade; and a moment later the crowd scrambled up the slope again, taking the tiger's victim with them. In that seething rabble I could pick out nothing, but all the kaffirs maintained they could see the mauled one dragged along by its arms by two others, much as a child might be helped uphill.

We were still looking excitedly about—trying to make out what the baboons were doing, watching the others still coming down the Berg, and peering anxiously for a sight of the tiger—when once more Jim's voice gave us a shock.

"Where are the dogs?" he asked; and the question turned us cold. If they had gone after the baboons they were as good as dead already—nothing could save

272

"*SCRAMBLING DOWN THE FACE CAME
MORE AND MORE BABOONS*"

them. Calling was useless: nothing could be heard in the roar and din that the enraged animals still kept up. We watched the other side of the ravine with something more than anxiety, and when Jock's reddish-looking form broke through the bracken near to the tiger's rock, I felt like shutting my eyes till all was over. We saw him move close under the rock and then disappear. We watched for some seconds—it may have been a minute, but it seemed an eternity—and then, feeling the utter futility of waiting there, jumped off the rock and ran down the slope in the hope that the dogs would hear us call from there.

From where the slope was steepest we looked down into the bed of the stream at the bottom of the ravine, and the two dogs were there: they were moving cautiously down the wide stony watercourse just as we had seen them move in the morning, their noses thrown up and heads turning slowly from side to side. We knew what was coming; there was no time to reach them through the bush below; the cries of the baboons made calling useless; and the three of us sat down with rifles levelled ready to fire at the first sight. With gun gripped and breath hard held, watching intently every bush and tree and rock, every spot of light and shade, we sat—not daring to move. Then, over the edge of a big rock overlooking the two dogs, appeared something round; and, smoothly yet swiftly and with a snake-like movement, the long spotted body followed the head and, flattened against the rock, crept stealthily forward until the tiger looked straight down upon Jess and Jock.

273   T

The three rifles cracked like one, and with a howl of rage and pain the tiger shot out over the dogs' heads, raced along the stony bed, and suddenly plunging its nose into the ground, pitched over—dead.

It was shot through the heart, and down the ribs on each side were the scraped marks of the trap.

BUFFALO
BUSHFIRE & WILD DOGS

THE summer slipped away—the full-pulsed ripeness of the year; beauty and passion; sunshine and storm; long spells of peace and gentleness, of springing life and radiant glory; short intervals of reckless tempest and destructive storm! Among the massed ever-greens of the woods there stood out here and there bright spots of colour, the careless dabs from Nature's artist hand; yellow and brown, orange and crimson, all vividly distinct, yet all in perfect harmony. The rivers, fed from the replenished mountains' stores, ran full but clear; the days were bright; the nights were cold; the grass was rank and seeding; and it was time to go.

Once more the Bushveld beckoned us away.

We picked a spot where grass and water were good, and waited for the rivers to fall; and it was while loitering there that a small hunting party from the fields making for the Sabi came across us and camped for the night. In the morning two of our party joined them for a few days to try for something big.

275

It was too early in the season for really good sport. The rank tropical grass—six to eight feet high in most places, twelve to fourteen in some— was too green to burn yet, and the stout stems and heavy seed heads made walking as difficult as in a field of tangled sugar cane; for long stretches it was not possible to see five yards, and the dew in the early mornings was so heavy that after a hundred yards of such going one was drenched to the skin.

We were forced into the more open parts—the higher, stonier, more barren ground where just then the bigger game was by no means plentiful.

On the third day two of us started out to try a new quarter in the hilly country rising towards the Berg. My companion, Francis, was an experienced hunter and his idea was that we should find the big game, not on the hot humid flats or the stony rises, but still higher up on the breezy hill-tops or in the cool shady kloofs running towards the mountains. We passed a quantity of smaller game that morning, and several times heard the stampede of big animals—wildebeeste and waterbuck, as we found by the spoor—but it was absolutely impossible to see them. The dew was so heavy that even our hats were soaking wet, and times out of number we had to stop to wipe the water out of our eyes in order to see our way; a complete ducking would not have made the least difference.

Jock fared better than we did, finding openings and game tracks at his own level, which were of no use to us; he also knew better than we did what was going on ahead, and it was tantalising in the extreme to

276

see him slow down and stand with his nose thrown up, giving quick soft sniffs and ranging his head from side to side, when he knew there was something quite close, and knew too that a few more toiling steps in that rank grass would be followed by a rush of something which we would never see.

Once we heard a foot stamp not twenty yards off, and stood for a couple of minutes on tip-toe trying to pierce the screen of grass in front, absolutely certain that eyes and ears were turned on us in death-like silence waiting for the last little proof of the intruder that would satisfy their owners and start them off before we could get a glimpse. The silence must have made them suspicious, for at some signal unknown to us the troop broke away and we had the mortification to see something which we had ignored as a branch tilt slowly back and disappear: there was no mistaking the koodoo bull's horns once they moved!

After two hours of this we struck a stream, and there we made somewhat better pace and less noise, often taking to the bed of the creek for easier going. There, too, we found plenty of drinking places and plenty of fresh spoor of the bigger game, and as the hills began to rise in view above the bush and trees, we found what Francis was looking for. Something caught his eye on the far side of the stream, and he waded in. I followed and when halfway through saw the contented look on his face and caught his words: "Buffalo! I thought so!"

We sat down then to think it out. The spoor told of a troop of a dozen to sixteen animals—bulls, cows,

and calves; and it was that morning's spoor: even in the soft moist ground at the stream's edge the water had not yet oozed into most of the prints. Fortunately there was a light breeze from the hills, and as it seemed probable that in any case they would make that way for the hot part of the day we decided to follow for some distance on the track and then make for the likeliest poort in the hills.

The buffalo had come up from the low country in the night on a course striking the creek diagonally in the drinking place; their departing spoor went off at a slight tangent from the stream—the two trails making a very wide angle at the drinking place and confirming the idea that after their night's feed in the rich grass lower down they were making for the hills again in the morning and had touched at the stream to drink.

Jock seemed to gather from our whispered conversation and silent movements that there was work to hand, and his eyes moved from one face to the other as we talked, much as a child watches the faces in a conversation it cannot quite follow. When we got up and began to move along the trail, he gave one of his little sideways bounds, as if he half-thought of throwing a somersault and restrained himself; and then with several approving waggings of his tail settled down at once to business.

Jock went in front: it was best so, and quite safe, for, whilst certain to spot anything long before we could, there was not the least risk of his rushing it or making any noise. The slightest whisper of a "Hst"

278

from me would have brought him to a breathless standstill at any moment; but even this was not likely to be needed, for he kept as close a watch on my face as I did on him.

There was, of course, no difficulty whatever in following the spoor; the animals were as big as cattle, and their trail through the rank grass was as plain as a road: our difficulty was to get near enough to see them without being heard. Under the down-trodden grass there were plenty of dry sticks to step on, any of which would have been as fatal to our chances as a pistol shot, and even the unavoidable rustle of the grass might betray us while the buffalo themselves remained hidden. Thus our progress was very slow, a particularly troublesome impediment being the grass stems thrown down across the trail by the animals crossing and re-crossing each other's spoor and stopping to crop a mouthful here and there or perhaps to play. The tambookie grass in these parts has a stem thicker than a lead pencil, more like a young bamboo than grass; and these stems thrown cross-ways by storms or game make an entanglement through which the foot cannot be forced: it means high stepping all the time.

We expected to follow the spoor for several miles before coming on the buffalo—probably right into the kloof towards which it appeared to lead—but were, nevertheless, quite prepared to drop on to them at any moment, knowing well how game will loiter on their way when undisturbed and vary their time and course, instinctively avoiding the too regular habits which would make them an easy prey.

279

Jock moved steadily along the trodden track, sliding easily through the grass or jumping softly and noiselessly over impediments, and we followed, looking ahead as far as the winding course of the trail permitted.

To right and left of us stood the screen of tall grass, bush and trees. Once Jock stopped, throwing up his nose, and stood for some seconds while we held our breath; but having satisfied himself that there was nothing of immediate consequence, he moved on again—rather more slowly, as it appeared to us. I looked at Francis's face; it was pale and set like marble, and his watchful grey eyes were large and wide like an antelope's, as though opened out to take in everything; and those moments of intense interest and expectation were the best part of a memorable day.

There was something near: we felt it! Jock was going more carefully than ever, with his head up most of the time; and the feeling of expectation grew stronger and stronger until it amounted to absolute certainty. Then Jock stopped, stopped in mid-stride, not with his nose up ranging for scent, but with head erect, ears cocked, and tail poised—dead still: he was looking at something.

We had reached the end of the grass where the bush and trees of the mountain slope had choked it out, and before us there was fairly thick bush mottled with black shadows and patches of bright sunlight in which it was most difficult to see anything. There we stood like statues, the dog in front with the two men abreast behind him, and all peering intently. Twice Jock

280

slowly turned his head and looked into my eyes, and I felt keenly the sense of hopeless inferiority. "There it is, what are you going to do?" was what the first look seemed to say; and the second: "Well, what are you waiting for?"

How long we stood thus it is not possible to say: time is no measure of such things, and to me it seemed unending suspense; but we stood our ground scarcely breathing, knowing that something was there, because he saw it and told us so, and knowing that as soon as we moved it would be gone. Then close to the ground there was a movement—something swung, and the full picture flashed upon us. It was a buffalo calf standing in the shade of a big bush with its back towards us, and it was the swishing of the tail that had betrayed it. We dared not breathe a word or pass a look—a face turned might have caught some glint of light and shown us up; so we stood like statues each knowing that the other was looking for the herd and would fire when he got a chance at one of the full-grown animals.

My eyes were strained and burning from the intensity of the effort to see; but except the calf I could not make out a living thing: the glare of the yellow grass in which we stood and the sun-splotched darkness beyond it beat me.

At last, in the corner of my eye, I saw Francis's rifle rise, as slowly—almost—as the mercury in a warmed thermometer. There was a long pause and then came the shot and wild snorts of alarm and rage. A dozen huge black forms started

281

into life for a second and as quickly vanished —scattering and crashing through the jungle.

The first clear impression was that of Jock, who after one swift run forward for a few yards stood ready to spring off in pursuit, looking back at me and waiting for the word to go; but at the sign of my raised hand, opened with palm towards him, he subsided slowly and lay down flat with his head resting on his paws.

"Did you see?" asked Francis.

"Not till you fired. I heard it strike. What was it?"

"Hanged if I know! I heard it too. It was one of the big 'uns; but bull or cow I don't know."

"Where did you get it?"

"Well, I couldn't make out more than a black patch in the bush. It moved once, but I couldn't see how it was standing—end on or across. It may be hit anywhere. I took for the middle of the patch and let drive. Bit risky, eh?"

"Seems like taking chances."

"Well, it was no use waiting: we came for this!" and then added with a careless laugh, "They always clear from the first shot if you get 'em at close quarters, but the fun'll begin now. Expect he'll lay for us in the track somewhere."

That is the way of the wounded buffalo—we all knew that; and old Rocky's advice came to mind with a good deal of point: "Keep cool and shoot straight—or stay right home"; and Jock's expectant watchful look smote me with another memory—"It was my dawg!"

282

A few yards from where the buffalo had stood we picked up the blood spoor. There was not very much of it, but we saw from the marks on the bushes here and there, and more distinctly on some grass further on, that the wound was pretty high up and on the right side. Crossing a small stretch of more open bush we reached the dense growth along the banks of the stream, and as this continued up into the kloof it was clear we had a tough job before us.

Animals when badly wounded nearly always leave the herd and very often go down wind so as to be able to scent and avoid their pursuers. This fellow had followed the herd up wind, and that rather puzzled us.

A wounded buffalo in thick bush is considered to be about as nasty a customer as any one may desire to tackle; for its vindictive indomitable courage and extraordinary cunning are a very formidable combination, as a long list of fatalities bears witness. Its favourite device—so old hunters will tell you—is to make off down wind when hit, and after going for some distance, come back again in a semicircle to intersect its own spoor, and there under good cover lie in wait for those who may follow up.

This makes the sport quite as interesting as need be, for the chances are more nearly even than they generally are in hunting. The buffalo chooses the ground that suits its purpose of ambushing its enemy, and naturally selects a spot where concealment is possible; but, making every allowance for this, it seems little short of a miracle that the huge black

283

beast is able to hide itself so effectually that it can charge from a distance of a dozen yards on to those who are searching for it.

The secret of it seems to lie in two things: first, absolute stillness; and second, breaking up the colour. No wild animal, except those protected by distance and open country, will stand against a background of light or of uniform colour, nor will it as a rule allow its own shape to form an unbroken patch against its chosen background.

They work on Nature's lines. Look at the ostrich—the cock, black and handsome, so strikingly different from the commonplace grey hen! Considering that for periods of six weeks at a stretch they are anchored to one spot hatching the eggs, turn and turn about, it seems that one or other must be an easy victim for the beast of prey, since the same background cannot possibly suit both. But they know that too; so the grey hen sits by day, and the black cock by night! And the ostrich is not the fool it is thought to be—burying its head in the sand! Knowing how the long stem of a neck will catch the eye, it lays it flat on the ground, as other birds do, when danger threatens the nest or brood, and concealment is better than flight. That tame chicks will do this in a bare paddock is only a laughable assertion of instinct.

Look at the zebra! There is nothing more striking, nothing that arrests the eye more sharply—in the Zoo—than this vivid contrast of colour; yet in the bush the wavy stripes of black and white are a protection, enabling him to hide at will.

I have seen a wildebeeste effectually hidden by a single blighted branch; a koodoo bull by a few twisty sticks; a crouching lion by a wisp of feathery grass no higher than one's knee, no bigger than a vase of flowers! Yet the marvel of it is always fresh.

After a couple of hundred yards of that sort of going, we changed our plan, taking to the creek again and making occasional cross-cuts to the trail, to be sure he was still ahead. It was certain then that the buffalo was following the herd and making for the poort, and as he had not stopped once on our account we took to the creek after the fourth cross-cut and made what pace we could to reach the narrow gorge where we reckoned to pick up the spoor again.

There are, however, few short cuts—and no certainties—in hunting; when we reached the poort there was no trace to be found of the wounded buffalo; the rest of the herd had passed in, but we failed to find blood or other trace of the wounded one, and Jock was clearly as much at fault as we were.

We had overshot the mark and there was nothing for it but to hark back to the last blood spoor and, by following it up, find out what had happened. This took over an hour, for we spoored him then with the utmost caution, being convinced that the buffalo, if not dead, was badly wounded and lying in wait for us.

We came on his 'stand,' in a well-chosen spot, where the game path took a sharp turn round some heavy bushes. The buffalo had stood, not where one would naturally expect it—in the dense cover which seemed just suited for his purpose—but among lighter bush on the *opposite* side and about twenty yards nearer to us. There was no room for doubt about his hostile intentions; and when we recalled how we had instantly picked out the thick bush on the left—to the exclusion of everything else —as the spot to be watched, his selection of more open ground on the other side, and nearer to us, seemed so fiendishly clever that it made one feel cold and creepy. One hesitates to say it was deliberately planned; yet—plan, instinct or accident—there was the fact.

The marks showed us he was badly hit; but there was no limb broken, and no doubt he was good for some hours yet. We followed along the spoor, more cautiously than ever; and when we reached the sharp turn beyond the thick bush we found that the path was only a few yards from the stream, so that on our way up the bed of the creek we had passed within twenty yards of where the buffalo was waiting for us. No doubt he had heard us then as we walked past, and had winded us later on when we got ahead of him into the poort.

What had he made of it? What had he done? Had he followed up to attack us? Was he waiting somewhere near? Or had he broken away into the bush on finding himself headed off? These were some of the questions we asked ourselves as we crept along.

Well! what he had done did not answer our question. On reaching the poort again we found his spoor, freshly made since we had been there, and he had walked right along through the gorge without

286

stopping again and gone into the kloof beyond. Whether he had followed us up when we got ahead of him—hoping to stalk us from behind; or had gone ahead, expecting to meet us coming down wind to look for him; or, when he heard us pass down stream again—and, it may be, thought we had given up pursuit—had simply walked on after the herd, were questions never answered.

A breeze had risen since morning, and as we approached the hills it grew stronger: in the poort itself it was far too strong for our purpose—the wind coming through the narrow opening like a forced draught. The herd would not stand there, and it was not probable that the wounded animal would stop until he joined the others or reached a more sheltered place. We were keen on the chase, and as he had about an hour's start of us and it was already midday, there was no time to waste.

Inside the poort the kloof opened out into a big valley away to our left—our left being the right bank of the stream—and bordering the valley on that side there were many miles of timbered kloofs and green slopes, with a few kaffir kraals visible in the distance; but to the right the formation was quite different, and rather peculiar. The stream—known to the natives as Hlamba-Nyati, or Buffalo's Bathing Place —had in the course of time shortened its course to the poort by eating into the left bank, thus leaving a high and in most places inaccessible terrace above it on the left side and a wide stretch of flat alluvium on the right. This terrace was bounded on one side

287

by the steep bank of the creek and walled in on the other side by the precipitous kranses of the mountains. At the top end it opened out like a fan which died away in a frayed edge in the numberless small kloofs and spurs fringing the amphitheatre of the hills. The shape was in fact something like the human arm and hand with the fingers outspread. The elbow was the poort, the arm the terrace—except that the terrace was irregularly curved—and the fingers the small kloofs in the mountains. No doubt the haunts of the buffalo were away in the 'fingers,' and we worked steadily along the spoor in that direction.

Game paths were numerous and very irregular, and the place was a perfect jungle of trees, bush, bramble and the tallest rankest grass. I have ridden in that valley many times since then through grass standing several feet above my head. It was desperately hard work, but we did want to get the buffalo; and although the place was full of game and we put up koo-doo, wildebeeste, rietbuck, bushbuck, and duiker, we held to the wounded buffalo's spoor, neglecting all else.

Just before ascending the terrace we had heard the curious far-travelling sound of kaffirs calling to each other from a distance, but, except for a passing comment, paid no heed to it, and passed on; later we heard it again and again, and at last, when we happened to pause in a more open portion of the bush after we had gone halfway along the terrace, the calling became so frequent and came from so many quarters that we stopped to take note. Francis, who

288

spoke Zulu like one of themselves, at last made out a word or two which gave the clue.

"They're after the wounded buffalo!" he said. "Come on, man, before they get their dogs, or we'll never see him again."

Knowing then that the buffalo was a long way ahead, we scrambled on as fast as we could whilst holding to his track; but it was very hot and very rough, and, to add to our troubles, smoke from a grass fire came driving into our faces.

"Niggers burning on the slopes; confound them!" Francis growled.

They habitually fire the grass in patches during the summer and autumn, as soon as it is dry enough to burn, in order to get young grass for the winter or the early spring, and although the smoke worried us there did not seem to be anything unusual about the fire. But ten minutes later we stopped again; the smoke was perceptibly thicker; birds were flying past us down wind, with numbers of locusts and other insects; two or three times we heard buck and other animals break back, and all were going the same way. Then the same thought struck us both—it was stamped in our faces: this was no ordinary mountain grass fire; it was the bush.

Francis was a quiet fellow, one of the sort it is well not to rouse. His grave is in the Bushveld where his unbeaten record among intrepid lion-hunters was made, and where he fell in the war, leaving another and greater record to his name. The blood rose slowly to his face, until it was bricky red, and he looked an ugly customer as he said:

289   U

"The black brutes have fired the valley to burn him out. Come on quick. We must get out of this on to the slopes!"

We did not know then that there were no slopes —only a precipitous face of rock with dense jungle to the foot of it; and after we had spent a quarter of an hour in that effort, we found our way blocked by the krans and a tangle of undergrowth much worse than that in the middle of the terrace. The noise made by the wind in the trees and our struggling through the grass and bush had prevented our hearing the fire at first, but now its ever-growing roar drowned all sounds. Ordinarily, there would have been no real difficulty in avoiding a bush fire; but, pinned in between the river and the precipice and with miles of dense bush behind us, it was not at all pleasant.

Had we turned back even then and made for the poort it is possible we might have travelled faster than the fire, but it would have been rough work indeed; moreover, that would have been going back— and we did want to get the buffalo—so we decided to make one more try, towards the river this time. It was not much of a try, however, and we had gone no further than the middle of the terrace again when it became alarmingly clear that this fire meant business.

The wind increased greatly, as it always does once a bush fire gets a start; the air was thick with smoke, and full of flying things; in the bush and grass about us there was a constant scurrying; the terror of stampede was in the very atmosphere. A few words

290

of consultation decided us, and we started to burn a patch for standing room and protection.

The hot sun and strong wind had long evaporated all the dew and moisture from the grass, but the sap was still up, and the fire—our fire—seemed cruelly long in catching on. With bunches of dry grass for brands we started burns in twenty places over a length of a hundred yards, and each little flame licked up, spread a little, and then hesitated or died out: it seemed as if ours would never take, while the other came on with roars and leaps, sweeping clouds of sparks and ash over us in the dense rolling mass of smoke.

At last a fierce rush of wind struck down on us, and in a few seconds each little flame became a living demon of destruction; another minute, and the stretch before us was a field of swaying flame. There was a sudden roar and crackle, as of musketry, and the whole mass seemed lifted into the air in one blazing sheet: it simply leaped into life and swept everything before it.

When we opened our scorched eyes the ground in front of us was all black, with only here and there odd lights and torches dotted about—like tapers on a pall; and on ahead, beyond the trellis work of bare scorched trees, the wall of flame swept on.

Then down on the wings of the wind came the other fire; and before it fled every living thing. Heaven only knows what passed us in those few minutes when a broken stream of terrified creatures dashed by, hardly swerving to avoid us. There is no coherent picture left of that scene—just a medley of impressions linked up by flashes of unforgettable vividness.

291

A herd of koodoo came crashing by; I know there was a herd, but only the first and last will come to mind—the space between seems blurred. The clear impressions are of the koodoo bull in front, with nose outthrust, eyes shut against the bush, and great horns laid back upon the withers, as he swept along opening the way for his herd; and then, as they vanished, the big ears, ewe neck, and tilting hindquarters of the last cow—between them nothing but a mass of moving grey!

The wildebeeste went by in Indian file, uniform in shape, colour and horns; and strangely uniform in their mechanical action, lowered heads, and fiercely determined rush.

A rietbuck ram stopped close to us, looked back wide-eyed and anxious, and whistled shrilly, and then cantered on with head erect and white tail flapping; but its mate neither answered nor came by. A terrified hare with its ears laid flat scuttled past within a yard of Francis and did not seem to see him. Above us scared birds swept or fluttered down wind; while others again came up swirling and swinging about, darting boldly through the smoke to catch the insects driven before the fire.

But what comes back with the suggestion of infinitely pathetic helplessness is the picture of a beetle. We stood on the edge of our burn, waiting for the ground to cool, and at my feet a pair of tock-tockie beetles, hump-backed and bandy-legged, came toiling slowly and earnestly along; they reached the edge of our burn, touched the warm ash, and turned patiently aside—to walk round it!

292

A school of chattering monkeys raced out on to the blackened flat, and screamed shrilly with terror as the hot earth and cinders burnt their feet.

Porcupine, antbear, meerkat! They are vague, so vague that nothing is left but the shadow of their passing; but there is one other thing—seen in a flash as brief as the others, for a second or two only, but never to be forgotten! Out of the yellow grass; high up in the waving tops, came sailing down on us the swaying head and glittering eyes of a black mamba— swiftest, most vicious, most deadly of snakes. Francis and I were not five yards apart and it passed between us, giving a quick chilly beady look at each—pitiless, and hateful—and one hiss as the slithering tongue shot out: that was all, and it sailed past with strange effortless movement. How much of the body was on the ground propelling it, I cannot even guess; but we had to look upwards to see the head as the snake passed between us.

The scorching breath of the fire drove us before it on to the baked ground, inches deep in ashes and glowing cinders, where we kept marking time to ease our blistering feet; our hats were pulled down to screen our necks as we stood with our backs to the coming flames; our flannel shirts were so hot that we kept shifting our shoulders for relief. Jock, who had no screen and whose feet had no protection, was in my arms; and we strove to shield ourselves from the furnace-blast with the branches we had used to beat out the fire round the big tree which was our main shelter.

The heat was awful! Live brands were

flying past all the time, and some struck us; myriads of sparks fell round and on us, burning numberless small holes in our clothing, and dotting blisters on our backs, great sheets of flame leaped out from the driving glare, and, detached by many yards from their source, were visible for quite a space in front of us. Then, just at its maddest and fiercest there came a gasp and sob, and the fire devil died behind us as it reached the black bare ground. Our burn divided it as an island splits the flood, and it swept along our flanks in two great walls of living leaping roaring flame.

Two hundred yards away there was a bare yellow place in a world of inky black, and to that haven we ran. It was strange to look about and see the naked country all round us, where but a few minutes earlier the tall grass had shut us in; but the big bare ant-heap was untouched, and there we flung ourselves down, utterly done.

Faint from heat and exhaustion—scorched and blistered, face and arms, back and feet; weary and footsore, and with boots burnt through—we reached camp long after dark, glad to be alive.

We had forgotten the wounded buffalo; he seemed part of another life!

*　　*　　*　　*　　*

There was no more hunting for us: our feet had 'gone in,' and we were well content to sleep and rest. The burnt stubbly ends of the grass had pierced the baked leather of our boots many times; and Jock, too, had suffered badly and could hardly bear to set foot

294

to the ground next day. The best we could hope for
was to be sound enough to return to our own waggons
in two or three days' time.

The camp was under a very large wild fig tree,
whose dense canopy gave us shade all through the day.
We had burnt the grass for some twenty or thirty
yards round as a protection against bush fires; and as
the trees and scrub were not thick just there it was
possible to see in various directions rather further than
one usually can in the Bushveld. The big tree was a
fair landmark by day, and at night we made a good
fire, which owing to the position of the camp one
could see from a considerable distance. These precautions were for the benefit of strayed or belated
members of the party; but I mention them because
the position of the camp and the fire brought us a
strange visitor the last night of our stay there.

There were, I think, seven white men; and the
moving spirit of the party—old Teddy Blacklow of
Ballarat—was one of the old alluvial diggers, a warm-
hearted, impulsive, ever-young old boy, and a rare
good sportsman. That was Teddy, the 'man in muddy
moleskins,' who stretched out the hand of friendship
when the Boy was down, and said "You come along
o' me!"; one of 'God's sort.'

Teddy's spirits were always up; his presence
breathed a cheery optimism on the blankest day;
his humour lighted everything; his stories kept us
going; and his language was a joy for ever. In a
community in which such things savoured of eccen-
tricity, Teddy was an abstainer and never swore;

but if actual profanity was avoided, the dear old boy all unconsciously afforded strong support to those who hold that a man must find relief in vigorous expression. To do this without violating his principles, he invented words and phrases, meaningless in themselves but in general outline, so to say, resembling the worst in vogue; and the effect produced by them upon the sensitive was simply horrifying. Teddy himself was blissfully unconscious of this, for his language, being scrupulously innocent, was deemed by him to be suited to all circumstances and to every company. The inevitable consequence was that the first impression produced by him on the few women he ever met was that of an abandoned old reprobate whose scant veil of disguise only made the outrage of his language more marked. Poor old Teddy! Kindest and gentlest and dearest of souls! How he would have stared at this, speechless with surprise; and how we used to laugh at what some one called his 'glittering parofanities!' Pity it is that they too must go; for one dare not reproduce the best of them.

It was between eight and nine o'clock on the last day of our stay; Francis and I were fit again, and Jock's feet, thanks to care and washing and plenty of castor oil, no longer troubled him; we were examining our boots—re-soled now with raw hide in the rough but effective veld fashion; Teddy was holding forth about the day's chase whilst he cut away the pith of a koodoo's horns and scraped the skull; others were busy on their trophies too; and the kaffirs round their own fire were keeping up the simultaneous

gabble characteristic of hunting boys after a good day and with plenty of meat in camp.

I was sitting on a small camp stool critically examining a boot and wondering if the dried hide would grip well enough to permit of the top lacings being removed, and Jock was lying in front of me, carefully licking the last sore spot on one fore-paw, when I saw his head switch up suddenly and his whole body set hard in a study of intense listening. Then he got up and trotted briskly off some ten or fifteen yards, and stood—a bright spot picked out by the glare of the camp fire—with his back towards me and his uneven ears topping him off.

I walked out to him, and silence fell on the camp; all watched and listened. At first we heard nothing, but soon the call of a wild dog explained Jock's movements; the sound, however, did not come from the direction in which he was looking, but a good deal to the right; and as he instantly looked to this new quarter I concluded that this was not the dog he had previously heard, or else it must have moved rapidly. There was another wait, and then there followed calls from other quarters.

There was nothing unusual in the presence of wild dogs: hyenas, jackals, wild dogs and all the smaller beasts of prey were heard nightly; what attracted attention in this case was the regular calling from different points. The boys said the wild dogs were hunting something and calling to each other to indicate the direction of the hunt, so that those in front might turn the buck and by keeping it in a circle

297

enable fresh or rested dogs to jump in from time to time and so, eventually, wear the poor hunted creature down. This, according to the natives, is the system of the wild pack. When they cannot find easy prey in the young, weak or wounded, and are forced by hunger to hunt hard, they first scatter widely over the chosen area where game is located, and then one buck is chosen—the easiest victim, a ewe with young for choice—and cutting it out from the herd, they follow that one and that alone with remorseless invincible persistency. They begin the hunt knowing that it will last for hours—knowing too that in speed they have no chance against the buck—and when the intended victim is cut out from the herd one or two of the dogs —so the natives say—take up the chase and with long easy gallop keep it going, giving no moment's rest for breath; from time to time they give their weird peculiar call and others of the pack—posted afar— head the buck off to turn it back again; the fresh ones then take up the chase, and the first pair drop out to rest and wait, or follow slowly until their chance and turn come round again. There is something so hateful in the calculated pitiless method that one feels it a duty to kill the cruel brutes whenever a chance occurs.

The hunt went on round us; sometimes near enough to hear the dogs' eager cries quite clearly; sometimes so far away that for a while nothing could be heard; and Jock moved from point to point in the outermost circle of the camp-fire's light nearest to the chase.

298

When at last hunters and hunted completed their wide circuit round the camp, and passed again the point where we had first heard them, the end seemed near; for there were no longer single calls widely separated, but the voices of the pack in hot close chase. They seemed to be passing half a mile away from us; but in the stillness of the night sound travels far, and one can only guess. Again a little while and the cries sounded nearer and as if coming from one quarter—not moving round us as before; and a few minutes more, and it was certain they were still nearer and coming straight towards us. We took our guns then, and I called Jock back to where we stood under the tree with our backs to the fire.

The growing sounds came on out of the night where all was hidden with the weird crescendo effect of a coming flood; we could pick them out then—the louder harsher cries; the crashing through bush; the rush in grass; the sobbing gasps in front; and the hungry panting after. The hunt came at us like a cyclone out of the stillness, and in the forefront of it there burst into the circle of light an impala ewe with open mouth and haunting hunted despairing eyes and widespread ears; and the last staggering strides brought her in among us, tumbling at our feet.

A kaffir jumped out with assegai aloft; but Teddy, with the spring of a tiger and a yell of rage, swung his rifle round and down on assegai arm and head, and dropped the boy in his tracks.

"Go-sh!—Da-ll! Cr-r-r-i-miny! What the Hex are you up to?" and the fiery soft-hearted old boy was

299

down on to his knees in a second, panting with anger and excitement, and threw his arms about the buck.

The foremost of the pack followed hot foot close behind the buck—oblivious of fire and men, seeing nothing but the quarry—and at a distance of five yards a mixed volley of bullets and assegais tumbled it over. Another followed, and again another: both fell where they had stopped, a dozen yards away, puzzled by the fire and the shooting; and still more and more came on, but, warned by the unexpected check in front, they stopped at the clearing's edge, until over twenty pairs of eyes reflecting the fire's light shone out at us in a rough semi-circle. The shotguns came in better then; and more than half the pack went under that night before the others cleared off. Perhaps they did not realise that the shots and flashes were not part of the camp fire from which they seemed to come; perhaps their system of never relinquishing a chase had not been tried against the white man before.

One of the wild dogs, wounded by a shot, seemed to go mad with agony and raced straight into the clearing towards the fire, uttering the strangest maniac-like yaps. Jock had all along been straining to go for them from where I had jammed him between my feet as I sat and fired, and the charge of this dog was more than he could bear: he shot out like a rocket and the collision sent the two flying apart; but he was on to the wild dog again and had it by the throat before it could recover. Instantly the row of lights went out, as if switched off—they were no longer looking at us; there was a rustle and a sound of padded feet, and dim grey-looking forms gathered at the edge of the clearing nearest where Jock and the wounded dog fought. I shouted to Jock to come back, and several of us ran out to help, just as another of the pack made a dash in. It seemed certain that Jock, gripping and worrying his enemy's throat, had neither time nor thought for anything else; yet as the fresh dog came at him he let go his grip of the other, and jumped to meet the new-comer; in mid-spring Jock caught the other by the ear and the two spun completely round—their positions being reversed; then, with another wrench as he landed, he flung the attacker behind him and jumped back at the wounded one which had already turned to go.

It looked like the clean and easy movement of a finished gymnast. It was an affair of a few seconds only, for of course the instant we got a chance at the dogs, without the risk to Jock, both were shot; and he, struggling to get at the others, was haled back to the tree.

While this was going on the impala stood with widespread legs, dazed and helpless, between Teddy's feet, just as he had placed it. Its breath came in broken choking sobs; the look of terror and despair had not yet faded from the staring eyes; the head swayed from side to side; the mouth hung open and the tongue lolled out; all told beyond the power of words the tale of desperate struggle and exhaustion. It drank greedily from the dish that Teddy held for it—emptied it,

and five minutes later drank it again and then lay down.

For half an hour it lay there, slowly recovering; sometimes for spells of a few minutes it appeared to breathe normally once more; then the heavy open-mouthed panting would return again; and all the time Teddy kept on stroking or patting it gently and talking to it as if he were comforting a child, and every now and then bursting out with sudden gusty execrations, in his own particular style, of wild dogs and kaffirs. At last it rose briskly, and standing between his knees looked about, taking no notice of Teddy's hands laid on either side and gently patting it. No one moved or spoke. Jock, at my feet, appeared most interested of all, but I am afraid his views differed considerably from ours on that occasion, and he must have been greatly puzzled; he remained watching intently with his head laid on his paws, his ears cocked, and his brown eyes fixed unblinkingly; and at each movement on the buck's part something stirred in him, drawing every muscle tense and ready for the spring— internal grips which were reflected in the twitching and stiffening of his neck and back; but each time as I laid a hand on him he slackened out again and subsided.

We sat like statues as the impala walked out from its stall between Teddy's knees, and stood looking about wonderingly at the white faces and black, at the strange figures, and at the fire. It stepped out quite quietly, much as it might have moved about here and there any peaceful morning in its usual haunts; the

"GOOD-BYE, AND—THANK YOU!"

head swung about briskly, but unalarmed; and ears and eyes were turned this way and that in easy confidence and mild curiosity.

With a few more steps it threaded its way close to one sitting figure and round a bucket; stepped daintily over Teddy's rifle; and passed the koodoo's head unnoticed.

It seemed to us—even to us, and at the moment—like a scene in fairyland in which some spell held us while the beautiful wild thing strolled about unfrightened.

A few yards away it stopped for perhaps a couple of minutes; its back was towards us and the fire; the silence was absolute; and it stood thus with eyes and ears for the bush alone. There was a warning whisk of the white tail and it started off again—this time at a brisk trot—and we thought it had gone; but at the edge of the clearing it once more stood and listened. Now and again the ears flickered and the head turned slightly one way or another, but no sound came from the bush; the out-thrust nose was raised with gentle tosses, but no taint reached it on the gentle breeze.

All was well!

It looked slowly round, giving one long full gaze back at us which seemed to be "Good-bye, and—thank you!" and cantered out into the dark.

SNOWBALL & TSETSE

SNOWBALL was an 'old soldier'—I say it with all respect! He had been through the wars; that is to say, he had seen the ups and downs of life and had learnt the equine equivalent of "God helps those who help themselves." For Snowball was a horse.

Tsetse was also an old soldier, but he was what you might call a gentleman old soldier, with a sense of duty; and in his case the discipline and honour of his calling were not garments for occasion but part of himself. Snowball was no gentleman: he was selfish and unscrupulous, a confirmed shirker, often absent without leave, and upon occasions a rank deserter—for which last he once narrowly escaped being shot.

Tsetse belonged to my friend Hall; but Snowball was mine! What I know about him was learnt with mortification of the spirit and flesh; and what he could not teach in that way was 'over the head' of the most indurated old dodger that ever lived.

Tsetse had his peculiarities and prejudices: like many old soldiers he was a stickler for etiquette and did not like departures from habit and routine; for

304

instance, he would not under any circumstances permit mounting on the wrong side—a most preposterous stand for an old salted shooting horse to take, and the cause of much inconvenience at times. On the mountains it often happened that the path was too narrow and the slope too steep to permit one to mount on the left side, whereas the sharp rise of the ground made it very easy on the right. But Tsetse made no allowance for this, and if the attempt were made he would stand quite still until the rider was off the ground but not yet in the saddle, and then buck continuously until the offender shot overhead and went skidding down the slope. To one encumbered with a rifle in hand, and a kettle or perhaps a couple of legs of buck slung on the saddle, Tsetse's protest was usually irresis ble.

Snowball had no unpractical prejudices: he objected to work—that was all. He was a pure white horse, goodness knows how old, with enormously long teeth; every vestige of grey or other tinge had faded out of him, and his eyes had an aged and resigned look: one warmed to him at sight as a "dear old pet of a Dobbin!" who ought to be passing his last years grazing contentedly in a meadow and giving bareback rides to little children. The reproach of his venerable look nearly put me off taking him—it seemed such a shame to make the dear old fellow work; but I hardened my heart, and, feeling rather a brute, bought him because he was 'salted' and would live in the Bushveld: beside that, all other considerations were trivial. Of course he was said to be a shooting

horse, and he certainly took no notice of a gun fired under his nose or from his back—which was all the test I could apply at the time; and then his legs were quite sound; his feet were excellent; he had lost no teeth yet; and he was in tiptop condition. What more could one want?

"He looks rather a fool of a horse!" I had remarked dubiously to Joey the Smith, who was 'willin' to let him go,' and I can recall now the peculiar glint in Joey's eye and the way he sort of steadied himself with a little cough before he answered feelingly:

"He's no fool, sonny! You won't want to get a cleverer horse as long as you live!"

And no more I did—as we used to say!

Snowball had one disfigurement, consisting of a large black swelling as big as a small orange behind his left eye, which must have annoyed him greatly; it could easily have been removed, and many suggestions were made on the subject but all of them were firmly declined. Without that lump I should have had no chance against him: it was the weak spot in his defence: it was the only cover under which it was possible to stalk him when he made one of his determined attempts to dodge or desert; for he could see nothing that came up behind him on the left side without turning his head completely round; hence one part of the country was always hidden from him, and of course it was from this quarter that we invariably made our approaches to attack.

So well did Snowball realise this that when the old villain intended giving trouble he would start off with

306

his head swung away to the right, and when far enough away to graze in security—a hundred yards or so was enough—would turn right about and face towards the waggons or camp, or wherever the danger-quarter was; then, keeping us well in view, he would either graze off sideways, or from time to time walk briskly off to occupy a new place, with the right eye swung round on us like a searchlight.

Against all this, however, it is only fair to admit that there were times when for days, and even weeks, at a stretch he would behave admirably, giving no more trouble than Jock did. Moreover he had qualities which were not to be despised: he was as sound as a bell, very clever on his feet, never lost his condition, and, although not fast, could last for ever at his own pace.

Experience taught me to take no chances with Snowball. After a hard day he was apt to think that 'enough was as good as a feast,' and then trouble might be expected. But there was really no safe rule with him; he seemed to have moods—to 'get out of bed on the wrong side'—on certain days and, for no reason in the world, behave with a calculated hostility that was simply maddening.

Hunting horses live almost entirely by grazing, as it is seldom possible to carry any grain or other foods for them and never possible to carry enough; and salted horses have therefore a particular value in that they can be turned out to graze at night or in the morning and evening dews when animals not immunised will contract horse-sickness; thus they

feed during the hours when hunting is not possible and keep their condition when an unsalted horse would fall away from sheer want of food.

According to their training, disposition, and knowledge of good and evil, horses are differently treated when 'offsaddled'; some may be trusted without even a halter, and can be caught and saddled when and where required; others are knee-haltered; others are hobbled by a strap coupling either both fore-feet, or one fore and one hind foot, with enough slack to allow walking, but not enough for the greater reach of a trot or gallop; whilst some incorrigibles are both knee-haltered and hobbled; and in this gallery Snowball figured upon occasion—a mournful and injured innocent, if appearances went for anything!

It was not, as a rule, at the outspan, where many hands were available, that Snowball gave trouble, but out hunting when I was alone or with only one companion. A trained shooting horse should stop as soon as his rider lays hand on mane to dismount, and should remain where he is left for any length of time until his master returns; some horses require the reins to be dropped over their heads to remind them of their duty but many can safely be left to themselves and will be found grazing quietly where left.

Snowball knew well what to do, but he pleased himself about doing it; sometimes he would stand; sometimes move off a little way, and keep moving— just out of reach—holding his head well on one side so that he should not tread on the trailing reins or the long weighted reimpje which was attached to his bit

308

for the purpose of hindering and catching him; sometimes, with a troop of buck moving on ahead or perhaps a wounded one to follow, this old sinner would right-about-face and simply walk off—only a few yards separating us—with his ears laid back, his tail tucked down ominously, and occasional little liftings of his hindquarters to let me know what to expect—and his right eye on me all the while; and, if I ran to head him off, he would break into a trot and leave me a little worse off than before; and sometimes, in familiar country, he would make straight away for the waggons without more ado.

It is demoralising in the extreme to be expecting a jerk when in the act of aiming—and Snowball, who cared no more for shooting than a deaf gunner, would plunge like a two-year-old when he was play-acting—and it is little better, while creeping forward for a shot, to hear your horse strolling off behind and realise that you will have to hunt for him and perhaps walk many miles back to camp without means of carrying anything you may shoot. The result of experience was that I had to choose between two alternatives: either to hook him up to a tree or bush each time or hobble him with his reins, and so lose many good chances of quick shots when coming unexpectedly on game; or to slip an arm through the reins and take chance of being plucked off my aim or jerked violently backwards as I fired. But it was at the 'offsaddles' on long journeys across country, or during the rest in a day's hunt, that trouble was most to be feared, and although hobbling is dangerous in a country so full of holes, stumps, and

all sorts of grass-hidden obstacles, there were times when consideration for Snowball seemed mighty like pure foolishness, and it would have been no grief to me if he had broken his neck!

To the credit of Snowball stand certain things, however, and it is but justice to say that, when once in the ranks, he played his part well; and it is due to him to say that during one hard season a camp of waggons with their complement of men had to be kept in meat, and it was Snowball who carried—for short and long distances, through dry rough country, at all times of day and night, hot, thirsty, and tired, and without a breakdown or a day's sickness—a bag that totalled many thousands of pounds in weight, and the man who made the bag.

"That wall-eyed brute of yours" was launched at me in bitterness of spirit on many occasions when Snowball led the normally well-behaved ones astray; and it is curious to note how strength of character or clear purpose will establish leadership among animals, as among men. Rooiland the restless, when dissatisfied with the grass or in want of water, would cast about up wind for a few minutes and then with his hot eyeballs staring and nostrils well distended choose his line, going resolutely along and only pausing from time to time to give a low moan for signal and allow the straggling string of unquestioning followers to catch up. When Rooiland had 'trek fever' there was no rest for herd boys. So too with old Snowball: he led the well-behaved astray and they followed him blindly. Had Snowball been a schoolboy, a wise headmaster would have expelled him—for the general good and discipline of the school.

On one long horseback journey through Swaziland to the coast, where few white men and no horses had yet been seen, we learned to know Snowball and Tsetse well, and found out what a horse can do when put to it. It was a curious experience on that trip to see whole villages flee in terror at the first sight of the new strange animals—one brown and one white; in some places not even the grown men would approach, but too proud to show fear, they stood their ground, their bronze faces blanching visibly and setting hard as we rode up; the women fled with half-stifled cries of alarm; and once, when we came unexpectedly upon a party of naked urchins playing on the banks of a stream, the whole pack set off full cry for the water and, jumping in like a school of alarmed frogs, disappeared. Infinitely amused by the stampede we rode up to see what had become of them, but the silence was absolute, and for a while they seemed to have vanished altogether; then a tell-tale ripple gave the clue, and under the banks among the ferns and exposed roots we picked out little black faces half sub-merged and pairs of frightened eyes staring at us from all sides. They were not to be reassured, either: the only effect produced by our laughing comments and friendly overtures being that the head which deemed itself pointedly addressed would dis-appear completely and remain so long out of sight as to make us feel quite smothery and criminally responsible.

It is in the rivers that a man feels the importance of a good horse with a stout heart, and his dependence on it. There were no roads, and not even known tracks, there; and when we reached the Black Umbelusi we picked a place where there was little current and apparently an easy way out on the opposite side. It was much deeper than it looked; however, we were prepared, and thirty yards of swimming did not trouble us; yet it certainly was a surprise to us when the horses swam right up to the other bank without finding bottom and, turning aside, began to swim up stream. Looking down into the clear depths we saw that there was a sheer wall of rock to within a few inches of the surface. Now, a horse with a man on his back swims low—only the head and half the neck showing above water—and by what instinct or means the horses realised the position I do not know, but, with little hesitation and apparently of one accord, they got back a yard or two from the ledge and, raising first one fore-foot and then the other, literally climbed out—exactly as a man or a dog does out of a swimming bath—hoisting their riders out with them without apparent difficulty. That was something which we had not thought possible, and to satisfy ourselves we dismounted and tried the depth; but the ten-foot reeds failed to reach bottom.

When it came to crossing the Crocodile River we chose the widest spot in the hope that it would be shallow and free of rocks. We fired some shots into the river to scare the crocodiles, and started to

312

cross; but to our surprise Tsetse, the strong-nerved and reliable, who always had the post of honour in front, absolutely refused to enter.

The water of the Crocodile is at its best of amber clearness and we could not see bottom, but the sloping grassy bank promised well enough and no hint reached us of what the horses knew quite well. All we had was on our horses—food, blankets, billy, rifles and ammunition. We were off on a long trip and, to vary or supplement the game diet, carried a small packet of tea, a little sugar, flour, and salt, and some beads with which to trade for native fowls and thick milk; the guns had to do the rest. Thus there were certain things we could not afford to wet, and these we used to wrap up in a mackintosh and carry high when it came to swimming, but this crossing looked so easy that it seemed sufficient to raise the packs instead of carrying part of them.

Tsetse, who in the ordinary way regarded the spur as part of the accepted discipline, promptly resented it when there seemed to him to be sufficient reason; and when Hall, astonished at Tsetse's unexpected obstinacy, gave him both heels, the old horse considerately swung round away from the river, and with a couple of neatly executed bucks shot his encumbered rider off the raised pack, yards away on to the soft grass—water-bottle, rifle, bandolier and man landing in a lovely tangle.

I then put old Snowball at it, fully expecting trouble; but the old soldier was quite at home; he walked quietly to the edge,

313

sat down comfortably, and slid into the water—launching himself with scarce a ripple just like an old hippo. That gave us the explanation of Tsetse's tantrum: the water came up to the seat of my saddle and walking was only just possible. I stopped at once, waiting for Tsetse to follow; and Hall, prepared for another refusal, sat back and again used his spurs. No doubt Tsetse, once he knew the depth, was quite satisfied and meant to go in quietly, and the prick of the spur must have been unexpected, for he gave a plunge forward, landing with his fore-feet in deep water and hindquarters still on the bank, and Hall shot out overhead, landing half across old Snowball's back. There was a moment of ludicrous but agonised suspense! Hall's legs were firmly gripping Tsetse behind the ears while he sprawled on his stomach on Snowball's crupper, with the reins still in one hand and the rifle in the other. Doubled up with suppressed laughter I grabbed a fistful of shirt and held on, every moment expecting Tsetse to hoist his head or pull back and complete the disaster, while Hall was spluttering out directions, entreaties and imprecations; but good old Tsetse never moved, and Hall, handing me the rifle, managed to swarm backwards on to Tsetse's withers and scramble on to the pack again.

Then, saddle-deep in the river—duckings and crocodiles forgotten—we sat looking at each other and laughed till we ached.

The river was about three hundred yards wide there with a good sandy bottom and of uniform depth,

314

"I GRABBED A FISTFUL OF SHIRT AND HELD ON"

but, to our disappointment, we found that the other bank which had appeared to slope gently to the water edge was in fact a sheer wall standing up several feet above the river level. The beautiful slope which we had seen consisted of water grass and reed tops; the bank itself was of firm moist clay; and the river bottom close under it was soft mud. We tried a little way up and down, but found deeper water, more mud and reeds, and no break in the bank; there was not even a lagavaan slide, a game path, or a drinking-place. There seemed to be nothing for it but to go back again and try somewhere else.

Hall was 'bad to beat' when he started on anything—he did not know how to give in; but when he looked at the bank and said, "We'll have a shot at this," I thought at first he was joking. Later, to my remark that "no horse ever born would face that," he answered that "any way we could try: it would be just as good as hunting for more places of the same sort!"

I do not know the height of the bank, as we were not thinking of records at that time, but there are certain facts which enable one to guess fairly closely.

Tsetse was ranged up beside the bank, and Hall standing in the saddle threw his rifle and bandolier up and scrambled out himself. I then loosened Tsetse's girths from my seat on Snowball, and handed up the packed saddle—Hall lying down on the bank to take it from me; and we did the same with Snowball's load, including my own clothes, for, as it was already sundown, a ducking was not desirable.

I loosened one side of Tsetse's reins, and after attaching one of mine in order to give the necessary length to them threw the end up to Hall, and he cut and handed me a long supple rod for a whip to stir Tsetse to his best endeavours. The water there was rather more than half saddle-flap high; I know that because it just left me a good expanse of hindquarters to aim at when the moment came.

"Now!" yelled Hall, "Up, Tsetse! Up!"; and whack went the stick! Tsetse reared up, right on end; he could not reach the top but struck his fore-feet into the moist bank near the top, and with a mighty plunge that soused Snowball and me, went out. The tug on the leading rein, on which Hall had thrown all his weight when Tsetse used it to lever himself up, had jerked Hall flat on his face; but he was up in a minute, and releasing Tsetse threw back the rein to get Snowball to face it while the example was fresh.

Then for the first time we thought of the crocodiles —and the river was full of them! But Snowball without some one behind him with a stick would never face that jump, and there was nothing for it but to fire some scaring shots, and slip into the water and get the job over as quickly as possible.

Snarleyow was with us—I had left Jock at the waggons fearing that we would get into fly country on the Umbelusi—and the bank was too high and too steep for him; he huddled up against it half-supported by reeds, and whined plaintively.

To our relief Snowball faced the jump quite readily; indeed, the old sinner did it with much less

316

effort and splash than the bigger Tsetse. But then came an extremely unpleasant spell. Snowball got a scare, because Hall in his anxiety to get me out rushed up to him on the warty side to get the reins off; and the old ruffian waltzed around, dragging Hall through the thorns, while Snarleyow and I waited in the water for help.

At that moment I had a poorer opinion of Snowball and Snarley than at any other I can remember. I wished Snarley dead twenty times in twenty seconds. Crocodiles love dogs; and it seemed to me a million to one that a pair of green eyes and a black snout must slide out of the water any moment, drawn to us by those advertising whines! And the worst of it was, I was outside Snarley, with my white legs gleaming in the open water, while his cringing form was tucked away half-hidden by the reeds. What an age it seemed! How each reed shaken by the river breeze caught the eye, giving me goose-flesh and sending waves of cold shudders creeping over me! How the cold smooth touch of a reed stem against my leg made me want to jump and to get out with one huge plunge as the horses had done! And even when I had passed the struggling yowling Snarley up, the few remaining seconds seemed painfully long. Hall had to lie flat and reach his furthest to grip my hand; and I nearly pulled him in, scrambling up that bank like a chased cat up a tree.

When one comes to think it out, the bank must have been nine feet high. It was mighty unpleasant; but it taught us what a horse can do when he puts his back into it!

JOCK'S·MISTAKE

Halfway between the Crocodile and Komati rivers, a few miles south of the old road. there are half a dozen or more small kopjes between which lie broad richly grassed depressions, too wide and flat to be called valleys. The fall of the country is slight, yet the rich loamy soil has been washed out in places into dongas of considerable depth. There is no running water there in winter, but there are a few big pools—long narrow irregularly shaped bits of water—with shady trees around them.

I came upon the place by accident one day, and thereafter we kept it dark as our own preserve; for it was full of game, and a most delightful spot. It was there that Snarleyow twice cleaned out the hunter's pot.

Apart from the discovery of this preserve, the day was memorable for the reason that it was my first experience of a big mixed herd; and I learned that day how difficult the work may be when several kinds of game run together. After a dry and warm morning the sight of the big pool had prompted an offsaddle;

318

Snowball was tethered in a patch of good grass, and Jock and I were lying in the shade.

When he began to sniff and walk up wind I took the rifle and followed, and only a little way off we came into dry vlei ground where there were few trees and the grass stood about waist high. Some two hundred yards away where the ground rose slightly and the bush became thicker there was a fair-sized troop of impala, perhaps a hundred or more, and just behind, and mostly to one side of them, were between twenty and thirty tsessebe. We saw them clearly and in time to avoid exposing ourselves: they were neither feeding nor resting, but simply standing about, and individual animals were moving unconcernedly from time to time with an air of idle loitering. I tried to pick out a good tsessebe ram, but the impala were in the way, and it was necessary to crawl for some distance to reach certain cover away on the right.

Crawling is hard work and very rough on both hands and knees in the Bushveld, frequent rests being necessary; and in one of the pauses I heard a curious sound of soft padded feet jumping behind me, and looking quickly about caught Jock in the act of taking his observations. The grass was too high for him to see over, even when he stood up on his hind legs, and he was giving jumps of slowly increasing strength to get the height which would enable him to see what was on. I shall never forget that first view of Jock's ballooning observations; it became a regular practice afterwards and I grew accustomed to seeing him stand on his hind legs or jump when his view was shut out—

319

indeed sometimes when we were having a slow time I used to draw him by pretending to stalk something; but it is that first view that remains a picture of him. I turned at the instant when he was at the top of his jump; his legs were all bunched up, his eyes staring eagerly and his ears had flapped out, giving him a look of comic astonishment. It was a most surprisingly unreal sight: he looked like a caricature of Jock shot into the air by a galvanic shock. A sign with my hand brought him flat on the ground, looking distinctly guilty, and we moved along again; but I was shaking with silent laughter.

At the next stop I had a look back to see how he was behaving, and to my surprise, although he was following carefully close behind me, he was looking steadily away to our immediate right. I subsided gently on to my left side to see what it was that interested him, and to my delight saw a troop of twenty to twenty-five blue wildebeeste. They too were 'standing any way' and evidently had not seen us.

I worked myself cautiously round to face them so as to be able to pick my shot and take it kneeling, thus clearing the tops of the grass; but whilst doing this another surprising development took place. Looking hard and carefully at the wildebeeste two hundred yards away, I became conscious of something else in between us, and only half the distance off, looking at me. It had the effect of a shock; the disagreeable effect produced by having a book or picture suddenly thrust close to the face; the feeling of wanting to get further away from it to re-focus one's sight.

320

What I saw was simply a dozen quagga, all exactly alike, all standing alike, all looking at me, all full face to me, their fore-feet together, their ears cocked, and their heads quite motionless—all gazing steadily at me, alive with interest and curiosity. There was something quite ludicrous in it, and something perplexing also; when I looked at the quagga the wildebeeste seemed to get out of focus and were lost to me; when I looked at the wildebeeste the quagga 'blurred' and faded out of sight. The difference in distance, perhaps as much as the very marked difference in the distinctive colourings, threw me out; and the effect of being watched also told. Of course I wanted to get a wildebeeste, but I was conscious of the watching quagga all the time, and, for the life of me, could not help constantly looking at them to see if they were going to start off and stampede the others.

Whilst trying to pick out the best of the wildebeeste a movement away on the left made me look that way: the impala jumped off like one animal, scaring the tsessebe into a scattering rout; the quagga switched round and thundered off like a stampede of horses; and the wildebeeste simply vanished. One signal in one troop had sent the whole lot off. Jock and I were left alone, still crouching, looking from side to side, staring at the slowly drifting dust, and listening to the distant dying sound of galloping feet.

It was a great disappointment, but the conviction that we had found a really good spot made some amends, and Snowball was left undisturbed to feed and rest for another two hours. We made for the waggons

along another route taking in some of the newly discovered country in the home sweep, and the promise of the morning was fulfilled. We had not been more than a few minutes on the way when a fine rietbuck ram jumped up within a dozen yards of Snowball's nose. Old Rocky had taught me to imitate the rietbuck's shrill whistle and this one fell to the first shot. He was a fine big fellow, and as Snowball put on airs and pretended to be nervous when it came to packing the meat, I had to blindfold him, and after hoisting the buck up to a horizontal branch lowered it on to his back.

Snowball was villainously slow and bad to lead. He knew that whilst being led neither whip nor spur could touch him, and when loaded up with meat he dragged along at a miserable walk: one had to haul him. Once —but only once—I had tried driving him before me, trusting to about 400 lb. weight of koodoo meat to keep him steady; but no sooner had I stepped behind with a switch than he went off with a cumbrous plunge and bucked like a frantic mule until he rid himself of his load, saddle and all. The fact is one person could not manage him on foot, it needed one at each end of him, and he knew it; thus it worked out at a compromise: he carried my load, and I went his pace!

We were labouring along in this fashion when we came on the wildebeeste again. A white man on foot seems to be recognised as an enemy; but if accompanied by animals, either on horseback, driving in a vehicle, leading a horse, or walking among cattle, he may pass unnoticed for a long while: attention seems to be fixed on the animals rather than the man, and frank curiosity instead of alarm is quite evidently the feeling aroused.

The wildebeeste had allowed me to get close up, and I picked out the big bull and took the shot kneeling, with my toe hooked in the reins to secure Snowball, taking the chance of being jerked off my aim rather than let him go; but he behaved like an angel, and once more that day a single shot was enough.

It was a long and tedious job skinning the big fellow, cutting him up, hauling the heavy limbs and the rest of the meat up into a suitable tree, and making all safe against the robbers of the earth and the air; and most troublesome of all was packing the head and skin on Snowball, who showed the profoundest mistrust of this dark ferocious-looking monster.

Snowball and I had had enough of it when we reached camp, well after dark; but Jock I am not so sure of: his invincible keenness seemed at times to have something in it of mute reproach—the tinge of disappointment in those they love which great hearts feel, and strive to hide! I never outstayed Jock, and never once knew him 'own up' that he had had enough.

No two days were quite alike; yet many were alike in the sense that they were successful without hitch and without interest to any but the hunters; many others were marked by chases in which Jock's part— most essential to success—too closely resembled that of other days to be worth repeating. On that day

323

he had, as usual, been the one to see the wildebeeste and had 'given the word' in time; the rest was only one straight shot. That was fair partnership in which both were happy; but there was nothing much to talk about.

There was very little wanton shooting with us, for when we had more fresh meat than was required, as often happened, it was dried as 'bultong' for the days of shortage which were sure to come.

I started off early next morning with the boys to bring in the meat, and went on foot, giving Snowball a rest, more or less deserved. By nine o'clock the boys were on their way back, and leaving them to take the direct route I struck away eastwards along the line of the pools, not expecting much and least of all dreaming that fate had one of the worst days in store for us: "From cloudless heavens her lightnings glance" did not occur to my mind as we moved silently along in the bright sunshine.

We passed the second pool, loitering a few minutes in the cool shade of the evergreens to watch the green pigeons feeding on the wild figs and peering down curiously at us; then moved briskly into more open ground. It is not wise to step too suddenly out of the dark shade into strong glare, and it may have been that act of carelessness that enabled the koodoo to get off before I saw them. They cantered away in a string with the cows in the rear, between me and two full-grown bulls. It was a running-shot—end on—and the last of the troop, a big cow, gave a stumble; but catching

324

herself up again she cantered off slowly. Her body was all bunched up and she was pitching greatly, and her hind legs kept flying out in irregular kicks, much as you may see a horse kick out when a blind fly is biting him.

There was no time for a second shot and we started off in hot pursuit; and fifty yards further on where there was a clear view I saw that the koodoo was going no faster than an easy canter, and Jock was close behind.

Whether he was misled by the curious action, and believed there was a broken leg to grip, or was simply over-bold, it is impossible to know. Whatever the reason, he jumped for one of the hind legs, and at the same moment the koodoo lashed out viciously. One foot struck him under the jaw close to the throat, 'whipped' his head and neck back like a bent switch, and hurled him somersaulting backwards.

I have the impression—as one sees oneself in a nightmare—of a person throwing up his arms and calling the name of his child as a train passed over it.

Jock lay limp and motionless, with the blood oozing from mouth, nose and eyes. I recollect feeling for his heart-beat and breath, and shaking him roughly and calling him by name; then, remembering the pool near by, I left him in the shade of a tree, filled my hat with water, ran back again and poured it over him and into his mouth, shaking him again to rouse him, and several times pressing his sides—bellows fashion— in a ridiculous effort to restore breathing.

The old hat was leaky and I had to grip the rough-cut ventilations to make it hold any water at all, and I was returning with a second supply when with a great big heart-jump I saw Jock heel over from his side and with his forelegs flat on the ground raise himself to a resting position, his head wagging groggily and his eyes blinking in a very dazed way.

He took no notice when I called his name, but at the touch of my hand his ears moved up and the stumpy tail scraped feebly in the dead leaves. He was stone deaf; but I did not know it then. He lapped a little of the water, sneezed the blood away and licked his chops; and then, with evident effort, stood up.

But this is the picture which it is impossible to forget. The dog was still so dazed and shaken that he reeled slightly, steadying himself by spreading his legs well apart, and there followed a few seconds' pause in which he stood thus; and then he began to walk forward with the uncertain staggery walk of a toddling child. His jaws were set close; his eyes were beady black, and he looked 'fight' all over. He took no notice of me; and I, never dreaming that he was after the koodoo, watched the walk quicken to a laboured trot before I moved or called; but he paid no heed to the call. For the first time in his life there was rank open defiance of orders, and he trotted slowly along with his nose to the ground. Then I understood; and, thinking he was maddened by the kick and not quite responsible for himself, and—more than that—admiring his pluck far too much to be angry, I ran to bring him back; but at a turn in

his course he saw me coming, and this time he obeyed the call and signal instantly, and with a limp air of disappointment followed quietly back to the tree.

The reason for Jock's persistent disobedience that day was not even suspected then; I put everything down to the kick; and he seemed to me to be 'all wrong,' but indeed there was excuse enough for him. Nevertheless it was puzzling that at times he should ignore me in positively contemptuous fashion, and at others obey with all his old readiness: I neither knew he was deaf, nor realised that the habit of using certain signs and gestures when I spoke to him—and even of using them in place of orders when silence was imperative—had made him almost independent of the word of mouth. From that day he depended wholly upon signs; for he never heard another sound.

Jock came back with me and lay down; but he was not content. Presently he rose again and remained standing with his back to me, looking steadily in the direction taken by the koodoo. It was fine to see the indomitable spirit, but I did not mean to let him try again; the koodoo was as good as dead no doubt, yet a hundred koodoo would not have tempted me to risk taking him out: to rest him and get him back to the camp was the only thought. I was feeling very soft about the dog then. And while I sat thus watching him and waiting for him to rest and recover, once more and almost within reach of me he started off again. But it was not as he had done before: this time he went with a spring and a rush, and with head lowered and meaning business. In vain I called

327

and followed: he outpaced me and left me in a few strides.

The koodoo had gone along the right bank of the donga which, commencing just below the pool, extended half a mile or more down the flat valley. Jock's rush was magnificent, but it was puzzling, and his direction was even more so; for he made straight for the donga.

I ran back for the rifle and followed, and he had already disappeared down the steep bank of the donga when, through the trees on the opposite side, I saw a koodoo cow moving along at a slow cramped walk. The donga was a deep one with perpendicular sides, and in places even overhanging crumbling banks, and I reached it as Jock, slipping and struggling, worked his way up the other wall writhing and climbing through the tree roots exposed by the floods. As he rushed out the koodoo saw him and turned; there was just a chance—a second of time: a foot of space—before he got in the line of fire; and I took it. One hind leg gave way, and in the short sidelong stagger that followed Jock jumped at the koodoo's throat and they went down together.

It took me several minutes to get through the donga, and by that time the koodoo was dead and Jock was standing, wide-mouthed and panting, on guard at its head: the second shot had been enough.

It was an unexpected and puzzling end; and, in a way, not a welcome one, as it meant delay in getting back. After the morning's experience there was not much inclination for the skinning and cutting

328

up of a big animal and I set to work gathering branches and grass to hide the carcass, meaning to send the boys back for it.

But the day's experiences were not over yet: a low growl from Jock made me look sharply round, to see half a dozen kaffirs coming through the bush with a string of mongrel hounds at their heels.

So that was the explanation of the koodoo's return to us! The natives, a hunting party, had heard the shot and coming along in hopes of meat had met and headed off the wounded koodoo, turning her back almost on her own tracks. There was satisfaction in having the puzzle solved, but the more practical point was that here was all the help I wanted; and the boys readily agreed to skin the animal and carry the four quarters to the camp for the gift of the rest.

Then my trouble began with Jock. He flew at the first of the kaffir dogs that sneaked up to sniff at the koodoo. Shouting at him produced no effect whatever, and before I could get hold of him he had mauled the animal pretty badly. After hauling him off I sat down in the shade, with him beside me; but there were many dogs, and a succession of affairs, and I, knowing nothing of his deafness, became thoroughly exasperated and surprised by poor old Jock's behaviour.

His instinct to defend our kills, which was always strong, was roused that day beyond control, and his hatred of kaffir dogs—an implacable one in any case—made a perfect fury of him; still, the sickening awful feeling that came over me as he lay limp and lifeless was too fresh, and it was not possible to be really

329

angry; and after half a dozen of the dogs had been badly handled there was something so comical in the way they sheered off and eyed Jock that I could only laugh. They sneaked behind bushes and tried to circumvent him in all sorts of ways, but fled precipitately as soon as he moved a step or lowered his head and humped his shoulders threateningly. Even the kaffir owners, who had begun to look glum, broke into appreciative laughter and shouts of admiration for the white man's dog.

Jock kept up an unbroken string of growls, not loud, of course, but I could feel them going all the while like a volcano's rumbling as my restraining hand rested on him, and when the boys came up to skin the koodoo I had to hold him down and shake him sharply. The dog was mad with fight; he bristled all over; and no patting or talking produced more than a flicker of his ears. The growling went on; the hair stood up; the tail was quite unresponsive; his jaws were set like a vice; and his eyes shone like two black diamonds. He had actually struggled to get free of my hand when the boys began to skin, and they were so scared by his resolute attempt that they would not start until I put him down between my knees and held him.

I was sitting against a tree only three or four yards from the koodoo, and the boys, who had lighted a fire in anticipation of early tit-bits which would grill while they worked, were getting along well with the skinning, when one of them saw fit to pause in order to hold forth in the native fashion on the glories of the chase and the might of the white man. Jock's

330

head lay on his paws and his mouth was shut like a rat-trap; his growling grew louder as the bombastic nigger, all unconscious of the wicked watching eyes behind him, waved his blood-stained knife and warmed to his theme.

"Great you thought yourself," proclaimed the orator, addressing the dead koodoo in a long rigmarole which was only partly understood by me but evidently much approved by the other boys as they stooped to their work, "Swift of foot and strong of limb. But the white man came, and—there!" I could not make out the words with any certainty; but whatever the last word was, it was intended as a dramatic climax, and to lend additional force to his point the orator let fly a resounding kick on the koodoo's stomach.

The effect was quite electrical! Like an arrow from the bow Jock flew at him! The warning shout came too late, and as Jock's teeth fastened in him behind the terrified boy gave a wild bound over the koodoo, carrying Jock like a streaming coat-tail behind him.

The work was stopped and the natives drew off in grave consultation. I thought that they had had enough of Jock for one day and that they would strike work and leave me, probably returning later on to steal the meat while I went for help from the waggons. But it turned out that the consultation was purely medical, and in a few minutes I had an interesting exhibition of native doctoring. They laid the late orator out face downwards, and one burly 'brother' straddled him across the small of the back; then after a little preliminary examination of the four

331

slits left by Jock's fangs, he proceeded to cauterise them with the glowing ends of sundry sticks which an assistant took from the fire and handed to him as required. The victim flapped his hands on the ground and hallooed out "My babo! My babo!" but he did not struggle; and the operator toasted away with methodical indifference.

The orator stood it well!

I took Jock away to the big tree near the pool: it was evident that he too had had enough of it for one day.

JANTJE

THERE was no hunting for several days after the affair with the koodoo cow. Jock looked worse the following day than he had done since recovering consciousness: his head and neck swelled up so that chewing was impossible and he could only lap a little soup or milk, and could hardly bend his neck at all.

On the morning of the second day Jim Makokel' came up with his hostile-looking swagger and a cross worried look on his face, and in a half-angry and wholly disgusted tone jerked out at me, "The dog is deaf. I say so! Me! Makokela! Jock is deaf. He does not hear when you speak. Deaf! yes, deaf!"

Jim's tone grew fiercer as he warmed up; he seemed to hold me responsible. The moment the boy spoke I knew it was true—it was the only possible explanation of many little things; nevertheless I jumped up hurriedly to try him in a dozen ways, hoping to find that he could hear something. Jim was right; he was really stone deaf. It was pathetic to find how each little subterfuge that drew his eyes from me left

333

him out of reach: it seemed as if a link had broken between us and I had lost my hold. That was wrong, however! In a few days he began to realise the loss of hearing; and after that, feeling so much greater dependence on sight, his watchfulness increased so that nothing escaped him. None of those who saw him in that year, when he was at his very best, could bring themselves to believe that he was deaf. With me it made differences both ways: something lost, and something gained. If he could hear nothing, he saw more; the language of signs developed; and taking it all round I believe the sense of mutual dependence for success and of mutual understanding was greater than ever.

Snowball went on to the retired list at the end of the next trip.

Joey the Smith stood at the forge one day, trimming a red-hot horse-shoe, when I rode up and dropping the reins over Snowball's head, sang out "Morning, Joey!"

Joey placed the chisel on the shoe with nice calculation of the amount he wanted to snip off; his assistant boy swung the big hammer, and an inch cube of red-hot iron dropped off. Then Joey looked up with, what seemed to me, a conflict of innocent surprise and stifled amusement in his face. The boy also turned to look, and—the insignificant incident is curiously unforgettable—trod upon the piece of hot iron. "Look where you're standing," said Joey reproachfully, as the smoke and smell of burning skin-welt rose up; and the boy with a grunt of disgust, such as we might give at a

334

burned boot, looked to see what damage had been done to his 'unders.' It gave me an even better idea of a nigger's feet than those thorn-digging operations when we had to cut through a solid whitish welt a third of an incn thick.

Joey grinned openly at the boy; but he was thinking of Snowball.

"I wonder you had the heart, Joey, I do indeed!" I said, shaking my head at him.

"You would have him, lad, there was no refusin' you! You arst so nice and wanted him so bad!"

"But how could you bear to part with him, Joey? It must have been like selling one of the family."

"'Es, Boy, 'es! We are a bit stoopid—our lot! Is he still such a fool, or has he improved any with you?"

"Joey, I've learned him—full up to the teeth. If he stops longer he will become wicked, like me; and you would not be the ruin of an innocent young thing trying to earn a living honestly, if he can?"

"Come round behind the shop, Boy. I got a pony 'll suit you proper!" He gave a hearty laugh, and added "You can always get what you arsk for—if it ain't worth having. Moril! Don't arsk! I never offered you Snowball. This one's different. You can have him at cost price; and that's an old twelve-month account! Ten pounds. He's worth four of it! Salted *an'* shootin'! Shake!" and I gripped

his grimy old fist gladly, knowing it was 'jonnick' and 'a square deal.'

That was Mungo Park—the long, strong, low-built, half-bred Basuto pony—well-trained and without guile.

I left Snowball with his previous owner, to use as required, and never called back for him; and if this should meet the eye of Joey the Smith he will know that I no longer hope his future life will be spent in stalking a wart-eyed white horse in a phantom Bush-veld. Mungo made amends.

There was a spot between the Komati and Crocodile rivers on the north side of the road where the white man seldom passed and nature was undisturbed; few knew of water there; it was too well concealed between deep banks and the dense growth of thorns and large trees.

The spot always had great attractions for me apart from the big game to be found there. I used to steal along the banks of this lone water and watch the smaller life of the bush. It was a delightful field for naturalist and artist, but unfortunately we thought little of such things, and knew even less; and now nothing is left from all the glorious opportunities but the memory of an endless fascination and a few facts that touch the human chord and will not submit to be forgotten.

There were plenty of birds—guinea-fowl, pheasant, partridge, knoorhaan and bush pauw. Jock accompanied me of course when I took the fowling-piece, but merely for companionship; for there was no need for him on these occasions. I shot birds to get a change of food and trusted to walking them up along the river banks and near drinking pools; but one evening Jock came forward of his own accord to help me—a sort of amused volunteer; and after that I always used him.

He had been at my heels, apparently taking little interest in the proceedings from the moment the first bird fell and he saw what the game was; probably he was intelligently interested all the time but considered it nothing to get excited about. After a time I saw him turn aside from the line we had been taking and stroll off at a walking pace, sniffing softly the while. When he had gone a dozen yards he stopped and looked back at me; then he looked in front again with his head slightly on one side, much as he would have done examining a beetle rolling his ball.

There were no signs of anything, yet the grass was short for those parts, scarce a foot high, and close, soft and curly. A brace of partridges rose a few feet from Jock, and he stood at ease calmly watching them, without a sign or a move to indicate more than amused interest. The birds were absurdly tame and sailed so quietly along that I hesitated at first to shoot; then the noise of the two shots put up the largest number of partridges I have ever seen in one lot, and a line of birds rose for perhaps sixty yards across our front. There was no wild whirr and confusion: they rose in leisurely fashion as if told to move on, sailing infinitely slowly down the slope to the thorns near the donga. Running my eye along the line I counted them in twos up to between thirty and forty; and that could not have been more than half. How many

337   z

coveys had packed there, and for what purpose, and whether they came every evening, were questions which one would like answered now; but they were not of sufficient interest then to encourage a second visit another evening. The birds sailed quietly into the little wood, and many of them alighted on branches of the larger trees. It is the only time I have seen a partridge in a tree; but when one comes to think it out, it seems common-sense that, in a country teeming with vermin and night-prowlers, all birds should sleep off the ground. Perhaps they do!

There were numbers of little squirrel-like creatures there too. Our fellows used to call them ground-squirrels and 'tree-rats,' because they live underground, yet climb trees readily in search of food; they were little fellows like meerkats, with bushy tails ringed in brown, black and white, of which the waggon boys made decorations for their slouch hats.

Jock wanted a go at them: they did not appear quite so much beneath notice as the birds.

Along the water's edge one came on the lagavaans, huge repulsive water-lizards three to four feet long, like crocodiles in miniature, sunning themselves in some favourite spot in the margin of the reeds or on the edge of the bank; they give one the jumps by the suddenness of their rush through the reeds and plunge into deep water.

There were otters, too, big black-brown fierce fellows, to be seen swimming silently close under the banks. I got a couple of them, but was always nervous of letting Jock into the water after things, as one never knew where the crocodile lurked. He got an ugly bite from one old dog-otter which I shot in shallow water; and, mortally wounded as he was, the otter put up a rare good fight before Jock finally hauled him out.

Then there were the cane-rats, considered by some most excellent and delicate of meats, as big and tender as small sucking-pigs. The cane-rat, living and dead, was one of the stock surprises, and the subject of jokes and tricks upon the unsuspecting: there seems to be no sort of ground for associating the extraordinary fat thing, gliding among the reeds or swimming silently under the banks, with either its live capacity of rat or its more attractive dead rôle of roast sucking-pig.

The hardened ones enjoyed setting this treat before the hungry and unsuspecting, and, after a hearty meal, announcing—"That was roast rat: good, isn't it?" The memory of one experience gives me water in the gills now! It was unpleasant, but not equal to the nausea and upheaval which supervened when, after a very savoury stew of delicate white meat, we were shown the fresh skin of a monkey hanging from the end of the buck-rails, with the head drooping forward eyes closed, arms dangling lifeless, and limp open hands—a ghastly caricature of some hanged human, shrivelled and shrunk within its clothes of skin. I felt like a cannibal.

The water tortoises in the silent pools, grotesque muddy fellows, were full of interest to the quiet watcher, and better that way than as the "turtle soup" which once or twice we ventured on and tried to think was good!

339

There were certain hours of the day when it was more pleasant and profitable to lie in the shade and rest. It is the time of rest for the Bushveld—that spell about middle-day; and yet if one remains quiet, there is generally something to see and something worth watching. There were the insects on the ground about one which would not otherwise be seen at all; there were caterpillars clad in spiky armour made of tiny fragments of grass—fair defence no doubt against some enemies and a most marvellous disguise; other caterpillars clad in bark, impossible to detect until they moved; there were grasshoppers like leaves, and irregularly shaped stick insects, with legs as bulky as the body, and all jointed by knots like irregular twigs —wonderful mimetic creatures.

Jock often found these things for me. Something would move and interest him; and when I saw him stand up and examine a thing at his feet, turning it over with his nose or giving it a scrape with his paw, it was usually worth joining in the inspection. The Hottentot-gods always attracted him as they reared up and 'prayed' before him; quaint things, with tiny heads and thin necks and enormous eyes, that sat up with forelegs raised to pray, as a pet dog sits up and begs.

One day I was watching the ants as they travelled along their route—sometimes stopping to hobnob with those they met, sometimes hurrying past, and sometimes turning as though sent back on a message or reminded of something forgotten—when a little dry brown bean lying in a spot of sunlight gave a jump of an inch or two. At first it seemed that I must have

340

nnknowingly moved some twig or grass stem that flicked it; but as I watched it there was another vigorous jump. I took it up and examined it but there was nothing unusual about it, it was just a common light brown bean with no peculiarities or marks ; it was a real puzzle, a most surprising and ridiculous one. I found half a dozen more in the same place; but it was some days before we discovered the secret. Domiciled in each of them was a very small but very energetic worm, with a trap-door or stopper on his one end, so artfully contrived that it was almost impossible with the naked eye to locate the spot where the hole was. The worm objected to too much heat and if the beans were placed in the sun or near the fire the weird astonishing jumping would commence.

The beans were good for jumping for several months, and once in Delagoa, one of our party put some on a plate in the sun beside a fellow who had been doing himself too well for some time previously: he had become a perfect nuisance to us and we could not get rid of him. He had a mouthful of bread, and a mug of coffee on the way to help it down, when the first bean jumped. He gave a sort of peck, blinked several times to clear his eyes, and then with his left hand pulled slightly at his collar, as though to ease it. Then came another jump, and his mouth opened slowly and his eyes got big. The plate being hollow and glazed was not a fair field for the jumpers—they could not escape; and in about half a minute eight or ten beans were having a rough-and-tumble.

With a white scared face our guest slowly lowered his mug, screened his eyes with the other hand, and after fighting down the mouthful of bread, got up and walked off without a word.

We tried to smother our laughter, but some one's choking made him look back and he saw the whole lot of us in various stages of convulsions. He made one rude remark, and went on; but every one he met that day made some allusion to beans, and he took the Durban steamer next morning.

The insect life was prodigious in its numbers and variety; and the birds, the beasts, and the reptiles were all interesting. There is a goodness-knows-what-will-turn-up-next atmosphere about the Bushveld which is, I fancy, unique. The story of the curate, armed with a butterfly net, coming face to face with a black-maned lion may or may not be true—in fact; but it is true enough as an illustration; and it is no more absurd or unlikely than the meeting at five yards of a lioness and a fever-stricken lad carrying a white green-lined umbrella—which is true! The boy stood and looked: the lioness did the same. "She seemed to think I was not worth eating, so she walked off," he used to say —and he was Trooper 242 of the Imperial Light Horse who went back under fire for wounded comrades and was killed as he brought the last one out.

I had an old cross-bred Hottentot-Bushman boy once—one could not tell which lot he favoured—who was full of the folklore stories and superstitions of his strange and dying race, which he half humorously and half seriously blended with his own knowledge and hunting experiences. Jantje had the ugly wrinkled dry-leather face of his breed, with hollow cheeks, high cheek bones, and little pinched eyes, so small and so deeply set that no one ever saw the colour of them; the peppercorns of tight wiry wool that did duty for hair were sparsely scattered over his head like the stunted bushes in the desert; and his face and head were seamed with scars too numerous to count, the souvenirs of his drunken brawls. He resembled a tame monkey rather than a human creature, being, like so many of his kind, without the moral side or qualities of human nature which go to mark the distinction between man and monkey. He was normally most cheery and obliging; but it meant nothing, for in a moment the monkey would peep out, vicious, treacherous and unrestrained. Honesty, sobriety, gratitude, truth, fidelity, and humanity were impossible to him: it seemed as if even the germs were not there to cultivate, and the material with which to work did not exist. He had certain make-believe substitutes, which had in a sense been grafted on to his nature, and appeared to work, while there was no real use for them; they made a show, until they were tested; one took them for granted, as long as they were not disproved: it was a skin graft only, and there seemed to be no real 'union' possible between them and the tough alien stock. He differed in character and nature from the Zulu as much as he did from the

343

white man; he was as void of principle as—well, as his next of kin, the monkey; yet, while without either shame of, or contempt for, cowardice; he was wholly without fear of physical danger, having a sort of fatalist's indifference to it; and that was something to set off against his moral deficit. I put Jantje on to wash clothes the day he turned up at the waggons to look for work, and as he knelt on the rocks stripped to the waist I noticed a very curious knotted line running up his right side from the lowest rib into the armpit. The line was whiter than his yellow skin; over each rib there was a knot or widening in the line; and under the arm there was a big splotchy star—all markings of some curious wound.

He laughed almost hysterically, his eyes disappearing altogether and every tooth showing, as I lifted his arm to investigate; and then in high-pitched falsetto tones he shouted in a sort of ecstasy of delight, "Die ouw buffels, Baas! Die buffels bull, Baas!"

"Buffalo! Did he toss you?" I asked.

Jantje seemed to think it the best joke in the world and with constant squeals of laughter and graphic gestures gabbled off his account.

His master, it appears, had shot at and slightly wounded the buffalo, and Jantje had been placed at one exit from the bush to prevent the herd from breaking away. As they came towards him he fired at the foremost one; but before he could reload the wounded bull made for him and he ran for dear life to the only tree near—one of the flat-topped thorns. He heard the thundering hoofs and the snorting breath behind,

344

"WITH ONE TOSS RIGHT ON TOP OF THE THORN TREE"

but raced on hoping to reach the tree and dodge behind it; a few yards short, however, the bull caught him, in spite of a jump aside, and flung him with one toss right on top of the thorn tree.

When he recovered consciousness he was lying face upwards in the sun, with nothing to rest his head on and only sticks and thorns around him. He did not know where he was or what had happened; he tried to move, but one arm was useless and the effort made him slip and sag, and he thought he was falling through the earth. Presently he heard regular tramping underneath him and the breath of a big animal: and the whole incident came back to him. By feeling about cautiously he at last located the biggest branch under him, and getting a grip on this he managed to turn over and ease his right side. He could then see the buffalo: it had tramped a circle round the tree and was doing sentry over him. Now and again the huge creature stopped to sniff, snort and stamp, and then resumed the round, perhaps the reverse way. The buffalo could not see him and never once looked up, but glared about at its own accustomed level; and, relying entirely on its sense of smell, it kept up the relentless vengeful watch for hours, always stopping in the same place, to leeward, to satisfy itself that the enemy had not escaped.

Late in the afternoon the buffalo, for the first time, suddenly came to a stand on the windward side of the tree, and after a good minute's silence, turned its tail on Jantje and with angry sniffs and tosses stepped swiftly and resolutely forward some paces.

345

 There was nothing to be seen; but Jantje judged the position and yelled out a warning to his master whom he guessed to be coming through the bush to look for him, and at the same time he made what noise he could in the-tree top to make the buffalo think he was coming down. The animal looked round from time to time with swings and tosses of the head and threatening angry sneezes, much as one sees a cow do when standing between her young calf and threatened danger: it was defending Jantje, for his own purposes, and facing the danger.

For many minutes there was dead silence: no answer came to Jantje's call, and the bull stood its ground glaring and sniffing towards the bush. At last there was a heavy thud below, instantly followed by the report of the rifle—the bullet came faster than the sound; the buffalo gave a heavy plunge and with a grunting sob slid forward on its chest.

Round the camp fire at night Jantje used to tell tales in which fact, fancy, and superstition were curiously mingled; and Jantje when not out of humour was free with his stories. The boys, for whose benefit they were told, listened open-mouthed; and I often stood outside the ring of gaping boys at their fire, an interested listener.

The tale of his experiences with the honey-bird which he had cheated of its share was the first I heard him tell. Who could say how much was fact, how much fancy, and how much the superstitions of his race? Not even Jantje knew that He believed it all.

346

The honey-bird met him one day with cheery cheep-cheep, and as he whistled in reply it led him to an old tree where the beehive was: it was a small hive, and Jantje was hungry; so he ate it all. All the time he was eating, the bird kept fluttering about, calling anxiously, and expecting some honey or fat young bees to be thrown out for it; and when he had finished, the bird came down and searched in vain for its share. As he walked away the guilty Jantje noticed that the indignant bird followed him with angry cries and threats.

All day long he failed to find game; whenever there seemed to be a chance an angry honey-bird would appear ahead of him and cry a warning to the game; and that night as he came back, empty-handed and hungry, all the portents of bad luck came to him in turn. An owl screeched three times over his head; a goat-sucker with its long wavy wings and tail flitted before him in swoops and rings in most ghostly silence—and there is nothing more ghostly than that flappy wavy soundless flitting of the goat-sucker; a jackal trotted persistently in front looking back at him; and a striped hyena, humpbacked, savage, and solitary, stalked by in silence, and glared.

At night as he lay unable to sleep the bats came and made faces at him; a night adder rose up before his face and slithered out its forked tongue—the two black beady eyes glinting the firelight back; and whichever way he looked there was a honey-bird, silent and angry, yet with a look of satisfaction, as it watched. So it went all night: no sleep for him; no rest!

347

In the morning he rose early and taking his gun and chopper set out in search of hives: he would give all to the honey-bird he had cheated, and thus make amends.

He had not gone far before, to his great delight, there came a welcome chattering in answer to his low whistle, and the busy little fellow flew up to show himself and promptly led the way, going ahead ten to twenty yards at a flight. Jantje followed eagerly until they came to a small donga with a sandy bottom, and then the honey-bird, calling briskly, fluttered from tree to tree on either bank, leading him on.

Jantje, thinking the hive must be near by, was walking slowly along the sandy bed and looking upwards in the trees when something on the ground caught his eye and he sprang back just as the head of a big puff-adder struck where his bare foot had been a moment before. With one swing of his chopper he killed it; he took the skin off for an ornament, the poison-glands for medicine, and the fangs for charms, and then whistled and looked about for the honey-bird; but it had gone.

A little later on, however, he came upon another, and it led him to a big and shady wild fig tree. The honey-bird flew to the trunk itself and cheeped and chattered there, and Jantje put down his gun and looked about for an easy place to climb. As he peered through the foliage he met a pair of large green eyes looking full into his: on a big limb of the tree lay a tiger, still as death, with its head resting on its paws, watching him with a cat-like eagerness for its

348

prey. Jantje hooked his toe in the reim sling of his old gun and slowly gathered it up without moving his eyes from the tiger's, and backing away slowly, foot by foot, he got out into the sunshine and made off as fast as he could.

It was the honey-bird's revenge: he knew it then!

He sat down on some bare ground to think what next to do; for he knew he must die if he did not find honey and make good a hundred times what he had cheated.

All day long he kept meeting honey-birds and following them; but he would no longer follow them into the bad places, for he could not tell whether they were new birds or the one he had robbed! Once he had nearly been caught; the bird had perched on an old ant-heap, and Jantje, thinking there was a ground hive there, walked boldly forward. A small misshapen tree grew out of the ant-heap, and one of the twisted branches caught his eye because of the thick ring around it: it was the coil of a long green mamba; and far below that, half-hidden by the leaves, hung the snake's head with the neck gathered in half-loop coils ready to strike at him.

After that Jantje kept in the open, searching for himself among rocks and in all the old dead trees for the tell-tale stains that mark the hive's entrance, but he had no luck, and when he reached the river in the early afternoon he was glad of a cool drink and a place to rest.

349

For a couple of hours he had seen no honey-birds, and it seemed that at last his pursuer had given him up, for that day at least. As he sat in the shade of the high bank, however, with the river only a few yards from his feet, he heard again a faint chattering: it came from the river-side beyond a turn in the bank, and it was too far away for the bird to have seen Jantje from where it called, so he had no doubt about this being a new bird. It seemed to him a glorious piece of luck that he should find honey by the aid of a strange bird, and be able to take half of it back to the hive he had emptied the day before and leave it there for the cheated bird.

There was a beach of pebbles and rocks between the high bank and the river, and as Jantje walked along it on the keen look-out for the bird, he spotted it sitting on a root halfway down the bank some twenty yards ahead. Close to where the chattering bird perched there was a break in the pebbly beach, and there shallow water extended up to the perpendicular bank. In the middle of this little stretch of water, and conveniently placed as a stepping-stone, there was a black rock, and the bare-footed Jantje stepped noiselessly from stone to stone towards it.

An alarmed cane-rat, cut off by Jantje from the river, ran along the foot of the bank to avoid him; but when it reached the little patch of shallow water it suddenly doubled back in fright and raced under the boy's feet into the river.

Jantje stopped! He did not know why; but there seemed to be something wrong. Something had

350

frightened the cane-rat back on to him, and he stared hard at the bank and the stretch of beach ahead of him. Then the rock he meant to step on to gave a heave, and a long blackish thing curved towards him; he sprang into the air as high as he could, and the crocodile's tail swept under his feet!

Jantje fled back like a buck—the rattle on the stones behind him and crash of reeds putting yards into every bound.

For four days he stayed in camp waiting for some one to find a hive and give him honey enough to make his peace; and then, for an old snuff-box and a little powder, he bought a huge basketful of comb, young and old, from a kaffir woman at one of the kraals some miles away, and put it all at the foot of the tree he had cleaned out.

Then he had peace.

The boys believed every word of that story: so, I am sure, did Jantje himself. The buffalo story was obviously true, and Jantje thought nothing of it: the honey-bird story was not, yet he gloried in it; it touched his superstitious nature, and it was impossible for him to tell the truth or to separate fact from fancy and superstition.

How much of fact there may have been in it I cannot say: honey-birds gave me many a wild-goose chase, but when they led to anything at all it was to hives, and not to snakes, tigers and crocodiles. Perhaps it is right to own up that I never cheated a honey-bird! We pretended to laugh at the superstition, but we left some honey all the same—just for luck! After

351

all, as we used to say, the bird earned its share and deserved encouragement.

Round the camp-fire at nights it was no uncommon thing to see some one jump up and let out with whatever was handiest at some poisonous intruder. There was always plenty of dead wood about and we piled on big branches and logs freely, and as the ends burnt to ashes in the heart of the fire we kept pushing the logs further in. Of course, dead trees are the home of all sorts of 'creepy-crawly' things, and as the log warmed up and the fire ate into the decayed heart and drove thick hot smoke through the cracks and corridors and secret places in the logs the occupants would come scuttling out at the butt ends. Small snakes were common—the big ones usually clearing when the log was first disturbed—and they slipped away into the darkness giving hard quick glances about them; but scorpions, centipedes and all sorts of spiders were by far the most numerous.

Occasionally in the mornings we found snakes under our blankets, where they had worked in during the night for the warmth of the human body; but no one was bitten, and one made a practice of getting up at once, and with one movement, so that unwelcome visitors should not be warned or provoked by any preliminary rolling. The scorpions, centipedes and tarantulas seemed to be more objectionable; but they were quite as anxious to get away as we were, and it is wonderful how little damage was done.

One night when we had been watching them coming out of a big honeycombed log like the animals from the

Ark, and were commenting on the astonishing number and variety of these things, I heard Jantje conveying in high-pitched tones fanciful bits of information to the credulous waggon boys. When he found that we too were listening—and Jantje had the storyteller's love for a 'gallery'—he turned our way and dropped into a jargon of broken English, helped out with Hottentot-Dutch, which is impossible to reproduce in intelligible form.

He had made some allusion to 'the great battle,' and when I asked for an explanation he told us the story. It is well enough known in South Africa, and similar stories are to be found in the folklore of other countries, but it had a special interest for us in that Jantje gave it as having come to him from his own people. He called it "The Great Battle between the Things of the Earth and the Things of the Air."

For a long time there had been jealousy between the Things of the Earth and the Things of the Air, each claiming superiority for themselves; each could do something the others could not do; and each thought their powers greater and their qualities superior. One day a number of them happened to meet on an open plain near the river's bank, and the game of brag began again as usual. At last the Lion, who was very cross, turned to the old Black Aasvogel, as he sat half-asleep on a dead tree, and challenged him.

"You only eat the dead: you steal where others kill. It is all talk with you; you will not fight!"

The Aasvogel said nothing, but let his bald head and bare neck settle down between his shoulders, and closed his eyes.

353   2A

"He wakes up soon enough when we find him squatting above the carcass," said the Jackal. "See him flop along then."

"When *we* find him!" the Aasvogel said, opening his eyes wide. "Sneaking prowler of the night! Little bastard of the Striped Thief!"

"Come down and fight," snarled the Hyena angrily. "Thief and scavenger yourself!"

So the Things of the Air gathered about and joined in backing the Black Aasvogel; and the Things of the Earth kept on challenging them to come down and have it out; but nobody could hear anything because the Jackal yapped incessantly and the Go'way bird, with its feathers all on end and its neck craned out, screamed itself drunk with passion.

Then the Eagle spoke out:

"You have talked enough. Strike—strike for the eyes!" and he swept down close to the Lion's head, but swerving to avoid the big paw that darted out at him, he struck in passing at the Jackal, and took off part of his ear.

"I am killed! I am killed!" screamed the Jackal, racing for a hole to hide in. But the other beasts laughed at him; and when the Lion called them up and bade them take their places in the field for the great battle, the Jackal walked close behind him holding his head on one side and showing each one what the Eagle had done.

"Where is my place?" asked the Crocodile, in a soft voice, from the bank where no one had noticed him come up.

354

The Things of the Earth that were near him moved quietly away.

"Your place is in the water," the Lion answered. "Coward and traitor whom no one trusts! Who would fight with his back to you?"

The Crocodile laughed softly and rolled his green eyes from one to another; and they moved still further away.

"What am I?" asked the Ostrich. "Kindred of the Birds, I am of the winged ones; yet I cannot fight with them!"

"Let him fly!" said the Jackal, grinning, "and we shall then see to whom he belongs! Fly, old Three Sticks! Fly!"

The Ostrich ran at him, waltzing and darting with wings outspread, but the Jackal dodged away under the Lion, and squealed out, "Take your feet off the ground, Clumsy, and fly!"

Then it was arranged that there should be two Umpires, one for each party, and that the Umpires should stand on two high hills where all could see them. The Ostrich was made Umpire for the Things of the Air, and as long as the fight went well with his party he was to hold his head high so that the Things of the Air might see the long thin neck upright and, knowing that all was well, fight on.

The Jackal asked that he might be Umpire for the Things of the Earth.

"You are too small to be seen!" objected the Lion gruffly.

"No! No!" urged the Jackal, "I will stand on

355

a big ant-heap and hold my bushy tail on high where all will see it shining silver and gold in the sunlight."

"Good!" said the Lion. "It is better so, perhaps, for you would never fight; and as soon as one begins to run, others follow!"

The Things of the Air gathered in their numbers, and the Eagle led them, showing them how to make up for their weakness by coming swiftly down in numbers where they found their enemies alone or weak; how to keep the sun behind them so that it would shine in their enemies' eyes, and blind them; and how the loud-voiced ones should attack on the rear and scream suddenly, while those with bill and claw swooped down in front and struck at the eyes.

And for a time it went well with the Things of the Air. The little birds and locusts and butterflies came in clouds about the Lion and he could see nothing as he moved from place to place; and the Things of the Earth were confused by these sudden attacks; and, giving up the fight, began to flee from their places.

Then the Jackal, believing that he would not be found out, cheated: he kept his tail up to make them think they were not beaten. The Lion roared to them, so that all could hear, to watch the hill where the Jackal stood and see the sign of victory; and the Things of the Earth, being strong, gathered together again and withstood the enemy and drove them off.

The battle was going against the Things of the Air when the Go'way bird came to the Eagle and said:

"It is the Jackal who has done this. Long ago we had won; but, Cheat and Coward, he kept his tail

356

aloft and his people have returned and are winning now."

Then the Eagle, looking round the field, said, "Send me the Bee."

And when the Bee came the Eagle told him what to do; and setting quietly about his work, as his habit is, he made a circuit through the trees that brought him to the hill where the Jackal watched from the ant-heap.

While the Jackal stood there with his mouth open and tongue out, laughing to see how his cheating had succeeded, the Bee came up quietly behind and, as Jantje put it, "stuck him from hereafter!"

The Jackal gave a scream of pain and, tucking his tail down, jumped from the ant-heap and ran away into the bush; and when the Things of the Earth saw the signal go down they thought that all was lost, and fled.

So was the Great Battle won!

MONKEYS & WILDEBEESTE

Mungo was not a perfect mount, but he was a great improvement on Snowball; he had a wretched walk, and led almost as badly as his predecessor; but this did not matter so much because he could be driven like a pack donkey and relied on not to play pranks. In a gallop after game he was much faster than Snowball, having a wonderfully long stride for so low a pony.

A horse made a good deal of difference in the hunting in many ways, not the least of which was that some sort of excursion was possible on most days. One could go further in the time available and, even if delayed, still be pretty sure of catching up to the waggons without much difficulty.

Sometimes after a long night's trekking I would start off after breakfast for some 'likely' spot, off-saddle there in a shady place, sleep during the heat of the day, and after a billy of tea start hunting towards the waggons in the afternoon.

358

It was in such a spot on the Komati River, a couple of hundred yards from the bank, that on one occasion I settled down to make up lost ground in the matter of sleep, and with Mungo knee-haltered in good grass and Jock beside me, I lay flat on my back with hat covering my eyes and was soon comfortably asleep.

The sleep had lasted a couple of hours when I began to dream that it was raining and woke up in the belief that a hail storm—following the rain—was just breaking over me. I started up to find all just as it had been, and the sunlight beyond the big tree so glaring as to make the eyes ache. Through half-closed lids I saw Mungo lying down asleep and made out Jock standing some yards away quietly watching me.

With a yawn and stretch I lay back again; sleep was over but a good lazy rest was welcome: it had been earned, and, most comforting of all, there was nothing else to be done. In the doze that followed I was surprised to feel quite distinctly something like a drop of rain strike my leg, and then another on my hat.

"Hang it all, it is raining," I said, sitting up again and quite wide awake this time. There was Jock still looking at me, but only for the moment of moving, it appears; for a minute later he looked up into the tree above me with ears cocked, head on one side, and tail held lazily on the horizontal and moving slowly from time to time.

It was his look of interested amusement.

A couple of leaves fluttered down, and then the half-eaten pip of a 'wooden orange' struck me in the face as I lay back again to see what was going on

359

above. The pip gave me the line, and away up among the thick dark foliage I saw a little old face looking down at me; the quick restless eyes were watchfully on the move, and the mouth partly opened in the shape of an O—face and attitude together a vivid expression of surprise and indignation combined with breathless interest.

As my eyes fairly met those above me, the monkey ducked its head forward and promptly 'made a face' at me without uttering a sound. Then others showed up in different places, and whole figures became visible now as the monkeys stole softly along the branches to get a better look at Jock and me: there were a couple of dozen of them of all sizes.

They are the liveliest, most restless, and most inquisitive of creatures; ludicrously nervous and excitable; quick to chattering anger and bursts of hysterical passion, which are intensely comical, especially when they have been scared. They are creatures whose method of progress most readily betrays them by the swaying of a branch or quivering of leaves, yet they can steal about and melt away at will, like small grey ghosts, silent as the grave.

I had often tried to trap them, but never succeeded: Jantje caught them, as he caught everything, with cunning that outmatched his wilder kindred; pitfalls, nooses, whip-traps, fall-traps, foot-snares, drags, slip-knots of all kinds, and tricks that I cannot now remember, were in his repertory; but he disliked showing his traps, and when told to explain he would half-sulkily show one of the common kind.

The day he caught the monkey he was well pleased, and may possibly have told the truth. Baboons and monkeys, he said, can count just like men, but they can only count two! If one man goes into a mealie field and waits for them with a gun, their sentry will see him, and he may wait for ever; if two go and one remains, it is useless, for they realise that only one has come out where two went in; but if three go in, one may remain behind to lie in wait for them, for the monkeys, seeing more than one return, will invade the mealie field as soon as the two are safely out of the way. That was only Jantje's explanation of the well-known fact that monkeys and baboons know the difference between one and more than one.

But, as Jantje explained, their cleverness helped him to catch them. He went alone and came away alone, leaving his trap behind, knowing that they were watching his every movement, but knowing also that their intense curiosity would draw them to it the moment it seemed safe. The trap he used was an old calabash or gourd with a round hole in it about an inch in diameter; and a few pumpkin seeds and mealies and a hard crust of bread, just small enough to get into the calabash, formed the bait.

After fastening the gourd by a cord to a small stump, he left it lying on its side on the ground where he had been sitting. A few crumbs and seeds were dropped near it and the rest placed in the gourd, with one or two showing in the mouth. Then he walked off on the side where he would be longest in view, and when well out of sight sped round in a circuit

361

to a previously selected spot where he could get close up again and watch.

The foremost monkey was already on the ground when he got back and others were hanging from low branches or clinging to the stems, ready to drop or retreat. Then began the grunts and careful timid approaches, such as one sees in a party of children hunting for the hidden 'ghost' who is expected to appear suddenly and chase them; next, the chattering garrulous warnings and protests from the timid ones—the females—in the upper branches; the sudden start and scurry of one of the youngsters; and the scare communicated to all, making even the leader jump back a pace; then his angry grunt and loud scolding of the frightened ones—angry because they had given him a fright, and loud because he was reassuring himself.

After a pause they began the careful roundabout approach and the squatting and waiting, making pretences of not being particularly interested, while their quick eyes watched everything; then the deft picking up of one thing—instantly dropped again, as one picks up a roasted chestnut and drops it in the same movement, in case it should be hot; and finally the greedy scramble and chatter.

I have seen all that, but not, alas, the successful ending, when trying to imitate Jantje's methods. Jantje waited until the tugs at the gourd became serious, and then, knowing that the smaller things had been taken out or shaken out and eaten and that some enterprising monkey had put its arm into the hole and grabbed the crust, he ran out.

362

A monkey rarely lets go any food it has grabbed, and when, as in this case, the hand is jammed in a narrow neck, the letting go cannot easily be done instinctively or inadvertently; the act requires a deliberate effort. So Jantje caught his monkey, and flinging his ragged coat over the captive sat down to make it safe. By pushing the monkey's arm deeper into the gourd the crust became released and the hand freed; he then gradually shifted the monkey about until he got the head into the shoulders of the loose old coat, and thence into the sleeve; and worked away at this until he had the creature as helpless as a mummy with the head appearing at the cuff-opening and the body jammed in the sleeve like a bulging over-stuffed sausage. The monkey struggled, screamed, chattered, made faces, and cried like a child; but Jantje gripping it between his knees worked away unmoved.

He next took the cord from the calabash and tied one end securely round the monkey's neck, to the shrinking horror of that individual, and the other end to a stout bush stick about seven or eight feet long; and then slipped monkey, cord and stick back through the sleeve and had his captive safe; the cord prevented it from getting away, and the stick from getting too close and biting him. When they sat opposite and pulled faces at each other the family likeness was surprising.

The grimacing little imps invariably tempt one to tease or chase them, just to see their antics and methods; and when I rose, openly watching them and stepping about for a better view, they abandoned the

363

silent methods and bounded freely from branch to branch for fresh cover, always ducking behind something if I pointed the gun or a stick or even my arm at them, and getting into paroxysms of rage and leaning over to slang and cheek me whenever it seemed safe.

Jock was full of excitement, thoroughly warmed up and anxious to be at them, running about from place to place to watch them, tacking and turning and jumping for better views, and now and then running to the trunk and scraping at it. Whenever he did this there was a moment's silence; the idea of playing a trick on them struck me and I caught Jock up and put him in the fork of a big main branch about six feet from the ground. The effect was magical: the whole of the top of the tree seemed to whip and rustle at once, and in two seconds there was not a monkey left.

Then a wave in the top of a small tree some distance off betrayed them and we gave chase—a useless romping school-boy chase. They were in the small trees away from the river and it was easy to see and follow them; and to add to the fun and excitement I threw stones at the branches behind them. Their excitement and alarm then became hysterical, and as we darted about to head them off they were several times obliged to scamper a few yards along the ground to avoid me and gain other trees. It was then that Jock enjoyed himself most: he ran at them and made flying leaps and snaps as they sprang up the trees out of reach. It was like a caricature of children in one of their make-believe chases; the screams, grimaces,

364

and actions were so human that it would have seemed like a tragedy had one of them been hurt. They got away into the big trees once more, to Jock's disappointment but greatly to my relief, for I was quite pumped from the romp and laughter.

The river at this point was broken into several sluices by islands formed of piles of rocks on which there were a few stunted trees and dense growths of tall reeds, and here and there little spits and fringes of white sand were visible. There was plenty of small game in that part, and it was a great place for crocodiles. As we were then about half a mile below where Mungo had been left I strolled along the bank on the look-ott for a shot, frequently stopping to examine suspicious-looki ig rocks on the sand spits or at the borders of the reed fringes on the little islands.

The shooting of crocodiles was an act of war: it was enmity and not sport or a desire for trophies that prompted it, and when it did not interfere with other chances we never missed a practice shot at these fellows. I picked out several 'rocks', so suspicious-looking that I would have had a shot at them had there been a clear chance, and twice, while I was trying to make them out, they slid silently into the water before there was time to fire.

However, further on there came a better chance than any: there was something so peculiar about the look of this 'rock' that I picked a good spot and sat down to watch it; and presently the part nearest me turned slightly, just enough to show that it was a crocodile lying on the flat sand with his nose towards me and his

365

tail hidden in the reeds. It was fifty yards away, and from where I sat there was not much to aim at, as a Martini bullet would glance from almost any part of that polished hard case if it struck at such an angle.

I was sitting on the bank above the shelving beach of the river on which a dense mass of reeds grew, and the waving feathery tops partly obscured the sight. I know the bullet hit him somewhere, because he bounded with astonishing strength and activity several feet in the air and his tail slashed through the reeds like a mighty scythe. The huge jaws opened and he gave a horrible angry bellow—something between a roar and a snarl—as he plunged into the river, sending masses of spray and water flying every way. He made straight across, apparently at me, swimming on top of the water at amazing speed and throwing up a wave on either side and a white swirl of foam from the propelling tail.

It was certainly a most surprising and unheard-of proceeding, and as he reached my side of the stream, and because hidden from me by the screen of reeds at my feet, I turned and bolted. It may be that he came at me with murderous intent; or it may be that, blinded by rage or pain, he came towards me simply because he happened to be facing that way; but, whatever the reason, it was painfully clear that if he meant business he would be on to me before it was possible to see him in the reeds. That was enough for me. It had never occurred to me that there was going to be any fun in this for the crocodile; but one's sense of humour and justice was always being stimulated in the Bushveld.

366

With twenty yards of open ground between us I
turned and waited; but no crocodile appeared, nor
was there a sound to be heard in the reeds. A few
minutes' wait; a cautious return; a careful scrutiny;
and then resort to sticks and stones; but all to no
purpose: there was neither sign nor sound of the
crocodile; and not being disposed to go into the
reeds to look for something which I did not want,
but might want me, I returned to Mungo—a little
wiser, it is true, but not unduly 'heady' on that
account.

Half an hour's jogging along the bank having failed
to propose anything, I struck away from the river
taking a line through the bush towards camp, and
eventually came across a small herd of blue wildebeeste.
Mungo's pricked ears and raised head warned me; but
the grass being high it was not easy to see enough of
them from the ground to place an effective shot, and
before a chance offered they moved off slowly. I
walked after them, leading Mungo and trying to get
a fair opening on slightly higher ground.

Presently half a dozen blackish things appeared
above the tall grass; they were the heads of the wildebeeste—all turned one way, and all looking at us with
ears widespread. Only the upper halves of the heads
were visible through the thinner tops of the grass, and
even an ordinary standing shot was not possible. I
had to go to a tree for support in order to tip-toe
for the shot, and whilst in the act of raising my rifle
the heads disappeared; but I took chance and fired
just below where the last one had shown up.

The wildebeeste were out of sight, hidden by grass six feet high, but a branch of the tree beside me served as a horizontal bar and hoisting myself chin high I was able to see them again. In front of us there was a dry vlei quite free of bush, some two hundred yards across and four hundred yards long, and the wildebeeste had gone away to the right and were skirting the vlei, apparently meaning to get round to the opposite side, avoiding the direct cut across the vlei for reasons of their own. It occurred to me that there must be a deep donga or perhaps a mud-hole in front which they were avoiding; but that it might be possible for me to get across, or even halfway across, in time to have another shot at them the next time they stopped to look back, as they were almost certain to do; so I ran straight on.

One does not have to reason things out like that in actual practice: the conclusion comes instantly, as if by instinct, and no time is lost. To drop from the branch, pick up the rifle, and start running were all parts of one movement. Stooping slightly to prevent my bobbing hat from showing up in the grass tops, and holding the rifle obliquely before me as a sort of snowplough to clear the grass from my eyes, I made as good pace as the ground would allow.

No doubt the rifle held in front of me made it difficult to notice anything on the ground; but the concentrated stare across the vlei in the direction of the galloping wildebeeste was quite as much the cause of what followed. Going fast and stooping low, with all my weight thrown forward, I ran right into a wildebeeste cow. My shot had wounded her through the

368

kidneys, completely paralysing the hindquarters, and she had instantly dropped out of sight in the grass. The only warning I got was a furious snort, and the black-looking monster with great blazing blood-shot eyes rose up on its front legs as I ran into it.

To charge into a wounded wildebeeste ready to go for you, just when your whole attention is concentrated upon others two hundred yards beyond, is nearly as unpleasant as it is unexpected; it becomes a question of what will happen to you, rather than of what you will do. That at any rate was my experience. The rifle, if it had hindered me, also helped: held out at arm's length it struck the wildebeeste across the forehead and the collision saved my chest from the horns. There was an angry toss of the big head and the rifle was twirled out of my hand, as one might flip a match away.

I do not know exactly what happened: the impression is of a breathless second's whirl and scramble, and then finding myself standing untouched five yards away, with the half-paralysed wildebeeste squatting like a dog and struggling to drag the useless hindquarters along in its furious efforts to get at Jock who had already intervened to help me.

The rifle lay within the circle of the big hooked horns; and the squatting animal, making a pivot of its hindquarters, slewed round and round,

making savage lunges at Jock and great heaves at me each time I tried to get the rifle.

It often happens that shots touching the kidneys produce a paralysis, temporarily severe, which passes off to a great extent after some minutes and leaves the wounded animal well able to charge: it happened to me some years later while trying to photograph a wounded sable.

I tried to hook the gun out with a stick but the wildebeeste swung round and faced me at once, snapping the sticks and twirling them out of my hands with surprising ease and quickness. I then tried another game, and by making feint attacks from the other side at last got the animal gradually worked away from my gun; and the next attempt at raking was successful.

When the excitement was over and there was a chance of taking stock of the position, I found that Jock had a pretty good 'gravel rash' on one hip and a nasty cut down one leg; he had caught the wildebeeste by the nose the instant I ran into it, and it had 'wiped the floor' with him and flung him aside.

I found my bandolier with a broken buckle lying on the grass; one shirt sleeve was ripped open; the back of the right hand cut across; hands and knees were well grated; and there were lumps and bruises about the legs for which there was no satisfactory explanation. I must have scrambled out like an unwilling participant in a dog fight.

It was a long job skinning,

cutting up, and packing the wildebeeste, and when we reached the outspan the waggons had already started and we had a long tramp before us to catch them.

I drove Mungo before me, keeping him at an easy jog. We had been going for possibly an hour and it was quite dark, except for the stars and the young moon low down on our right; the road was soft and Mungo's jogging paces sounded like floppy pats; there was no other sound at all, not even a distant rumble from the waggons to cheer us; Mungo must have been sick of it and one might have thought him jogging in his sleep but for the occasional pricking of his ears—a trick that always makes me wonder how much more do horses see in the dark than we do. I walked like a machine, with rifle on shoulder and glad to be rid of the broken bandolier, then transferred to Mungo; and Jock trotted at my heels.

This tired monotonous progress was disturbed by Mungo: his ears pricked; his head went up; and he stopped, looking hard at a big low bush on our left. I gave him a tap with the switch, and without an instant hesitation he dashed off to the right making a half-circle through the veld and coming into the road again fifty yards ahead, and galloped away leaving a rising column of dust behind him.

I stood and faced the bush that Mungo had shied at, and the first thing that occurred to me was that my bandolier and cartridges were with the pony. Then Jock growled low and moved a few steps forward and slightly to the right, also sheering off from that

371

bush. I felt that he was bristling all over, but there was neither time nor light to watch him. I stepped slowly sideways after him, gripping the rifle and looking hard at the bush.

Our line was much the same as Mungo's and would take us some seven or eight paces off the road—more than that was not possible owing to the barrier of thorns on that side. When we got abreast of the bush two large spots of pale light appeared in the middle of it, apparently waist high from the ground.

It is impossible to forget the tense creepy feeling caused by the dead stillness, the soft light, and the pale expressionless glow of those eyes—the haunting mystery of eyes and nothing more!

It is not unusual to see eyes in the night; but this was a 'nervy' occasion, and there is no other that comes back with all the vividness and reality of the experience itself, as this one does. And I was not the only nervous one. Mungo incontinently bolted— probably what he saw warranted it; Jock, as ever, faced it; but when my foot touched his hind leg as we sidled away he flew around with a convulsive jump. He too was strung to concert pitch.

As we moved on and passed the reflecting angle of the moon, the light of the eyes went out as suddenly and silently as it had appeared. There was nothing then to show me where danger lay; but Jock knew, and I kept a watch on him. He jogged beside me, lagging slightly as if to cover our retreat, always looking back. A couple of times he stopped entirely and stood in the road, facing straight back and

*"THE HAUNTING MYSTERY OF EYES AND
NOTHING MORE"*

growling; and I followed suit. He was in command; he knew!

There was nothing more. Gradually Jock's subdued purring growl died down and the glances back became fewer. I found Mungo a long way on, brought to a standstill by the slipping of his load; and we caught up to the waggons at the next outspan.

THE OLD CROCODILE

WE reached the Crocodile River drift on a Sunday morning after a particularly dry and dusty night trek. 'Wanting a wash' did not on such occasions mean a mild inclination for a luxury: it meant that washing was badly needed. The dust lay inches deep on the one worn veld road, and the long strings of oxen toiling along kicked up suffocating clouds of fine dust which there was seldom any breeze to carry off: it powdered white man and black to an equal level of yellowy red. The waggons were a couple of hundred yards from the river; and, taking a complete change, I went off for a real clean up.

We generally managed to get in a couple of bathes at the rivers—real swims—but that was only done in the regular drifts and when there were people about or waggons crossing. In such conditions crocodiles rarely appeared; they prefer solitude and silence. The swims were very delightful but somewhat different from ordinary bathes; however remote may have been the risk of meeting a crocodile when you dived, or of being grabbed by one as you swam, the idea was always there and made it more interesting.

Being alone that day I had no intention of having a swim or of going into the open river, and I took a little trouble to pick a suitable pool with a rock on which to stand and dress. The water was clear and I could see the bottom of the pool. It was quite shallow--three feet deep at most—made by a scour in the sandy bed and divided from the main stream by a narrow spit of sand a couple of yards wide and twenty long. At the top end of the sand spit was a flat rock—my dressing-table.

After a dip in the pool I stood on the sand spit to scrub off the brown dust, keeping one unsoaped eye roving round for intrusive crocodiles, and the loaded rifle lying beside me. The brutes slide out so silently and unexpectedly that in that exposed position, with water all round, one could not afford to turn one's back on any quarter for long. There is something laughable—it seemed faintly humorous even then— in the idea of a naked man hastily washing soap out of his eyes and squeezing away the water to take a hurried look behind him, and then after careful survey, doing an 'altogether' dowse just as hastily—blowing and spluttering all the time like a boy after his first dive.

The bath was successful and ended without incident —not a sign of a crocodile the whole time! Breakfast was ready when I reached the waggons, and feeling very fit and clean in a fresh flannel shirt and white moleskins, I sat down to it. Jim Makokel' brought the kettle of coffee from the fire and was in the act of pouring some into a big mug when he stopped with

a grunt of surprise and, looking towards the river, called out sharply, "What is it?"

One of the herd boys was coming at a trot towards us, and the drivers, thinking something had happened to the oxen, called a question to him. He did not answer until he reached them and even then spoke in so quiet a tone that I could not catch what he said. But Jim, putting down the kettle, ran to his waggon and, grabbing his sticks and assegais, called to me in a husky shouting whisper—which imperfectly describes Jim's way of relieving his feelings, without making the whole world echo: "Ingwenye, Inkos! Ingwenye Umkulu! Big Clocodile! Groot Krokodil, Baas!"

Then abandoning his excited polyglot he gabbled off in pure Zulu and at incredible speed a long account of the big crocodile: it had carried off four boys going to the gold-fields that year; it had taken a woman and a baby from the kraal near by, but a white man had beaten it off with a bucket; it had taken all the dogs, and even calves and goats, at the drinking place; and goodness knows how much more. How Jim got his news, and when he made his friends, were puzzles never solved.

Hunting stories, like travellers' tales, are proverbially dangerous to reputations, however literally true they may be; and this is necessarily so, partly because only exceptional things are worth telling, and partly because the conditions of the country or the life referred to are unfamiliar and cannot be grasped. It is a depressing but accepted fact that the ideal, lurid—

and, I suppose, convincing—pictures of wild life are done in London, where the author is unhampered by fact or experience.

"Stick to the impossible, and you will be believed: keep clear of fact and commonplace, and you cannot be checked."

Such was the cynical advice given many years ago by one who had bought his experience in childhood and could not forget it. Sent home as a small boy from a mission station in Zululand to be educated by his grandparents, he found the demand for marvels among his simple country relatives so great that his small experience of snakes and wild animals was soon used up; but the eager suggestive questions of the good people, old and young, led him on, and he shyly crossed the border. The Fields of Fancy were fair and free; there were no fences there; and he stepped out gaily into the Little People's country—The Land of Let's Pretendia! He became very popular.

One day, however, whilst looking at the cows, he remarked that in Zululand a cow would not yield her milk unless the calf stood by.

The old farmer stopped in his walk, gave him one suspicious look, and asked coldly, "What do they do when a calf is killed or dies?"

"They never kill the calves there," the boy answered "but once when one died father stuffed the skin with grass and showed it to the cow, because they said that would do."

The old man, red with anger, took the boy to his room, saying that as long as he spoke

of the lions, tigers and snakes that he knew about, they believed him; but when it came to farming! No! Downright lying he would not have; and there was nothing for it but larruping.

"It was the only piece of solid truth they had allowed me to tell for months," he added thoughtfully, "and I got a first-class hiding for it."

And was there no one who doubted Du Chaillu and Stanley and others? Did no one question Gordon Cumming's story of the herd of elephants caught and killed in a little kloof? And did not we of Barberton many years later locate the spot by the enormous pile of bones, and name it Elephants' Kloof?

There are two crocodile incidents well known to those whom time has now made old hands, but believed by no one else; even in the day of their happening they divided men into believers and unbelievers. The one was of 'Mad' Owen—only mad because utterly reckless—riding through Komati Drift one moonlight night alone and unarmed, who, riding, found his horse brought to a stop, plunging, kicking and struggling on the sand bank in mid-stream where the water was not waist deep. Owen looking back saw that a crocodile had his horse by the leg. All he had was a leaded hunting-crop, but, jumping into the water he laid on so vigorously that the crocodile made off, and Owen remounted and rode out.

There are many who say that it is not true—that it cannot be true; for no man would do it. But there are others who have an open mind, because they knew Owen—Mad Owen, who for a wager bandaged

378

his horse's eyes and galloped him over a twenty-foot bank headlong into the Jew's Hole in Lydenburg; Owen, who when driving four young horses in a Cape cart flung the reins away and whipped up the team, bellowing with laughter, because his nervous companion said he had never been upset and did not want to be; Owen, who—— But too many things rise up that earned him his title and blow the 'impossible' to the winds.

Mad Owen deserves a book to himself; but here is my little testimony on his behalf, given shame-faced at the thought of how he would roar to think it needed.

I crossed that same drift one evening and on riding up the bank to Furley's store saw a horse standing in a dejected attitude with one hind leg clothed in 'trousers' made of sacking and held up by a suspender ingeniously fastened across his back.

During the evening something reminded me of the horse, and I asked a question; and the end of Furley's answer was, "They say it's all a yarn about 'horse-whipping' a crocodile: all we know is that one night, a week ago, he turned up here dripping wet, and after having a drink told us the yarn. He had the leaded hunting-crop in his hand; and that's the horse he was riding. You can make what you like of it. We've been doctoring the horse ever since, but I doubt if it will pull through!"

I have no doubt about the incident. Owen did not invent: he had no need to; and Furley himself was no mean judge of crocodiles and men. Furley kept a ferry boat for the use of natives and others when the river was up, at half a crown a trip. The business ran itself and went strong during the summer floods, but in winter when the river was low and fordable it needed pushing; and then Furley's boatman, an intelligent native, would loiter about the drift and interest travellers in his crocodile stories, and if they proved over-confident or sceptical, would manœuvre them a little way down stream where, from the bank, they would usually see a big crocodile sunning himself on a sand spit below the drift. The boys always took the boat. One day some police entered the store and joyously announced that they had got him— "bagged the old villain at last!"; and Furley dropped on a sack of mealies groaning out, "Glory, boys! The ferry's ruined. Why, I've preserved him for years!"

The other crocodile incident concerns "Lying Tom" —brave, merry-faced blue-eyed Tom; bubbling with good humour; overflowing with kindness; and full of the wildest yarns, always good and amusing, but so steep that they made the most case-hardened draw a long breath.

The name Lying Tom was understood and accepted by every one in the place, barring Tom himself; for, oddly enough, there was another Tom of the same surname, but no relation, and once when his name cropped up I heard the real Simon Pure refer to him as "my namesake—the chap they call Lying Tom." To the day of his death Tom believed that it was the other Tom who was esteemed the liar.

Tom was a prospector who 'came in' occasionally for supplies or licences; and there came a day when Barberton was convulsed by Lying Tom's latest.

He had been walking along the bank of the Crocodile River, and on hearing screams ran down just in time to see a kaffir woman with a child on her back dragged off through the shallow water by a crocodile. Tom ran in to help—"I kicked the dashed thing on the head and in the eyes," he said, "and punched its ribs and then grabbed the bucket that the woman had in her hand and hammered the blamed thing over the head till it let go. By Jimminy, boys, the woman was in a mess: never saw any one in such a fright!"

Poor Tom suffered from consumption in the throat and talked in husky jerks broken by coughs and laughter. Is there one among them who knew him who does not remember the breezy cheeriness, the indomitable pluck, the merry blue eyes, so limpidly clear, the expressive bushy eyebrows, and the teeth, too perfect to be wasted on a man, and ever flashing with his unfailing smiles?

Tom would end up with—"Niggers said I was 'takati': asked for some of my medicine! Blamed niggers; got no pluck: would've let the woman go!"

Of course this story went the rounds as Tom's latest and best; but one day we turned up in Barberton to deliver our loads, and that evening a whisper went about and men with faces humorously puzzled looked at one another and said

381

"Lying Tom's a fraud: the crocodile story is true!"

For our party, shooting guinea-fowl in the kaffir lands along the river, came upon a kraal where there sat a woman with an arm so scarred and marked that we could not but ask what had caused it. There was no difference in the stories, except that the kaffirs after saying that the white man had kicked the crocodile and beaten it with the bucket, added "and he kicked and beat with the bucket the two men who were there, saying that they were not men but dogs, who would not go in and help the woman. But he was bewitched: the crocodile could not touch him!"

Some of Tom's stories were truly incredible, but not those in which he figured to advantage: he was too brave a man to have consciously gained credit he did not deserve. He died, slowly starved to death by the cruel disease—the brave, kindly, cheery spirit, smiling unbeaten to the end.

That was what Jim referred to when he called me to kill the murderer of women and children. It pleased him and others to say that this was the same crocodile; and I believe it was. The locality was the same, and the kraal boys said that it was in the old place from which all its murderous raids had been made; and that was all we knew.

I took the rifle and went with the herd boy; Jim followed close behind, walking on his toes with the waltzy springy movement of an ostrich, eager to get ahead and repeatedly silenced and driven back by me in the few hundred yards' walk to the river.

382

A queer premonitory feeling came over me as I saw we were making straight for the bathing pool; but before reaching the bank the herd boy squatted down, indicating that somewhere in front and below us the enemy would be found. An easy crawl brought me to the river bank and, sure enough, on the very spot where I had stood to wash, only fifty yards from us, there was an enormous crocodile. He was lying along the sand spit with his full length exposed to me. Such a shot would have been a moral certainty, but as I brought the rifle slowly up it may have glinted in the sun, or perhaps the crocodile had been watching us all the time, for with one easy turn and no splash at all he slid into the river and was gone.

It was very disgusting and I pitched into Jim and the other boys behind for having made a noise and shown themselves; but they were still squatting when I reached them and vowed they had neither moved nor spoken. We had already turned to go when there came a distant call from beyond the river. To me it was merely a kaffir's voice and a sound quite meaningless: but to the boys' trained ears it spoke clearly. Jim pressed me downwards and we all squatted again.

"He is coming out on another sand-bank," Jim explained.

Again I crawled to the bank and lay flat, with the rifle ready. There was another sand streak a hundred yards out in the stream with two out-croppings of

383

black rock at the upper end of it—they were rocks right enough, for I had examined them carefully when bathing. This was the only other sandbank in sight: it was higher than it appeared to be from a distance and the crocodile whilst hidden from us was visible to the natives on the opposite bank as it lay in the shallow water and emerged inch by inch to resume its morning sun bath. The crocodile was so slow in showing up that I quite thought it had been scared off again, and I turned to examine other objects and spots up and down the stream; but presently glancing back at the bank again I saw what appeared to be a third rock, no bigger than a loaf of bread. This object I watched until my eyes ached and swam; it was the only possible crocodile; yet it was so small, so motionless, so permanent-looking, it seemed absurd to doubt that it really was a stone which had passed unnoticed before.

As I watched unblinkingly it seemed to grow bigger and again contract with regular swing, as if it swelled and shrank with breathing; and knowing that this must be merely an optical delusion caused by staring too long, I shut my eyes for a minute. The effect was excellent: the rock was much bigger; and after that it was easy to lie still and wait for the cunning old reptile to show himself.

It took half an hour of this cautious manœuvring and edging on the part of the crocodile before he was comfortably settled on the sand with the sun warming all his back. In the meantime the waggon boys behind me had not stirred; on the opposite side

384

of the river kaffirs from the neighbouring kraal had
gathered to the number of thirty or forty men, women,
and children, and they stood loosely grouped, instinctively still, silent and watchful, like a little scattered
herd of deer. All on both sides were watching me and
waiting for the shot. It seemed useless to delay
longer; the whole length of the body was showing,
but it looked so wanting in thickness, so shallow
in fact, that it was evident the crocodile was lying,
not on the top, but on the other slope of the sand spit;
and probably not more than six or eight inches—in
depth—of body was visible.

It was little enough to aim at, and the bullet seemed
to strike the top of the bank first, sending up a
column of sand, and then, probably knocked all out
of shape, ploughed into the body with a tremendous
thump.

The crocodile threw a back somersault—that is,
it seemed to rear up on its tail and spring backwards;
the jaws divided into a huge fork as, for a second, it
stood up on end; and it let out an enraged roar,
seemingly aimed at the heavens. It was a very sudden
and dramatic effect, following on the long silence.

Then the whole world seemed to burst into indescribable turmoil; shouts and yells burst out on
all sides; the kaffirs rushed down to the banks—
the men armed with sticks and assegais, and the
women and children with nothing more formidable
than their voices; the crocodile was alive—very
much alive—and in the water; the waggon boys,
headed by Jim, were all round me and all yelling

385   2C

out together what should or should not be done, and what would happen if we did or did not do it. It was Babel and Bedlam let loose.

With the first plunge the crocodile disappeared, but it came up again ten yards away thrashing the water into foam and going up stream like a paddle-boat gone reeling roaring mad—if one can imagine such a thing! I had another shot at him the instant he reappeared, but one could neither see nor hear where it struck; and again and again I fired whenever he showed up for a second. He appeared to be shot through the lungs; at any rate the kaffirs on the other bank, who were then quite close enough to see, said that it was so. The waggon boys had run down the bank out on to the first sand spit and I followed them, shouting to the kaffirs opposite to get out of the line of fire, as I could no longer shoot without risk of hitting them.

The crocodile after his first straight dash up stream had tacked about in all directions during the next few minutes, disappearing for short spells and plunging out again in unexpected places. One of these sudden reappearances brought him once more abreast, and quite near to us, and Jim with a fierce yell and with his assegai held high in his right hand dashed into the water, going through the shallows in wild leaps. I called to him to come back but against his yells and the excited shouts of the ever-increasing crowd my voice could not live; and Jim, mad with excitement, went on. Twenty yards out, where increasing depth steadied him, he turned for a moment and seeing

386

himself alone in the water called to me with eager confidence, "Come on, Baas."

It had never occurred to me that any one would be such an idiot as to go into water after a wounded crocodile. There was no need to finish off this one, for it was bound to die, and no one wanted the meat or skin. Who, then, would be so mad as to think of such a thing? Five minutes earlier I would have answered very confidently for myself; but there are times when one cannot afford to be sensible. There was a world of unconscious irony in Jim's choice of words, "*Come* on!" and "*Baas!*"

The boy giving the lead to his master was too much for me; and in I went!

I cannot say that there was much enjoyment in it for the first few moments—not until the excitement took hold and all else was forgotten. The first thing that struck me was that in the deep water my rifle was worth no more than a walking-stick, and not nearly as useful as an assegai; but what drove this and many other thoughts from my mind in a second was the appearance of Jock on the stage and his sudden jump into the leading place.

In the first confusion he had passed unnoticed, probably at my heels as usual, but the instant I answered Jim's challenge by jumping into the water he gave one whimpering yelp of excitement and plunged in too; and in a few seconds he had outdistanced us all and was leading straight for the crocodile. I shouted to him, of course in vain—he heard nothing; and Jim and I plunged and struggled along to head the dog off.

387

As the crocodile came up Jock went straight for him—his eyes gleaming, his shoulders up, his nose out, his neck stretched to the utmost in his eagerness—and he ploughed along straining every muscle to catch up. When the crocodile went under he slackened and looked anxiously about, but each fresh rise was greeted by the whimpering yelps of intense suppressed excitement as he fairly hoisted himself out of the water with the vigour of his swimming.

The water was now breast-high for us, and we were far out in the stream, beyond the sand spit where the crocodile had lain, when the kaffirs on the bank got their first chance and a flight of assegais went at the enemy as he rose. Several struck and two remained in him; he rose again a few yards from Jim, and that sportsman let fly one that struck well home. Jock, who had been toiling close behind for some time, and gaining slowly, was not five yards off then; the floundering and lashing of the crocodile were bewildering, but on he went as grimly and eagerly as ever. I fired again—not more than eight yards away—but the water was then up to my arms, and it was impossible to pick a vital part; the brain and neck were the only spots to finish him, but one could see nothing beyond a great upheaval of water and clouds of spray and blood-stained foam.

The crocodile turned from the shot and dived up stream, heading straight for Jock: the din of yelling voices stopped instantly as the huge open-mouthed thing plunged towards the dog; and for one sick horrified moment I stood and watched—helpless.

388

"THE LASHING TAIL SENT THE DOG UP WITH A COLUMN OF WATER"

Had the crocodile risen in front of Jock that would have been the end—one snap would have done it; but it passed clear underneath, and, coming up just beyond him, the great lashing tail sent the dog up with the column of water a couple of feet in the air. He did as he had done when the koodoo bull tossed him: his head was round straining to get at the crocodile before he was able to turn his body in the water; and the silence was broken by a yell of wild delight and approval from the bank.

Before us the water was too deep and the stream too strong to stand in; Jim in his eagerness had gone in shoulder high, and my rifle when aimed only just cleared the water. The crocodile was the mark for more assegais from the bank as it charged up stream again, with Jock tailing behind, and it was then easy enough to follow its movements by the shafts that were never all submerged. The struggles became perceptibly weaker, and as it turned again to go with the stream every effort was concentrated on killing and landing it before it reached the rocks and rapids.

I moved back for higher ground and, finding that the bed shelved up rapidly down stream, made for a position where there would be enough elevation to put in a brain shot. The water was not more than waist high then, and as the crocodile came rolling and thrashing down I waited for his head to show up clearly. My right foot touched a sloping rock which rose almost to the surface of the water close above the rapids, and anxious to get the best possible position for a last shot, I took my stand there. The rock was

389

the ordinary shelving bedrock, uptilted at an easy angle and cut off sheer on the exposed side, and the wave in the current would have shown this to any one not wholly occupied with other things; but I had eyes for nothing except the crocodile which was then less than a dozen yards off, and in my anxiety to secure a firm footing for the shot I moved the right foot again a few inches—over the edge of the rock. The result was as complete a spill as if one unthinkingly stepped backwards off a diving board: I disappeared in deep water, with the knowledge that the crocodile would join me there in a few seconds.

One never knows how these things are done or how long they take: I was back on the rock—without the rifle—and had the water out of my eyes in time to see the crocodile roll helplessly by, six feet away, with Jock behind making excited but ridiculously futile attempts to get hold of the tail; Jim—swimming, plunging and blowing like a maddened hippo—formed the tail of the procession, which was headed by my water-logged hat floating heavily a yard or so in front of the crocodile.

While a crowd of yelling niggers under the general-ship of Jim were landing the crocodile, I had time to do some diving, and managed to fish out my rifle.

My Sunday change was wasted. But we got the old crocodile; and that was something, after all.

THE FIGHTING·BABOON

On the way to Lydenburg, not many treks from Paradise Camp, we were outspanned for the day. Those were the settled parts; on the hills and in the valleys about us were the widely scattered workings of the gold diggers or the white tents of occasional prospectors.

The place was a well-known and much-frequented public outspan, and a fair-sized wayside store marked its importance. After breakfast we went to the store to 'swap' news with the men on the spot and a couple of horsemen who had offsaddled there.

There were several other houses of sorts; they were rough wattle and daub erections which were called houses, as an acknowledgment of pretensions expressed in the rectangular shape and corrugated iron roof. One of these belonged to Seedling, the Field Cornet and only official in the district. He was the petty local Justice who was supposed to administer minor laws, collect certain revenues and taxes, and issue passes. The salary was nominal, but the position bristled with opportunities for one who was not very

391

particular; and the then occupant of the office seemed well enough pleased with the arrangement, whatever the public may have thought of it.

He was neither popular nor trusted: many tales of great harshness and injustice to the natives, and of corruption and favouritism in dealing with the whites, added to habitual drunkenness and uncertain temper, made a formidable tally in the account against him; he was also a bully and a coward, and all knew it; but unfortunately he was the law—as it stood for us!

Seedling, although an official of the Boer Government, was an Englishman; there were several of them on the goldfields in those days, and for the most part, they were good fellows and good officials—this one was an exception. We all knew him personally: he was effusively friendly; and we suffered him and—paid for the drinks. That was in his public capacity: in his private capacity he was the owner of the fighting baboon of evil and cruel repute.

If ever fate's instruments moved unconscious of their mission and the part they were to play, it is certain that Jock and Jim Makokel' did so that day —the day that was the beginning of Seedling's fall and end.

It is not very clear how the trouble began. We had been sitting on the little store-counter and talking for over an hour, a group of half a dozen, swapping off the news of the goldfields and the big world against that from Delagoa and the Bushveld; Seedling had joined us early

392

and, as usual, began the morning with drinks. We were not used to that on the road, or out hunting; indeed, we rarely took any drink, and most of us never touched a drop except in the towns. The transport rider had opportunities which might easily become temptations—the load often consisting of liquor, easy to broach and only to be paid for at the end of the trip; but we had always before us the lesson of the failures. Apart from this, however, we did not take liquor because we could not work as well or last as long, run as fast or shoot as straight, if we did. And that was reason enough!

We had one round of drinks which was 'called' by one of the horsemen, and then, to return the compliment, another round called by one of us. A few minutes later Seedling announced effusively that it was his 'shout.' But it was only ten in the morning, and those who had taken spirits had had enough; indeed, several had only taken a sip of the second round in order to comply with a stupid and vicious custom; I would not and could not attack another bottle of sour gingerbeer; and thus Seedling's round was reduced to himself and the proprietor. No man however thirsty would drink alone in those days—it was taken a mark of meanness or evidence of 'soaking' —and the proprietor had to be ready at any time to 'take one for the good of the house.'

A quarter of an hour passed, and Seedling, who had said nothing since his 'shout' was declined, turned away and strolled out, with hands thrust deep in the pockets of his riding breeches and a long heavy

sjambok dangling from one wrist. There was silence as he moved through the doorway, and when the square patch of sunlight on the earth floor was again unbroken the man behind the counter remarked.

"Too long between drinks for him! Gone for a pull at the private bottle."

"Is that how it's going?"

"Yah! all day long. Drinks here as long as any one'll call, but don't do much shoutin' on his own, I tell you! That's the first time I seen him call for a week. He wanted to get you chaps on the go, I reckon. He'll be wrong all day to-day. I know him!"

"Cost him two bob for nothing, eh!"

"Well, it ain't so much that; ye see, he reckoned you'd all shout your turns, and drinks 'd come regular; but he sees you're not on. Twig? I'm not complainin' mind you—Lord no! He don't pay anyway! It's all 'chalked up' for him, an' I got to wipe it off the slate when the next loads comes and he collects my customs duties. His liquor's took him wrong to-day —you'll see!"

We did see; and that before very long. We had forgotten Seedling, and were hearing all about the new finds reported from Barberton district, when one of the waggon boys came running into the store calling to me by my kaffir name and shouting excitedly, "Baas, Baas! come quickly! The baboon has got Jock: it will kill him!"

I had known all about the vicious brute, and had often heard of Seedling's fiendish delight in arranging fights or enticing dogs up to attack it for the pleasure

394

of seeing the beast kill the over matched dogs. The dog had no chance at all, for the baboon remained out of reach in his house on the pole as long as it chose, if the dog was too big or the opening not a good one, and made its rush when it would tell best. But apart from this the baboon was an exceptionally big and powerful one, and it is very doubtful if any dog could have tackled it successfully in an open fight. The creature was as clever as even they can be; its enormous jaws and teeth were quite equal to the biggest dog's, and it had the advantage of four 'hands.' Its tactics in a fight were quite simple and most effective: with its front feet it caught the dog by the ears or neck, holding the head so that there was no risk of being bitten, and then gripping the body lower down with the hind feet, it tore lumps out of the throat, breast, and stomach—pushing with all four feet and tearing with the terrible teeth. The poor dogs were hopelessly outmatched.

I did not see the beginning of Jock's encounter, but the boys' stories pieced together told everything. It appears that when Seedling left the store he went into his own hut and remained there some little time; on coming out again he strolled over to the baboon's pole about halfway between the two houses and began teasing it, throwing pebbles at it to see it dodge and duck behind the pole, and then flicking at it with the sjambok, amused by its frightened and angry protests. While he was doing this, Jock, who had followed me to the store, strolled out again making his way towards the waggons. He was not interested in our talk; he

395

had twice been accidentally trodden on by men stepping back as he lay stretched out on the floor behind them; and doubtless he felt that it was no place for him: his deafness prevented him from hearing movements, except such as caused vibration in the ground, and, poor old fellow, he was always at a disadvantage in houses and towns.

The baboon had then taken refuge in its box on top of the pole to escape the sjambok, and when Seedling saw Jock come out he commenced whistling and calling softly to him. Jock, of course, heard nothing: he may have responded mildly to the friendly overtures conveyed by the extended hand and patting of legs, or more probably simply took the nearest way to the waggon where he might sleep in peace, since there was nothing else to do. What the boys agree on is that as Jock passed the pole Seedling patted and held him, at the same time calling the baboon, and then gave the dog a push which did not quite roll him over but upset his balance; and Jock, recovering himself, naturally jumped round and faced Seedling, standing almost directly between him and the baboon. He could not hear the rattle of the chain on the box and pole, and saw nothing of the charging brute, and it was the purest accident that the dog stood a few inches out of reach. The baboon—chained by the neck instead of the waist, because it used to bite through all loin straps—made its rush, but the chain brought it up before its hands could reach Jock and threw the hindquarters round with such force against him that he was sent rolling yards away.

396

I can well believe that this second attack from a different and wholly unexpected quarter thoroughly roused him, and can picture how he turned to face it.

It was at this moment that Jim first noticed what was going on. The other boys had not expected anything when Seedling called the dog, and they were taken completely by surprise by what followed. Jim would have known what to expect: his kraal was in the neighbourhood; he knew Seedling well, and had already suffered in fines and confiscations at his hands; he also knew about the baboon; but he was ignorant, just as I was, of the fact that Seedling had left his old place across the river and come to live in the new hut, bringing his pet with him.

It was the hoarse threatening shout of the baboon as it jumped at Jock, as much as the exclamations of the boys, that roused Jim. He knew instantly what was on, and grabbing a stick made a dash to save the dog, with the other boys following him.

When Jock was sent spinning in the dust the baboon recovered itself first, and standing up on its hind legs reached out its long ungainly arms towards him, and let out a shout of defiance. Jock regaining his feet dashed in, jumped aside, feinted again and again, as he had learnt to do when big horns swished at him; and he kept out of reach just as he had done ever since the duiker taught him the use of its hoofs. He knew what to do, just as he had known how to swing the porcupine: the dog—for all the fighting fury that possessed him—took the measure of the chain and kept

outside it. Round and round he flew, darting in, jumping back, snapping and dodging, but never getting right home. The baboon was as clever as he was: at times it jumped several feet in the air, straight up, in the hope that Jock would run underneath; at others, it would make a sudden lunge with the long arms, or a more surprising reach out with the hind legs to grab him. Then the baboon began gradually to reduce its circle, leaving behind it slack chain enough for a spring; but Jock was not to be drawn. In cleverness they were well matched—neither scored in attack; neither made or lost a point.

When Jim rushed up to save Jock, it was with eager anxious shouts of the dog's name that warned Seedling and made him turn; and as the boy ran forward the white man stepped out to stop him.

"Leave the dog alone!" he shouted, pale with anger.

"Baas, Baas, the dog will be killed," Jim called excitedly, as he tried to get round; but the white man made a jump towards him, and with a backhand slash of the sjambok struck him across the face, shouting at him again:

"Leave him, I tell you."

Jim jumped back, thrusting out his stick to guard another vicious cut; and so it went on with alternate slash and guard, and the big Zulu danced round with nimble bounds, guarding, dodging, or bearing the sjambok cuts, to save the dog. Seedling was mad with rage; for who had ever heard of a nigger standing up to a Field Cornet? Still Jim would not give way;

398

he kept trying to get in front of Jock, to head him off the fight, and all the while shouting to the other boys to call me. But Seedling was the Field Cornet, and not one of them dared to move against him.

At last the baboon, finding that Jock would not come on, tried other tactics; it made a sudden retreat and, rushing for the pole, hid behind it as for protection. Jock made a jump and the baboon leaped out to meet him, but the dog stopped at the chain's limit,  and the baboon—just as in the first dash of all—overshot the mark; it was brought up by the jerk of the collar, and for one second sprawled on its back. That was the first chance for Jock and he took it. With one spring he was in; his head shot between the baboon's hind legs, and with his teeth buried in the soft stomach he lay back and pulled—pulled for dear life, as he had pulled and dragged on the legs of wounded game; tugged as he had tugged at the porcupine; held on as he had held when the koodoo bull wrenched and strained every bone and muscle in his body.

Then came the sudden turn! As Jock fastened on to the baboon, dragging taut the chain while the screaming brute struggled on its back, Seedling stood for a second irresolute, and then with a stride forward raised his sjambok to strike the dog. That was too much for Jim; he made a spring in and grasping the raised sjambok with his left hand held Seedling powerless, while in his right the boy raised his stick on guard.

"Let him fight, Baas! You said it! Let the dog fight!" he panted, hoarse with excitement.

The white man, livid with fury, struggled and

kicked, but the wrist loop of his sjambok held him prisoner and he could do nothing.

That was the moment when a panic-stricken boy plucked up courage enough to call me; and that was the scene we saw as we ran out of the little shop. Jim would not strike the white man: but his face was a muddy grey, and it was written there that he would rather die than give up the dog.

Before I reached them it was clear to us all what had happened; Jim was protesting to Seedling and at the same time calling to me; it was a jumble, but a jumble eloquent enough for us, and all intelligible. Jim's excited gabble was addressed with reckless incoherence to Seedling, to me, and to Jock!

"You threw him in; you tried to kill him. He did it. It was not the dog. Kill him, Jock, kill him. Leave him, let him fight. You said it—Let him fight! Kill him, Jock! Kill! Kill! Kill!"

Then Seedling did the worst thing possible; he turned on me with,

"Call off your dog, I tell you, or I'll shoot him and your —— nigger too!"

"We'll see about that! They can fight it out now," and I took the sjambok from Jim's hand, and cut it from the white man's wrist.

"Now! Stand back!"

And he stood back.

The baboon was quite helpless. Powerful as the brute was, and formidable as were the arms and gripping feet, it had no chance while Jock could keep his feet and had strength to drag and hold the chain tight. The collar was choking it, and the grip on the stomach—the baboon's own favourite and most successful device—was fatal.

I set my teeth and thought of the poor helpless dogs that had been decoyed in and treated the same way. Jim danced about, the white seam of froth on his lips, hoarse gusts of encouragement bursting from him as he leant over Jock, and his whole body vibrating like an overheated boiler. And Jock hung on in grim earnest, the silence on his side broken only by grunting efforts as the deadly tug—tug—tug went on. Each pull caused his feet to slip a little on the smooth worn ground; but each time he set them back again, and the grunting tugs went on.

*   *   *   *   *

It was not justice to call Jock off; but I did it. The cruel brute deserved killing, but the human look and cries and behaviour of the baboon were too sickening; and Seedling went into his hut without even a look at his stricken champion

Jock stood off, with his mouth open from ear to ear and his red tongue dangling, blood-stained and panting, but with eager feet ever on the move shifting from spot to spot, ears going back and forward, and eyes—now on the baboon and now on me—pleading for the sign to go in again.

Before evening the baboon was dead.

*   *   *   *   *

The day's excitement was too much for Jim. After singing and dancing himself into a frenzy round Jock, after shouting the whole story of the fight in violent

401   2D

and incessant gabble over and over again to those who had witnessed it, after making every ear ring and every head swim with his mad din, he grabbed his sticks once more and made off for one the kraals, there to find drink for which he thirsted body and soul.

In the afternoon the sudden scattering of the inhabitants of a small kraal on the hillside opposite, and some lusty shouting, drew attention that way. At distances of from two to five hundred yards from the huts there stood figures, singly or grouped in twos and threes, up to the highest slopes; they formed a sort of crescent above the kraal; and on the lower side of it, hiding under the bank of the river, were a dozen or more whose heads only were visible. They were all looking towards the kraal like a startled herd of buck. Now and then a burly figure would dart out from the huts with wild bounds and blood-curdling yells, and the watchers on that side would scatter like chaff and flee for dear life up the mountainside or duck instantly and disappear in the river. Then he would stalk back again and disappear, to repeat the performance on another side a little later on.

It was all painfully clear to me. Jim had broken out.

We were loaded for Lydenburg—another week's trekking through and over the mountains—and as we intended coming back the same way a fortnight later I decided at once to leave Jim at his kraal, which was only a little further on, and pick him up on the return journey.

I nearly always paid him off in live stock or sheep: he had good wages, and for many months at a time would draw no money; the boy was a splendid worker and as true as steel; so that, in spite of all the awful worry I had a soft spot for Jim and had taken a good deal of trouble on his account. He got his pay at the end of the trip or the season, but not in cash. It was invested for him—greatly to his disgust at the time I am bound to say—in live stock, so that he would not be able to squander it in drink or be robbed of it while incapable.

Jim's gloomy dignity was colossal when it came to squaring up and I invited him to state what he wished me to buy for him. To be treated like an irresponsible child; to be chaffed and cheerfully warned by me; to be met by the giggles and squirts of laughter of the other boys, for whom he had the most profound contempt; to see the respectable Sam counting out with awkward eager hands and gleaming eyes the good red gold, while he, Makokela the Zulu, was treated like a piccanin—Ugh! It was horrible! Intolerable!

Jim would hold aloof in injured gloomy silence, not once looking at me, but standing sideways and staring stonily past me into the far distance, and not relaxing for a second the expression of profound displeasure on his weather-beaten face. No joke or chaff, no question or reason, would move him to even look my way. All he would do was, now and again, give a click of disgust, a quick shake of the head, and say, "Aug! Ang-a-funa!" ("I do not desire it!").

403

We had the same fight over and over again, but I always won in the end. Once, when he would not make up his mind what to buy, I offered him instead of cash two of the worst oxen in his span at the highest possible valuation, and the effect was excellent; but the usual lever was to announce that if he could not make his choice and bargain for himself I would do it for him. In the end he invariably gave way and bargained with his kaffir friends for a deal, venting on them by his hard driving and browbeating some of the accumulated indignation which ought to have gone elsewhere.

When it was all over Jim recovered rapidly, and at parting time there was the broadest of grins and a stentorian shout of "Hlala Kahle! Inkos!" and Jim went off with his springy walk, swinging his sticks and jabbering his thoughts aloud, evidently about me, for every now and again he would spring lightly into the air, twirl the stick, and shout a deep-throated "Inkos!" full of the joy of living. A boy going home for his holiday!

This time Jim was too fully wound up to be dealt with as before, and I simply turned him off, telling him to come to the camp in a fortnight's time.

*   *   *   *   *

I was a day behind the waggons returning, and riding up to the camp towards midday found Jim waiting for me. He looked ill and shrunken, wrapped in an old coat and squatting against the wall of the little hut. As I passed he rose slowly and gave his "Sakubona! Inkos!" with that curious controlled

404

air by which the kaffir manages to suggest a kind of fatalist resignation or indifference touched with disgust. There was something wrong; so I rode past without stopping—one learns from them to find out how the land lies before doing anything.

It was a bad story, almost as bad as one would think possible where civilised beings are concerned. Jim's own story lacked certain details of which he was necessarily ignorant, it also omitted the fact that he had been drunk; but in the main it was quite true.

This is what happened, as gleaned from several sources: several days after our departure Jim went down to the store again and raised some liquor; he was not fighting, but he was noisy, and was the centre of a small knot of shouting, arguing boys near the store when Seedling returned after a two days' absence. No doubt it was unfortunate that the very first thing he saw on his return was the boy who had defied him and who was the cause of his humiliation; and that that boy should by his behaviour give the slenderest excuse for interference was in the last degree unlucky. Seedling's mind was made up from the moment he set eyes on Jim. Throwing the reins over his horse's head he walked into the excited gabbling knot, all unconscious of his advent, and laid about him with the sjambok, scattering and silencing them instantly; he then took Jim by the wrist saying, "I want you"; he called to one of his own boys to bring a reim, and leading Jim over to the side of the store tied him up to the horse rail with arms at full stretch. Taking out his knife he cut the boy's

clothing down the back so that it fell away in two halves in front of him; then he took off his own coat and flogged the boy with his sjambok.

I would like to tell all that happened for one reason: it would explain the murderous man-hunting feeling that possessed us when we heard it! But it was too cruel: let it be! Only one thing to show the spirit: twice during the flogging Seedling stopped to go into the store for a drink.

Jim crawled home to find his kraal ransacked and deserted, and his wives and children driven off in panic. In addition to the flogging Seedling had, in accordance with his practice, imposed fines far beyond the boy's means in cash, so as to provide an excuse for seizing what he wanted. The police boys had raided the kraal; and the cattle and goats—his only property—were gone.

He told it all in a dull monotone: for the time the life and fire were gone out of him; but he was not cowed, not broken. There was a curl of contempt on his mouth and in his tone that whipped the white skin on my own back and made it all a disgrace unbearable. That this should be the reward for his courageous defence of Jock seemed too awful. We went inside to talk it over and make our plans. The waggons should go on next day as if nothing had happened, Jim remaining in one of the half-tents or elsewhere out of sight of passers-by. I was to ride into Lydenburg and lodge information —for in such a case the authorities would surely act. That was the best, or at any rate the first, course to be tried.

There was no difficulty about the warrant, for there were many counts in the indictment against Seedling; but even so worthless a brute as that seemed to have one friend, or perhaps an accomplice, to give him warning, and before we reached his quarters with the police he had cleared on horseback for Portuguese territory, taking with him a led horse.

We got most of Jim's cattle back for him—which he seemed to consider the main thing—but we were sorely disgusted at the man's escape.

That was the year of the 'rush.' Thousands of new-comers poured into the country on the strength of the gold discoveries; materials and provisions of all kinds were almost unprocurable and stood at famine prices; and consequently we—the transport riders—reaped a golden harvest. Never had there been such times; waggons and spans were paid for in single trips; and so great was the demand for supplies that some refused transport and bought their own goods, which they re-sold on the goldfields at prices twice as profitable as the highest rates of transport.

Thus the days lost in the attempt to catch Seedling were valuable days. The season was limited, and as early rains might cut us off, a few days thrown away might mean the loss of a whole trip. We hurried down, therefore, for the Bay, doing little hunting that time.

Near the Crocodile on our way down we heard from men coming up that Seedling had been there some days before but that, hearing we were on the way

down and had sworn to shoot him, he had ridden on to Komati, leaving one horse behind bad with horse-sickness. The report about shooting him was, of course ridiculous—probably his own imagination—but it was some comfort to know that he was in such a state of terror that his own fancies were hunting him down.

At Komati we learned that he had stayed three days at the store of that Goanese murderer, Antonio—the same Antonio who on one occasion had tried to drug and hand over to the enemy two of our men who had got into trouble defending themselves against raiding natives; the same Antonio who afterwards made an ill-judged attempt to stab one Mickey O'Connor in a Barberton canteen and happily got brained with a bottle of his own doctored spirit for his pains.

Antonio, suspecting something wrong about a white man who came on horseback and dawdled aimlessly three days at Komati Drift, going indoors whenever a stranger appeared, wormed the secret out with liquor and sympathy; and when he had got most of Seedling's money out of him, by pretence of bribing the Portuguese officials and getting news, made a bold bid for the rest by saying that a warrant was out for him in Delagoa and he must on no account go on. The evil-looking half-caste no doubt hoped to get the horse, saddle and bridle, as well as the cash, and was quite prepared to drug Seedling when the time came, and slip him quietly into the Komati at night where the crocodiles would take care of the evidence.

Antonio, however, overshot the mark; Seedling, who knew all about him, took fright, saddled up and

bolted up the river meaning to make for the Lebombo, near the Tembe Drift, where Bob McNab and his merry comrades ran free of Governments and were a law unto themselves. It was no place for a nervous man, but Seedling had no choice, and he went on. He had liquor in his saddle bags and food for several days; but he was not used to the bush, and at the end of the first day he had lost his way and was beyond the river district where the kaffirs lived.

So much is believed, though not positively known; at any rate he left the last kraal in those parts about noon, and was next heard of two days later at a kraal under the Lebombo. There he learnt that the Black Umbelusi, which it would be necessary to swim—as Snowball and Tsetse had done—lay before him, and that it was yet a great distance to Sebougwaans, and even then he would be only halfway to Bob's. Seedling could not face it alone, and turned back for the nearest store.

The natives said that before leaving the kraal he bought beer from them, but did not want food; for he looked sick; he was red and swollen in the face; and his eyes were wild; the horse was weak and also looked sick, being very thin and empty; but they showed him the footpath over the hills which would take him to Tom's—a white man's store on the road to Delagoa— and he left them! That was Tom Barnett's at Piscene, where we always stopped; for Tom was a good friend of ours.

That was how we came to meet Seedling again. He had made a loop of a hundred and fifty miles in four

days in his efforts to avoid us; but he was waiting for us when we arrived at Tom Barnett's. We who had hurried on to catch him, believing that the vengeance of justice depended on us, forgot that it had been otherwise decreed.

Tom stood in the doorway of his store as we walked up—five feet one in his boots, but every inch of it a man—with his hands resting idly on his hips and a queer smile on his face as he nodded welcome.

"Did a white man come here on horseback during the last few days from the Drift?"

"No!"

"On foot?"

"No, not the whole way."

"Is he here now?"

Tom nodded.

"You know about him, Tom?"

"Seedling! the chap you're after, isn't it?"

"Yes," we answered, lowering our voices.

Tom looked from one to the other with the same queer smile, and then making a move to let us into the store said quietly, "He won't clear, boys; he's dead!"

Some kaffirs coming along the footpath from the 'Bombo had found the horse dead of horse-sickness half a day away, and further on—only a mile or so from the store—the rider lying on his back in the sun, dying of thirst. He died before they got him in.

He was buried under a big fig tree where another and more honoured grave was made later on.

* * * * *

Jim sat by himself the whole evening and never spoke a word.

THE·LAST·TREK

It was Pettigrew's Road that brought home to me, and to others, the wisdom of the old transport riders' maxim: 'Take no risks.' We all knew that there were 'fly' belts on the old main road but we rushed these at night, for we knew enough of the tsetse fly to avoid it; however, the discovery of the new road to Barberton, a short cut with plenty of water and grass, which offered the chance of working an extra trip into the short Delagoa season, tempted me, among others, to take a risk. We had seen no 'fly' when riding through to spy out the land, and again on the trip down with empty waggons all had seemed to be well; but I had good reason afterwards to recall that hurried trip down and the night spent at Low's Creek. It was a lovely moonlight night, cool and still, and the grass was splendid; after many weeks of poor feeding and drought the cattle revelled in the land of plenty. We had timed our treks so as to get through the suspected parts of the road at night, believing that the fly did not trouble after dark, and thus we were that night outspanned in the worst spot

411

of all—a tropical garden of clear streams, tree ferns, foliage plants, mosses, maidenhair, and sweet grass! I moved among the cattle myself, watching them feed greedily and waiting to see them satisfied before in-spanning again to trek through the night to some higher and more open ground. I noticed then that their tails were rather busy. At first it seemed the usual accompaniment of a good feed, an expression of satis-faction; after a while, however, the swishing became too vigorous for this, and when heads began to swing round and legs also were made use of, it seemed clear that something was worrying them. The older hands were so positive that at night cattle were safe from fly that it did not even then occur to me to suspect anything seriously wrong. Weeks passed by, and although the cattle became poorer, it was reasonable enough to put it down to the exceptional drought.

It was late in the season when we loaded up for the last time in Delagoa and ploughed our way through the Matolla swamp and the heavy sands at Piscene; but late as it was, there was no sign of rain, and the rain that we usually wanted to avoid would have been very welcome then. The roads were all blistering stones or powdery dust, and it was cruel work for man and beast. The heat was intense, and there was no breeze; the dust moved along slowly apace with us in a dense cloud—men, waggons, and animals, all toned to the same hue; and the poor oxen toiling slowly along drew in the finely powdered stuff at every breath. At the outspan they stood about exhausted and pant-ing, with rings and lines of brown marking where the moisture from nostrils, eyes and mouths had caught the dust and turned it into mud. At Matolla Poort, where the Lebombo Range runs low, where the polished black rocks shone like anvils, where the stones and baked earth scorched the feet of man and beast to aching, the world was like an oven; the heat came from above, below, around—a thousand glistening surfaces flashing back with intensity the sun's fierce rays. And there, at Matolla Poort, the big pool had given out!

Our stand-by was gone! There, in the deep cleft in the rocks where the feeding spring, cool and constant, had trickled down a smooth black rock beneath another overhanging slab, and where ferns and mosses had clustered in one little spot in all the miles of blistering rocks, there was nothing left but mud and slime. The water was as green and thick as pea-soup; filth of all kinds lay in it and on it; half a dozen rotting carcasses stuck in the mud round the one small wet spot where the pool had been—just where they fell and died; the coat had dropped away from some, and mats of hair, black brown and white, helped to thicken the green water. But we drank it. Sinking a handkerchief where the water looked thinnest and making a little well into which the moisture slowly filtered, we drank it greedily.

The next water on the road was Komati River, but the cattle were too weak to reach it in one trek, and remembering another pool off the road—a small lagoon found by accident when out hunting the year before—we moved on that night out on to the flats

413

and made through the bush for several miles to look for water and grass.

We found the place just after dawn. There was a string of half a dozen pools ringed with yellow-plumed reeds—like a bracelet of sapphires set in gold—deep deep pools of beautiful water in the midst of acres and acres of rich buffalo grass. It was too incredibly good!

I was trekking alone that trip, the only white man there, and—tired out by the all-night's work, the long ride, and the searching in the bush for the lagoon—I had gone to sleep after seeing the cattle to the water and grass. Before midday I was back among them again; some odd movements struck a chord of memory and the night at Low's Creek flashed back. Tails were swishing freely, and the bullock nearest me kicked up sharply at its side and swung its head round to brush something away. I moved closer up to see what was causing the trouble: in a few minutes I heard a thin sing of wings, different from a mosquito's, and there settled on my shirt a grey fly, very like and not much larger than a common house-fly, whose wings folded over like a pair of scissors. That was the "mark of the beast." I knew then why this oasis had been left by transport-rider and trekker, as nature made it, untrodden and untouched.

Not a moment was lost in getting away from the 'fly.' But the mischief was already done; the cattle must have been bitten at Low's Creek weeks before, and again that morning during the time I slept; and it was clear that, not drought and poverty, but 'fly'

414

was the cause of their weakness. After the first rains they would begin to die, and the right thing to do now was to press on as fast as possible and deliver the loads. Barberton was booming and short of supplies, and the rates were the highest ever paid; but I had done better still, having bought my own goods, and the certain profit looked a fortune to me. Even if all the cattle became unfit for use or died, the loads would pay for everything and the right course therefore was to press on; for delay would mean losing both cattle and loads—all I had in the world—and starting again penniless with the years of hard work thrown away.

So the last hard struggle began. And it was work and puzzle day and night, without peace or rest; trying to nurse the cattle in their daily failing strength, and yet to push them for all they could do; watching the sky cloud over every afternoon, promising rain that never came, and not knowing whether to call it promise or threat; for although rain would bring grass and water to save the cattle, it also meant death to the fly-bitten.

We crossed the Komati with three spans—forty-four oxen—to a waggon, for the drift was deep in two places and the weakened cattle could not keep their feet. It was a hard day, and by nightfall it was easy to pick out the oxen who would not last out a week. That night Zole lay down and did not get up again—Zole, the little fat schoolboy, always out of breath, always good-tempered and quiet, as tame as a pet dog.

415

He was only the first to go; day by day others followed. Some were only cattle: others were old friends and comrades on many a trek. The two big after-oxen Achmoed and Bakir went down early; the Komati Drift had over-tried them, and the weight and jolting of the heavy disselboom on the bad roads finished them off. These were the two inseparables who worked and grazed, walked and slept, side by side—never more than a few yards apart day or night since the day they became yoke-fellows. They died on consecutive days.

But the living wonder of that last trek was still old Zwaartland the front ox! With his steady sober air, perfect understanding of his work, and firm clean buck-like tread, he still led the front span. Before we reached the Crocodile his mate gave in—worn to death by the ebbing of his own strength and by the steady indomitable courage of his comrade. Old Zwaartland pulled on; but my heart sank as I looked at him and noted the slightly 'staring' coat, the falling flanks, the tread less sure and brisk, and a look in his eyes that made me think he knew what was coming but would do his best.

The gallant-hearted old fellow held on. One after another we tried with him in the lead, half a dozen or more; but he wore them all down. In the dongas and spruits, where the crossings were often very bad and steep, the waggons would stick for hours, and the wear and strain on the exhausted cattle was killing: it was bad enough for the man who drove them. To see old Zwaartland then holding his ground, never for

one moment turning or wavering while the others backed, jibbed and swayed and dragged him staggering backwards, made one's heart ache. The end was sure: flesh and blood will not last for ever; the stoutest heart can be broken.

The worst of it was that with all the work and strain we accomplished less than we used to do before in a quarter of the time. Distances formerly covered in one trek took three, four, and even five now. Water, never too plentiful in certain parts, was sadly diminished by the drought, and it sometimes took us three or even four treks to get from water to water. Thus we had at times to drive the oxen back to the last place or on to the next one for their drinks, and by the time the poor beasts got back to the waggons to begin their trek they had done nearly as much as they were able to do.

And trouble begot trouble, as usual! Sam the respectable, who had drawn all his pay in Delagoa, gave up after one hard day and deserted me. He said that the hand of the Lord had smitten me and mine, and great misfortune would come to all; so he left in the dark at Crocodile Drift, taking one of the leaders with him, and joined some waggons making for Lydenburg. The work was too hard for him; it was late in the season; he feared the rains and fever; and he had no pluck or loyalty, and cared for no one but himself.

I was left with three leaders and two drivers to manage four waggons. It was Jim who told me of Sam's desertion. He had the cross, defiant, pre-

occupied look of old: but there was also something of satisfaction in his air as he walked up to me and stood to deliver the great vindication of his own unerring judgment:

"Sam has deserted you and taken his voorlooper." He jerked the words out at me, speaking in Zulu.

I said nothing. It was just about Sam's form; it annoyed but did not surprise me. Jim favoured me with a hard searching look, a subdued grunt, and a click expressive of things he could not put into words, and without another word he turned and walked back towards his waggon. But halfway to it he broke silence: facing me once more, he thumped his chest and hurled at me in mixed Zulu and English: "I said so! Sam lead a Bible. Sam no good. Umph! M'Shangaan! I said so! I always said so!"

When Jim helped me to inspan Sam's waggon, he did it to an accompaniment of Zulu imprecations which only a Zulu could properly appreciate. They were quite 'above my head,' but every now and then I caught one sentence repeated like the responses in a litany: "I'll kill that Shangaan when I see him again!"

At Lion Spruit there was more bad luck. Lions had been troublesome there in former years, but for a couple of seasons nothing had been seen of them. Their return was probably due to the fact that, because of the drought and consequent failure of other waters, the game on which they preyed had moved down towards the river. At any rate, they returned unexpectedly and we had one bad night when the cattle were unmanageable, and their nerves all on edge.

418

The herd-boys had seen spoor in the afternoon; at dusk we heard the distant roaring, and later on, the nearer and more ominous grunting. I fastened Jock up in the tent waggon lest the sight of him should prove too tempting; he was bristling like a hedgehog and constantly working out beyond the cattle, glaring and growling incessantly towards the bush. We had four big fires at the four corners of the outspan, and no doubt this saved a bad stampede, for in the morning we found a circle of spoor where the lions had walked round and round the outspan. There were scores of footprints—the tracks of at least four or five animals.

In the Bushveld the oxen were invariably tied up at night, picketed to the trek-chain, each pair at its yoke ready to be inspanned for the early morning trek. Ordinarily the weight of the chain and yokes was sufficient to keep them in place, but when there were lions about, and the cattle liable to be scared and all to sway off together in the same direction, we took the extra precaution of pegging down the chain and anchoring the front yoke to a tree or stake We had a lot of trouble that night, as one of the lions persistently took his stand to windward of the cattle to scare them with his scent. We knew well enough when he was there, although unable to see anything, as all the oxen would face up-wind, staring with bulging eye-balls in that direction and braced up tense with excitement. If one of them made a sudden move, the whole lot jumped in response and swayed off down wind away from the danger, dragging the gear with them and straining until the heavy

waggons yielded to the tug. We had to run out and then drive them up again to stay the stampede. It is a favourite device of lions, when tackling camps and outspans, for one of them to go to windward so that the terrified animals on winding him may stampede in the opposite direction where the other lions are lying in wait.

Two oxen broke away that night and were never seen again. Once I saw a low light-coloured form steal across the road, and took a shot at it; but rifle-shooting at night is a gamble, and there was no sign of a hit.

I was too short-handed and too pressed for time to make a real try for the lions next day, and after a morning spent in fruitless search for the lost bullocks we went on again.

Instead of fifteen to eighteen miles a day, as we should have done, we were then making between four and eight—and sometimes not one. The heat and the drought were awful; but at last we reached the Crocodile and struck up the right bank for the short cut—Pettigrew's Road—to Barberton, and there we had good water and some pickings of grass and young reeds along the river bank.

The clouds piled up every afternoon; the air grew still and sultry; the thunder growled and rumbled; a few drops of rain pitted the dusty road and pattered on the dry leaves; and that was all. Anything seemed preferable to the intolerable heat and dust and drought. and each day I hoped the rain would come, cost what it might to the fly-bitten cattle; but the days dragged on, and still the rain held off.

Then came one black day as we crawled slowly along the river bank, which is not to be forgotten. In one of the cross-spruits cutting sharply down to the river the second waggon stuck: the poor tired-out cattle were too weak and dispirited to pull it out. Being short of drivers and leaders it was necessary to do the work in turns, that is, after getting one waggon through a bad place, to go back for another. We had to double-span this waggon, taking the span from the front waggon back to hook on in front of the other; and on this occasion I led the span while Jim drove. We were all tired out by the work and heat, and I lay down in the dusty road in front of the oxen to rest while the chains were being coupled up. I looked up into old Zwaartland's eyes, deep, placid, constant, dark grey eyes—the ox-eyes of which so many speak and write and so few really know. There was trouble in them; he looked anxious and hunted; and it made me heart-sick to see it.

When the pull came, the back span, already disheartened and out of hand, swayed and turned every way, straining the front oxen to the utmost; yet Zwaartland took the strain and pulled. For a few moments both front oxen stood firm; then his mate cut it and turned; the team swung away with a rush, and the old fellow was jerked backwards and rolled over on his side. He struggled gamely, but it was some minutes before he could rise; and then his eye looked wilder and more despairing; his legs were planted apart to balance him, and his flanks were quivering.

421

Jim straightened up the double span again. Zwaartland leaned forward once more, and the others followed his lead; the waggon moved a little and they managed to pull it out. But I, walking in front, felt the brave old fellow stagger, and saw him, with head lowered, plod blindly like one stricken to death.

We outspanned on the rise, and I told Jim to leave the reim on Zwaartland's head. Many a good turn from him deserved one more from me—the last. I sent Jim for the rifle, and led the old front ox to the edge of the donga where a bleached tree lay across it. . . . He dropped into the donga under the dead tree; and I packed the dry branches over him and set fire to the pile. It looks absurd now; but to leave him to the wolf and the jackal seemed like going back on a friend; and the queer looks of the boys, and what they would think of me, were easier to bear. Jim watched, but said nothing: with a single grunt and a shrug of his shoulders he stalked back to the waggons.

The talk that night at the boys' fire went on in low-pitched tones—not a single word audible to me; but I knew what it was about. As Jim stood up to get his blanket off the waggon, he stretched himself and closed off the evening's talk with his Zulu click and the remark that "All white men are mad, in some way."

So we crawled on until we reached the turn where the road turned between the mountain range and the river and where the railway runs to-day. There, where afterwards Cassidy did his work, we outspanned one day when the heat became so great that it was no longer possible to go on. For weeks the storm-clouds had gathered, threatened, and dispersed; thunder had come half-heartedly, little spots of rain enough to pock-mark the dust; but there had been no break in the drought.

It was past noon that day when everything grew still; the birds and insects hushed their sound; the dry leaves did not give a whisper. There was the warning in the air that one knows but cannot explain; and it struck me and the boys together that it was time to spread and tie down the buck-sails which we had not unfolded for months.

While we were busy at this there came an unheralded flash and crash; then a few drops as big as florins; and then the flood-gates were opened and the reservoir of the long months of drought was turned loose on us. Crouching under the waggon where I had crept to lash down the sail, I looked out at the deluge, hesitating whether to make a dash for my tent-waggon or remain there.

All along the surface of the earth there lay for a minute or so a two-feet screen of mingled dust and splash: long spikes of rain drove down and dashed into spray, each bursting its little column of dust from the powdery earth. There was an indescribable and unforgettable progression in sounds and smells and sights—a growth and change—rapid yet steady, inevitable, breathless, overwhelming. Little enough could one realise in those first few minutes and in the few square yards around; yet there are details, unnoticed at the time, which come back quite vividly when the bewildering rush is over, and there are impressions which it is not possible to forget.

There were the sounds and the smells and the sights! The sounds that began with the sudden crash of thunder; the dead silence that followed it; the first great drops that fell with such pats on the dust; then more and faster—yet still so big and separate as to make one look round to see where they fell; the sound on the waggon-sail—at first as of bouncing marbles, then the 'devil's tattoo,' and then the roar!

And outside there was the muffled puff and patter in the dust; the rustle as the drops struck dead leaves and grass and sticks; the blend of many notes that made one great sound, always growing, changing and moving on—full of weird significance—until there came the steady swish and hiss of water upon water, when the earth had ceased to stand up against the rain and was swamped. But even that did not last; for then the fallen rain raised its voice against the rest, and little sounds of trickling scurrying waters came o tone the ceaseless hiss, and grew and grew until rom every side the chorus of rushing tumbling waters illed the air with the steady roar of the flood.

And the smells! The smell of the baked drought-bound earth; the faint clearing and purifying by the first few drops; the mingled dust and damp; the rinsed air; the clean sense of water, water everywhere; and in the end the bracing sensation in nostrils and head of, not wind exactly, but of swirling air thrust out to make room for the falling rain; and, when all was over, the sense of glorious clarified air and scoured earth—the smell of a new-washed world!

And the things that one saw went with the rest, marking the stages of the storm's short vivid life. The first puffs of dust, where drops struck like bullets; the cloud that rose to meet them; the drops themselves that streaked slanting down like a flight of steel ramrods; the dust dissolved in a dado of splash. I had seen the yellow-brown ground change colour; in a few seconds it was damp; then mud; then all asheen. A minute more, and busy little trickles started everywhere—tiny things a few inches long; and while one watched them they joined and merged, hurrying on with twist and turn, but ever onward to a given point—to meet like the veins in a leaf. Each tuft of grass became a fountain-head: each space between, a little rivulet: swelling rapidly, racing away with its burden of leaf and twig and dust and foam until in a few minutes all were lost in one sheet of moving water.

Crouching under the waggon I watched it and saw the little streamlets, dirty and débris-laden, steal slowly on like sluggard snakes down to my feet and, winding round me, meet beyond and hasten on. Soon the grass-tufts and higher spots were wet; and as the water rose on my boots and the splash beat up to my knees, it seemed worth while making for the tent of the waggon. But in there the roar was deafening; the rain beat down with such force that it drove through the canvas-covered waggon-tent and greased buck-sail in fine mist. In there it was black dark,

the tarpaulin covering all, and I slipped out again back to my place under the waggon to watch the storm.

We were on high ground which fell gently away on three sides—a long spur running down to the river between two of the numberless small watercourses scoring the flanks of the hills. Mere gutters they were, easy corrugations in the slope from the range to the river, insignificant drains in which no water ever ran except during the heavy rains. One would walk through scores of them with easy swinging stride and never notice their existence. Yet, when the half-hour's storm was over and it was possible to get out and look round, they were rushing boiling torrents, twenty to thirty feet across and six to ten feet deep, foaming and plunging towards the river, red with the soil of the stripped earth, and laden with leaves, grass, sticks, and branches—water-furies, wild and ungovernable, against which neither man nor beast could stand for a moment.

When the rain ceased the air was full of the roar of waters, growing louder and nearer all the time. I walked down the long low spur to look at the river, expecting much, and was grievously disappointed. It was no fuller and not much changed. On either side of me the once dry dongas emptied their soil-stained and débris-laden contents in foaming cataracts, each deepening the yellowy red of the river at its banks; but out in mid-stream the river was undisturbed, and its normal colour—the clear yellow of some ambers—was unchanged. How small the great storm seemed then! How puny the flooded creeks and dongas—yet each master of man and his work! How many of them are needed to make a real flood!

There are few things more deceptive than the tropical storm. To one caught in it, all the world seems deluged and overwhelmed; yet a mile away it may be all peace and sunshine. I looked at the river and laughed—at myself! The revelation seemed complete; it was humiliating; one felt so small. Still, the drought was broken; the rains had come; and in spite of disappointment I stayed to watch, drawn by the scores of little things caught up and carried by—the first harvest garnered by the rains.

A quarter of an hour or more may have been spent thus, when amid all the chorus of the rushing waters there stole in a duller murmur. Murmur it was at first, but it grew steadily into a low-toned, monotoned, distant roar; and it caught and held one like the roar of coming hail or hurricane. It was the river coming down.

The sun was out again, and in the straight reach above the bend there was every chance to watch the flood from the bank where I stood. It seemed strangely long in coming, but come it did at last, in waves like the half-spent breakers on a sandy beach—a slope of foam and broken waters in the van, an ugly wall with spray-tipped feathered crest behind, and tier on tier to follow. Heavens, what a scene! The force of waters, and the utter hopeless puniness of man! The racing waves, each dashing for the foremost place only to force the further on; the tall reeds caught

427

waist high and then laid low, their silvery tops dipped, hidden, and drowned in the flood; the trees yielding, and the branches snapping like matches and twirling like feathers down the stream; the rumbling thunder of big boulders loosed and tumbled, rolled like marbles on the rocks below; whole trees brought down, and turning helplessly in the flood—drowned giants with their branches swinging slowly over like nerveless arms. It was tremendous; and one had to stay and watch.

Then the waves ceased; and behind the opposite bank another stream began to make its way, winding like a huge snake, spreading wider as it went across the flats beyond, until the two rejoined and the river became one again. The roar of waters gradually lessened; the two cataracts beside me were silent; and looking down I saw the the fall was gone and that water ran to water—swift as ever, but voiceless now—and was lost in the river itself. Inch by inch the water rose towards my feet; tufts of grass trembled, wavered, and went down; little wavelets flipped and licked like tongues against the remaining bank of soft earth below me; piece after piece of it leant gently forward, and toppled headlong in the eager creeping tide; deltas of yellow scum-flecked water worked silently up the dongas, reaching out with stealthy feelers to enclose the place where I was standing; and then it was time to go!

*   *   *   *   *

The cattle had turned their tails to the storm, and stood it out. They too were washed clean and looked

428

fresher and brighter; but there was nothing in that! Two of them had been seen by the boys moving slowly, foot by foot, before the driving rain down the slope from the outspan, stung by the heavy drops and yielding in their weakness to the easy gradient. Only fifty yards away they should have stopped in the hollow— the shallow dry donga of the morning; but they were gone! Unwilling to turn back and face the rain, they had no doubt been caught in the rush of storm-water and swirled away, and their bodies were bobbing in the Crocodile many miles below by the time we missed them.

In a couple of hours the water had run off; the flooded dongas were almost dry again; and we moved on.

It was then that the real 'rot' set in. Next morning there were half a dozen oxen unable to stand up; and so again the following day. It was no longer possible to take the four waggons; all the spare cattle had been used up and it was better to face the worst at once; so I distributed the best of the load on the other three waggons and abandoned the rest of it with the fourth waggon in the bush. But day by day the oxen dropped out, and when we reached the Junction and branched up the Kaap, there were not enough left for three waggons.

This time it meant abandoning both waggon and load; and I gave the cattle a day's rest then, hoping that they would pick up strength on good grass to face the eight drifts that lay between us and Barberton.

OUR·LAST·HUNT

WE had not touched fresh meat for many days, as there had been no time for shooting; but I knew that game was plentiful across the river in the rough country between the Kaap and Crocodile, and I started off to make the best of the day's delay, little dreaming that it was to be the last time Jock and I would hunt together.

Weeks had passed without a hunt, and Jock must have thought there was a sad falling away on the part of his master; he no longer expected anything; the rifle was never taken down now except for an odd shot from the outspan or to put some poor animal out of its misery. Since the night with the lions, when he had been ignominiously cooped up, there had been nothing to stir his blood and make life worth living; and this morning as he saw me rise from breakfast and proceed to potter about the waggons in the way he had come to regard as inevitable, he looked on indifferently for a few minutes and then stretched out full length in the sun and went to sleep.

I could not take him with me across the river, as the 'fly' was said to be bad there, and it was no place to risk horse or dog. The best of prospects would not have tempted me to take chance with him, but I hated ordering him to stay behind, as it hurt his dignity and sense of comradeship, so it seemed a happy accident that he was asleep and I could slip away unseen. As the cattle were grazing along the river-bank only a few hundred yards off, I took a turn that way to have a look at them, with natural but quite fruitless concern for their welfare, and a moment later met the herd-boy running towards me and calling out excitedly something which I made out to be:

"Crocodile! Crocodile, Inkos! A crocodile has taken one of the oxen." The waggon-boys heard it also, and armed with assegais and sticks were on the bank almost as soon as I was; but there was no sign of crocodile or bullock. The boy showed us the place where the weakened animal had gone down to drink—the hoof slides were plain enough—and told how, as it drank, the long black coffin-head had appeared out of the water. He described stolidly how the big jaws had opened and gripped the bullock's nose; how he, a few yards away, had seen the struggle; how he had shouted and hurled his sticks and stones and tufts of grass, and feinted to rush down at it; and how, after a muffled bellow, and a weak staggering effort to pull back, the poor beast had slid out into the deep water and disappeared. It seemed to be

431

a quite unnecessary addition to my troubles: misfortunes were coming thick and fast!

Half an hour was wasted in watching and searching; but we saw no more of crocodile or bullock, and as there was nothing to be done I turned up stream to find a shallower and a safer crossing.

At best it was not pleasant: the water was waist-high and racing in narrow channels between and over boulders and loose slippery stones, and I was glad to get through without a tumble and a swim.

The country was rough on the other side, and the old grass was high and dense, for no one went there in those days, and the grass stood unburnt from season to season. Climbing over rocks and stony ground, crunching dry sticks underfoot, and driving a path through the rank tambookie grass, it seemed wellnigh hopeless to look for a shot; several times I heard buck start up and dash off only a few yards away, and it began to look as if the wiser course would be to turn back. At last I got out of the valley into more level and more open ground, and came out upon a ledge or plateau a hundred yards or more wide, with a low ridge of rocks and some thorns on the far side—quite a likely spot. I searched the open ground from my cover, and seeing nothing there crossed over to the rocks, threading my way silently between them and expecting to find another clear space beyond. The snort of a buck brought me to a standstill among the rocks, and as I listened it was followed by another and another from the same quarter, delivered at irregular intervals; and each snort was accompanied by the

'THE BRAVE MOTHER STOOD BETWEEN
HER YOUNG AND DEATH"

sound of trampling feet, sometimes like stamps of anger and at other times seemingly a hasty movement.

I had on several occasions interrupted fights between angry rivals: once two splendid koodoo bulls were at it; a second time it was two sables, and the vicious and incredibly swift sweep of the scimitar horns still lives in memory, along with the wonderful nimbleness of the other fellow who dodged it; and another time they were blue wildebeeste; but some interruption had occurred each time, and I had no more than a glimpse of what might have been a rare scene to witness.

I was determined not to spoil it this time: no doubt it was a fight, and probably they were fencing and circling for an opening, as there was no bump of heads or clash of horns and no tearing scramble of feet to indicate the real struggle. I crept on through the rocks and found before me a tangle of thorns and dead wood, impossible to pass through in silence; it was better to work back again and try the other side of the rocks. The way was clearer there, and I crept up to a rock four or five feet high, feeling certain from the sound that the fight would be in full view a few yards beyond. With the rifle ready I raised myself slowly until my eyes were over the top of the rock. Some twenty yards off, in an open flat of downtrodden grass, I saw a sable cow: she was standing with feet firmly and widely planted, looking fiercely in front of her, ducking her head in threatening manner every few seconds, and giving angry snorts; and behind, and huddled up against her, was her scared bewildered little red-brown calf.

It seems stupid not to have guessed what it all meant, yet the fact is that for the few remaining seconds I was simply puzzled and fascinated by the behaviour of the two sables. Then in the corner of my eye I saw, away on my right, another red-brown thing come into the open: it was Jock, casting about with nose to ground for my trail which he had overrun at the point where I had turned back near the deadwood on the other side of the rocks.

What happened then was a matter of a second or two. As I turned to look at him he raised his head, bristled up all over, and made one jump forward; then a long low yellowish thing moved in the unbeaten grass in front of the sable cow, raised its head sharply, and looked full into my eyes; and before I could move a finger it shot away in one streak-like bound. A wild shot at the lioness, as I jumped up full height; a shout at Jock to come back; a scramble of black and brown on my left; and it was all over: I was standing in the open ground, breathless with excitement, and Jock, a few yards off, with hind-legs crouched ready for a dash, looking back at me for leave to go!

The spoor told the tale: there was the outer circle made by the lioness in the grass, broken in places where she had feinted to rush in and stopped before the lowered horns; and inside this there was the smaller circle, a tangle of trampled grass and spoor, where the

434

brave mother had stood between her young and death.

* * * * *

Any attempt to follow the lioness after that would have been waste of time. We struck off in a new direction, and in crossing a stretch of level ground where the thorn trees were well scattered and the grass fairly short my eye caught a movement in front that brought me to instant standstill. It was as if the stem of a young thorn tree had suddenly waved itself and settled back again, and it meant that some long-horned buck, perhaps a koodoo or a sable bull, was lying down and had swung his head; and it meant also that he was comfortably settled, quite unconscious of danger. I marked and watched the spot, or rather, the line, for the glimpse was too brief to tell more than the direction; but there was no other move. The air was almost still, with just a faint drift from him to us, and I examined every stick and branch, every stump and ant-heap, every bush and tussock, without stirring a foot. But I could make out nothing: I could trace no outline and see no patch of colour, dark or light, to betray him.

It was an incident very characteristic of Bushveld hunting. There I stood minute after minute—not risking a move, which would be certain to reveal me— staring and searching for some big animal lying half-asleep within eighty yards of me on ground that you would not call good cover for a rabbit. We were in the sunlight; he lay somewhere beyond, where a few scattered thorn trees threw dabs of shade, marbling

with dappled shade and light the already mottled surface of earth and grass. I was hopelessly beaten, but Jock could see him well enough; he crouched beside me with ears cocked, and his eyes, all ablaze, were fixed intently on the spot, except for an occasional swift look up to me to see what on earth was wrong and why the shot did not come; his hind-legs were tucked under him and he was trembling with excitement. Only those will realise it who have been through the tantalising humiliating experience. There was nothing to be done but wait, leaving the buck to make the first move.

And at last it came: there was another slight shake of the horns, and the whole figure stood out in bold relief. It was a fine sable bull lying in the shadow of one of the thorn trees with his back towards us, and there was a small ant-heap close behind him, making a greyish blot against his black back and shoulder, and breaking the expanse of colour which the eye would otherwise easily have picked up.

The ant-heap made a certain shot impossible, so I lowered myself slowly to the ground to wait until he should begin feeding or change his position for comfort or shade, as they often do: this might mean waiting for half an hour or more, but it was better than risking a shot in the position in which he was lying. I settled down for a long wait with the rifle resting on my knees, confidently expecting that when the time came to move he would get up slowly, stretch himself, and have a good look round. But he did nothing of the kind; a turn or eddy of the faint breeze must have given him my wind; for there was one twitch of the horns, as his nose was laid to windward, and without an instant's pause he dashed off. It was the quickest thing imaginable in a big animal: it looked as though he started racing from his lying position. The bush was not close enough to save him, however, in spite of his start, and through the thin veil of smoke I saw him plunge and stumble, and then dash off again; and Jock, seeing me give chase, went ahead and in half a minute I was left well behind, but still in sight of the hunt.

I shouted at Jock to come back, just as one murmurs good-day to a passing friend in the din of traffic—from force of habit: of course, he could hear nothing. It was his first and only go at a sable; he knew nothing of the terrible horns and the deadly scythe-like sweep that makes the wounded sable so dangerous—even the lioness had fought shy of them—and great as was my faith in him, the risk in this case was not one I would have taken. There was nothing to do but follow. A quarter of a mile on I drew closer up and found them standing face to face among the thorns. It was the first of three or four stands; the sable, with a watchful eye on me, always moved on as I drew near enough to shoot. The beautiful black and white bull stood facing his little red enemy and the fence and play of feint and thrust, guard and dodge, was wonderful to see. Not once did either touch the other; at Jock's least movement the sable's head would go down

437

with his nose into his chest and the magnificent horns arched forward and poised so as to strike either right or left, and if Jock feinted a rush either way the scythe-sweep came with lightning quickness, covering more than half a circle and carrying the gleaming points with a swing right over the sable's own back. Then he would advance slowly and menacingly, with horns well forward ready to strike and eyes blazing through his eyebrows, driving Jock before him.

There were three or four of these encounters in which I could take no hand: the distance, the intervening thorns and grass, and the quickness of their movements, made a safe shot impossible; and there was always the risk of hitting Jock, for a hard run does not make for good shooting. Each time as the sable drove him back there would be a short vicious rush suddenly following the first deliberate advance, and as Jock scrambled back out of the way the bull would swing round with incredible quickness and be off full gallop in another direction. Evidently the final rush was a manœuvre to get Jock clear of his heels and flanks as he started, and thus secure a lead for the next run.

Since the day he was kicked by the koodoo cow, Jock had never tackled an unbroken hind-leg; a dangling one he never missed; but the lesson of the flying heels had been too severe to be forgotten, and he never made that mistake again. In this chase I saw him time after time try at the sable's flanks and run up abreast of his shoulder and make flying leaps at the throat; but he never got in front where the

438

horns could reach him, and although he passed and repassed behind to try on the other side when he had failed at the one, and looked up eagerly at the hind-legs as he passed them, he made no attempt at them.

It must have been at the fourth or fifth stand that Jock got through the guard at last. The sable was badly wounded in the body and doubtless strength was failing, but there was little evidence of this yet. In the pauses Jock's tongue shot and slithered about, a glittering red streak, but after short spells of panting, his head would shut up with a snap like a steel trap and his face set with that look of invincible resolution which it got in part from the pursed-up mouth and in part from the intensity of the beady black-brown eyes: he was good for hours of this sort of work.

This time the sable drove him back towards a big thorn tree. It may have been done without design, or it may have been done with the idea of pinning him up against the trunk. But Jock was not to be caught that way; in a fight he took in the whole field, behind as well as in front—as he had shown the night the second wild dog tackled him. On his side, too, there may or may not have been design in backing towards the tree; who knows? I thought that he scored, not by a manœuvre, but simply because of his unrelaxing watchfulness and his resolute unhesitating courage, He seemed to know instinctively that the jump aside, so safe with the straight-charging animals, was no game to play against the side sweep of a sable's horns, and at each charge of the enemy he had scrambled back out of range without the least pretence of taking liberties.

This time the sable drove him steadily back towards the tree, but in the last step, just as the bull made his rush, Jock jumped past the tree and instead of scrambling back out of reach as before, dodged round and was in the rear of the buck before it could turn on him. There were no flying heels to fear then, and without an instant's hesitation he fastened on one of the hindlegs above the hock. With a snort of rage and indignation the sable spun round and round, kicking and plunging wildly and making vicious sweeps with his horns; but Jock, although swung about and shaken like a rat, was out of reach, and kept his grip. It was a quick and furious struggle, in which I was altogether forgotten, and as one more desperate plunge brought the bull down in a struggling kicking heap with Jock completely hidden under him, I ran up and ended the fight.

It always took him some time to calm down after these tussles: he became so wound up by the excitement of the struggle that time was needed to run down again, so to say. While I was busy on the double precaution of fixing up a scare for the aasvogels and cutting grass and branches to cover the buck, Jock moved restlessly round the sable, ever ready to pounce on him again at the least sign of life. The slithering tongue and wide-open mouth looked like a big red gash splitting his head in two; he was so blown, his breath came and went like the puffing of a diminutive

440

steam-engine at full speed, and his eyes with all the wickedness of fight—but none of the watchfulness—gone out of them, flickered incessantly from the buck to me: one sign from either would have been enough! It was the same old scene, the same old performance, that I had watched scores of times; but it never grew stale or failed to draw a laugh, a word of cheer, and pat of affection; and from him there came always the same response, the friendly wagging of that stumpy tail, a splashy lick, a soft upward look, and a wider split of the mouth that was a laugh as plain as if one heard it. But that was only an interruption—a few seconds' distraction: it did not put him off or satisfy him that all was well. His attention went back to the buck, and the everlasting footwork went on again. With his front to the fallen enemy and his fore-legs well apart he kept ever on the move forwards and backwards, in quick steps of a few inches each, and at the same time edging round in his zigzag circle, making a track round the buck like a weather chart with the glass at 'Changeable.'

"Silly old fusser! Can't you see he's finished?" He could not hear anything, but the responsive wag showed that he knew I was talking to him; and, dodging the piece of bark I threw at him, he resumed his ridiculous round.

I was still laughing at him, when he stopped and turning sharply round made a snap at his side; and a few seconds later he did it again. Then there was a thin sing of insect wings; and I knew that the tsetse fly were on us.

 The only thought then was for Jock, who was still working busily round the sable. For some minutes I sat with him between my legs, wisping away the flies with a small branch and wondering what to do. It soon became clear that there was nothing to be gained by waiting: instead of passing away the fly became more numerous, and there was not a moment's peace or comfort to be had, for they were tackling me on the neck, arms and legs, where the thorn-ripped pants left them bare to the knees; so, slinging the rifle over my shoulder, I picked Jock up, greatly to his discomfort, and carried him off in my arms at the best pace possible under the circumstances. Half a mile of that was enough, however: the weight, the awkwardness of the position, the effort to screen him, and the difficulty of picking my way in very rough country at the same time, were too much for me. A tumble into a grass-hidden hole laid us both out sprawling, and I sat down again to rest and think, swishing the flies off as before.

Then an idea came which, in spite of all the anxiety, made me laugh, and ended in putting poor old Jock in quite the most undignified and ridiculous plight he had known since the days of his puppyhood when his head stuck in the bully-beef tin or the hen pecked him on the nose. I ripped off as much of my shirt as was not needed to protect me against the flies, and making holes in it for his legs and tail fitted him out with a home-made suit in about five minutes. Time was everything: it was impossible to run with him in my arms, but we could run together until we got out of the fly belt, and there was not much risk of being bitten as long as we kept up the running in the long grass. It was a long spell, and what with the rough country and the uncontrollable laughter at the sight of Jock, I was pretty well done by the time we were safely out of the 'fly.' We pulled up when the country began to fall away sharply towards the river, and there, to Jock's evident satisfaction, I took off his suit—by that time very much tattered and awry.

It was there, lying between two rocks in the shade of a marula tree, that I got one of those chances to see game at close quarters of which most men only hear or dream. There were no snapshot cameras then!

We had been lying there it may be for half an hour or more, Jock asleep and I spread out on my back, when a slight but distinct click, as of a hoof against a stone, made me turn quietly over on my side and listen. The rock beside me was about four feet high, and on the other side of it a buck of some kind, and a big one too, was walking with easy stride towards the river. Every footstep was perfectly clear; the walk was firm and confident: evidently there was not the least suspicion of danger. It was only a matter of yards between us, and what little breeze there was drifted across his course towards me, as he too made for the river, holding a course parallel with the two long rocks between which we were lying. The footsteps came abreast of us and then stopped, just as I was expecting him to walk on past the rock and down the hill in front of me. The sudden halt seemed to mean that some warning instinct had arrested him, or some least taint upon the pure air softly eddying between the

443

rocks had reached him. I could hear his sniffs, and pictured him looking about, silent but alarmed, before deciding which way to make his rush.

I raised myself by inches, close to the rock, until I could see over it. A magnificent waterbuck bull, full-grown and in perfect coat and condition, was standing less than five yards away and a little to the right, having already passed me when he came to a stop: he was so close that I could see the waves and partings in his heavy coat; the rise and fall in his flanks as he breathed; the ruff on his shaggy bearded throat, that gave such an air of grandeur to the head; the noble carriage, as with head held high and slightly turned to windward he sniffed the breeze from the valley, the nostrils, mobile and sensitive, searching for the least hint of danger; and the eye, large and full and soft, luminous with watchful intelligence, and yet mild and calm—so free was it from all trace of a disturbing thought. And yet I was so close, it seemed almost possible to reach out and touch him. There was no thought of shooting: it was a moment of supreme enjoyment. Just to watch him: that was enough.

In a little while he seemed satisfied that all was well, and with head thrown slightly forward and the sure clean tread of his kind, he took his line unhesitatingly down the hill. As he neared the thicker bush twenty yards away a sudden impulse made me give a shout. In a single bound he was lost among the trees, and the clattering of loose stones and the crackle of sticks in his path had ceased before the cold shiver-down-the-back, which my spell-breaking shout provoked, had

444

"JUST TO WATCH HIM, THAT WAS ENOUGH"

passed away. When I turned round Jock was still asleep: little incidents like that brought his deafness home.

*   *   *   *   *

It was our last day's hunting together; and I went back to the dreary round of hard, hopeless, useless struggle and daily loss.

One day, a calm cloudless day, there came without warning a tremendous booming roar that left the air vibrating and seemed to shake the very earth, as a thousand echoes called and answered from hill to hill down the long valley. There was nothing to explain it; the kaffirs turned a sickly grey, and appealed to me; but I could give them no explanation—it was something beyond my ken—and they seemed to think it an evil omen of still greater ill-luck. But, as it turned out, the luck was not all bad: some days passed before the mystery was solved, and then we came to where Coombes, with whom a week earlier I had tried—and failed—to keep pace, had been blown to pieces with his boys, waggon, oxen, and three tons of dynamite: there was no fragment of waggon bigger than one's hand; and the trees all around were barked on one side. We turned out to avoid the huge hole in the drift, and passed on.

There were only twenty oxen left when we reached the drift below Fig Tree. The water was nearly breast high and we carried three-fourths of the loads through on our heads, case by case, to make the pull as easy as possible for the oxen, as they could only crawl then.

445

We got one waggon through with some difficulty, but at nightfall the second was still in the river; we had carried out everything removable, even to the buck-sails, but the weakened bullocks could not move the empty waggon.

The thunder-clouds were piling up ahead, and distant lightning gave warning of a storm away up river; so we wound the trek-chain round a big tree on the bank, to anchor the waggon in case of flood, and reeling from work and weariness, too tired to think of food, I flung myself down in my blankets under the other waggon which was outspanned where we had stopped it in the double-rutted veld road, and settling comfortably into the sandy furrow cut by many wheels, was 'dead to the world' in a few minutes. Near midnight the storm awoke me and a curious coldness about the neck and shoulders made me turn over to pull the blankets up. The road had served as a storm-water drain, converting the two wheel furrows into running streams, and I, rolled in my blankets, had dammed up one of them. The prompt flow of the released water as soon as I turned over, told plainly what had happened. I looked out at the driving rain and the glistening earth, as shown up by constant flashes of lightning: it was a world of rain and spray and running water. It seemed that there was neither hope nor mercy anywhere; I was too tired to care, and dropping back into the trough, slept the night out in water.

In the morning we found the waggon still in the drift, although

446

partly hidden by the flood, but the force of the stream had half-floated and half-forced it round on to higher ground; only the anchoring chain had saved it. We had to wait some hours for the river to run down, and then to my relief the rested but staggering oxen pulled it out at the first attempt.

Rooiland, the light red ox with blazing yellow eyes and topped horns, fierce and untamable to the end, was in the lead then. I saw him as he took the strain in that last pull, and it was pitiful to see the restless eager spirit fighting against the failing strength: he looked desperate. The thought seems fanciful—about a dumb animal—and perhaps it is; but what happened just afterwards makes it still vivid and fitted in very curiously with the superstitious notions of the boys. We outspanned in order to repack the loads, and Rooiland, who as front ox was the last to be released, stood for a few moments alone while the rest of the cattle moved away; then turning his back on them he gave a couple of low moaning bellows and walked down the road back to the drift again. I had no doubt it was to drink; but the boys stopped their work and watched him curiously, and some remarks passed which were inaudible to me. As the ox disappeared down the slope into the drift, Jim called to his leader to bring him back, and then turning to me, added with his usual positiveness, "Rooiland is mad. Umtagati! Bewitched! He is looking for the dead ones. He is going to die to-day!"

The boy came back presently—

447

alone. When he reached the drift, he said, Rooiland was standing breast-high in the river, and then in a moment, whether by step or slip, he was into the flood and swept away. The leader's account was received by the others in absolute silence: a little tightening of the jaws and a little brightening of the eyes, perhaps, were all I could detect. They were saturated with superstition, and as pagan fatalists they accepted the position without a word. I suggested to Jim that it was nothing but a return of Rooiland's old straying habit, and probed him with questions, but could get nothing out of him; finally he walked off with an expressive shake of the head and the repetition of his former remark, without a shade of triumph, surprise, or excitement in his voice: "He is looking for the dead ones!"

We were out of the fly then, and the next day we reached Fig Tree.

That was the end of the last trek. Only three oxen reached Barberton, and they died within the week: the ruin was complete.

OUR·VARIOUS·WAYS

WHEN the trip was squared off and the boys paid, there was nothing left. Jim went home with waggons returning to Spitzkop: once more—for the last time—grievously hurt in dignity because his money was handed to my friend the owner of the waggons to be paid out to him when he reached his kraal; but his gloomy resentment melted as I handed over to him things for which there was no further need. The waggons moved off, and Jim with them; but twice he broke back again to dance and shout his gratitude; for it was wealth to him to have the reims and voor-slag, the odd yokes and strops and waggon tools, the baking pot and pan and billies; and they were little to me when all else was gone. And Jim, with all his faults, had earned some title to remembrance for his loyalty. My way **had** been his way; and the hardest day had **never** been too hard for him: he had seen it all through to the finish, without a grumble and without a shirk.

His last shout, like the bellow of a bull, was an up-roarious good-bye to Jock. And Jock seemed **to know**

it was something of an occasion, for, as he stood before me looking down the road at the receding waggons and the dancing figure of Jim, his ears were cocked, his head was tilted a little sideways, and his tail stirred gently. It was at least a friendly nod in return!

A couple of weeks later I heard from my friend: "You will be interested to hear that that lunatic of yours reached his kraal all right; but that's not *his* fault. He is a holy terror. I have never known such a restless animal: he is like a change in the weather—you seem to feel him everywhere, upsetting everything and every one the whole time. I suppose you hammered him into his place and kept him there; but I wouldn't have him at a gift. It is not that there was anything really wrong; only there was no rest, no peace.

"But he's a gay fighter! That was a treat: I never laughed so much in my life. Below the Devil's Kantoor we met a lot of waggons from Lydenburg, and he had a row with one of the drivers, a lanky nigger with dandy-patched clothes. The boy wouldn't fight—just yelled blue murder while Jim walloped him. I heard the yells and the whacks, like the beating of carpets, and there was Jim laying it on all over him—legs, head, back, and arms—with a sort of ferocious satisfaction, every whack being accompanied by a husky suppressed shout: 'Fight, Shangaan! Fight!' But the other fellow was not on for fighting; he floundered about, yelled for mercy and help, and tried to run away; but Jim simply played round him—one spring put him alongside each time. I felt

450

sorry for the long nigger and was going to interfere and save him, but just then one of his pals called out to their gang to come along and help, and ran for his sticks. It was rare fun then. Jim dropped the patched fellow and went like a charging lion straight for the waggons where the gang were swarming for their sticks, letting out right and left whenever he saw a nigger, whether they wanted to fight or not; and in about five seconds the whole lot were heading for the bush with Jim in full chase.

"Goodness knows what the row was about. As far as I can make out from your heathen, it is because the other boy is a Shangaan and reads the Bible. Jim says this boy—Sam is his name—worked for you and ran away. Sam says it is not true, and that he never even heard of you, and that Jim is a stranger to him. There's something wrong in this, though, because when the row began, Sam first tried to pacify your lunatic, and I heard him sing out in answer to the first few licks, 'Kahle, Umganaam; Kahle, Makokel'!' (Gently, friend; gently, Makokel'.) 'Wow, Makokela, y' ou bulala mena!' (Wow, Makokela, you will kill me.) He knew Jim right enough; that was evident. But it didn't help him; he had to skip for it all the same. I was glad to pay the noble Jim off and drop him at his kraal. Sam was laid up when we left."

It is better to skip the change from the old life to the new—when the luck, as we called it, was all out, when each straw seemed the last for the camel's breaking back, and there was always still another to come. But the turn came at last, and the 'long arm of coincidence' reached out to make the 'impossible' a matter of fact. It is better to skip all that: for it is not the story of Jock, and it concerns him only so far that in the end it made our parting unavoidable.

When the turn did come it was strange, and at times almost bewildering, to realise that the things one had struggled hardest against and regarded as the worst of bad luck were blessings in disguise and were all for the best. So the new life began and the old was put away; but the new life, for all its brighter and wider outlook and work of another class, for all the charm that makes Barberton now a cherished memory to all who knew the early days, was not all happy. The new life had its hours of darkness too; of almost unbearable 'trek fever'; of restless, sleepless longing for the old life; of 'home-sickness' for the veld, the freedom, the roaming, the nights by the fire, and the days in the bush! Now and again would come a sleepless night with its endless procession of scenes, in which some remembered from the past were interlinked with others imagined for the future; and here and there in these long waking dreams came stabs of memory—flashes of lightning vividness: the head and staring eyes of the koodoo bull, as we had stood for a portion of a second face to face; the yawning mouth of the maddened crocodile; the mamba and its beady hateful eyes, as it swept by before the bushfire. And there were others too that struck another chord: the cattle, the poor dumb beasts that had worked and died: stepping-stones in a man's career; the 'books,' the 'chalk and blackboard' of the school—used, discarded, and forgotten! No, they were not forgotten; and the memory of the last trek was one long mute reproach on their behalf: they had paved the roadway for the Juggernaut man.

All that was left of the old life was Jock; and soon there was no place for him. He could not always be with me; and when left behind he was miserable, leading a life that was utterly strange to him, without interest and among strangers. While I was in Barberton he accompanied me everywhere, but—absurd as it seems—there was a constant danger for him there, greater though less glorious than those he faced so lightly in the veld. His deafness, which passed almost unnoticed and did not seem to handicap him at all in the veld, became a serious danger in camp. For a long time he had been unable to hear a sound, but he could *feel* sounds: that is to say, he was quick to notice anything that caused a vibration. In the early days of his deafness I had been worried by the thought that he would be run over while lying asleep near or under the waggons, and the boys were always on the look-out to stir him up; but we soon found that this was not necessary. At the first movement he would feel the vibration and jump up. Jim realised this well enough, for when wishing to direct his attention to strange dogs or Shangaans, the villain could always dodge me by stamping or hammering on the ground, and Jock always looked up: he seemed to know the difference between the sounds he could ignore, such as chopping wood, and those that he ought to notice.

In camp—Barberton in those days was reckoned

453

a mining camp, and was always referred to as 'camp' —the danger was due to the number of sounds. He would stand behind me as I stopped in the street, and sometimes lie down and snooze if the wait was a long one; and the poor old fellow must have thought it a sad falling off, a weary monotonous change from the real life of the veld. At first he was very watchful, and every rumbling wheel or horse's footfall drew his alert little eyes round to the danger point; but the traffic and noise were almost continuous and one sound ran into another; and thus he became careless or puzzled and on several occasions had narrowly escaped being run over or trodden on.

Once, in desperation after a bad scare, I tried chaining him up, and although his injured reproachful look hurt, it did not weaken me: I had hardened my heart to do it, and it was for his own sake. At lunchtime he was still squatting at the full length of the chain, off the mat and straw, and with his head hanging in the most hopeless dejected attitude one could imagine. It was too much for me—the dog really felt it; and when I released him there was no rejoicing in his freedom as the hated collar and chain dropped off: he turned from me without a sign or sound of any sort, and walking off slowly, lay down some ten yards away with his head resting on his paws! He went to think—not to sleep.

I felt abominably guilty, and was conscious of wanting to make up for it all the afternoon.

Once I took him out to Fig Tree Creek fifteen miles away, and left him with a prospector friend at whose

camp in the hills it seemed he would be much better off and much happier. When I got back to Barberton that night he was waiting for me, with a tag of chewed rope hanging round his neck, not the least ashamed of himself, but openly rejoicing in the meeting and evidently never doubting that I was equally pleased. And he was quite right there.

But it could not go on. One day as he lay asleep behind me, a loaded waggon coming sharply round a corner as nearly as possible passed over him. The wheel was within inches of his back as he lay asleep in the sand: there was no chance to grab—it was a rush and a kick that saved him; and he rolled over under the waggon, and found his own way out between the wheels.

A few days after this Ted passed through Barberton, and I handed Jock over to him, to keep and to care for until I had a better and safer home for him.

*　　*　　*　　*　　*

One day some two years later there turned up at my quarters an old friend of the transport days— Harry Williams—he had been away on a long trek 'up north' to look for some supposed mine of fabulous richness of which there had been vague and secret reports from natives. He stayed with me for some days and one evening after the bout of fever and ague had passed off and rest and good feeding had begun to pull him round, he told us the story of their search. It was a trip of much adventure, but it was the end of his story that interested me most; and that is all that need be told here.

455

They had failed to find the mine; the native who was supposed to know all about it had deserted, with all he could carry off; they were short of food and money, and out of medicines; the delays had been great; they were two hundred miles from any white men; there was no road but their own erratic track through the bush; the rains had begun and the fever season set in; the cattle—they had one waggon and span—were worn out; the fever had gripped them, and of the six white men, three were dead, one dying and two only able to crawl; most of their boys had deserted; one umfaan fit for work, and the driver—then delirious with fever—completed the party.

The long journey was almost over; and they were only a few treks from the store and camp for which they were making; but they were so stricken and helpless it seemed as though that little was too much and they must die within reach of help. The driver, a big Zulu, was then raving mad; he had twice run off into the bush and been lost for hours. Precious time and waning strength were spent in the search, and with infinite effort and much good luck they had found him and induced him to return. On the second occasion they had enticed him on to the waggon, and as he lay half-unconscious between bursts of delirium, had tied him down flat on his back, with wrists and ankles fastened to the buckrails. It was all they could do to save him: they had barely strength to climb up and pour water into his mouth from time to time.

It was midday then, and their dying comrade was so far gone that they decided to abandon one trek and wait for evening, to allow him to die in peace. Later on, when they thought it was all over, they tried to scrape out a grave for him, and began to pull out one old blanket to wrap round him in place of a shroud and coffin. It was then that the man opened his eyes and faintly shook his head; so they inspanned as best they could and made another trek. I met the man some years afterwards, and he told me he had heard all they said, but could only remember one thing, and that was Harry's remark, that 'two gin-cases were not enough for a coffin, so they would have to take one of the blankets instead.'

In the morning they went on again. It was then at most two treks more to their destination; but they were too weak to work or walk, and the cattle were left to crawl along undriven; but after half an hour's trekking they reached a bad drift where the waggon stuck; the cattle would not face the pull. The two tottering trembling white men did their best, but neither had strength to use the whip; the umfaan led the oxen this way and that, but there was no more effort in them. The water had given out, and the despairing helpless men saw death from thirst awaiting them within a few hours' trek of help; and to add to the horror of it all the Zulu driver, with thirst aggravating his delirium, was a raving lunatic—struggling and wrenching at his bonds until the waggon rattled, and uttering maniac yells and gabbling incessantly.

457

Hours had gone by in hopeless effort; but the oxen stood out at all angles, and no two would pull together in answer to the feeble efforts of the fainting men. Then there came a lull in the shouts from the waggon and in answer to the little voorlooper's warning shout, "Pas op, Baas!" (Look out, Master!) the white men looked round and saw the Zulu driver up on his knees freeing himself from the reims. In another moment he was standing up full height— a magnificent but most unwelcome sight: there was a thin line of froth along the half-opened mouth; the deep-set eyes glared out under eyebrows and forehead bunched into frowning wrinkles, as for a few seconds he leaned forward like a lion about to spring and scanned the men and oxen before him; and then as they watched him in breathless silence, he sprang lightly off the waggon, picked up a small dry stick as he landed, and ran up along the span.

He spoke to the after-ox by name as he passed; called to another, and touched it into place; thrust his way between the next one and the dazed white man standing near it, tossing him aside with a brush of his arm, as a ploughshare spurns a sod; and then they saw how the boy's madness had taken him. His work and his span had called to him in his delirium; and he had answered. With low mutterings, short words hissed out, and all the sounds and terms the cattle knew shot at them—low pitched and with intense repression—he ran along the span, crouching low all the time like a savage stealing up for murderous attack.

458

The two white men stood back and watched.
Reaching the front oxen, he grasped the leading
reim and pulled them round until they stood level
for the straight pull out; then down the other side
of the span he ran with cat-like tread and activity,
talking to each and straightening them up as he had
done with the others; and when he reached the
waggon again, he turned sharply and overlooked the
span. One ox had swung round and stood out of
line; there was a pause of seconds, and then the big
Zulu called to the ox by name—not loudly but in a
deep low tone, husky with intensity—and the animal
swung back into line again.

Then out of the silence that followed came an
electrifying yell to the span: every bullock leaned to
its yoke, and the waggon went out with a rush.

And he drove them at a half-trot all the way to the
store: without water; without help; without consciousness; the little dry twig still in his hand, and
only his masterful intensity and knowledge of his work
and span to see him through.

"A mad troublesome savage," said Harry Williams,
"but one of the very best. Anyhow, we thought so;
he saved us!"

There was something very familiar in this, and it
was with a queer feeling of pride and excitement that
I asked:

"Did he ever say to you, 'My catchum lion
'live'?"

"By gum! You know him? Jim: Jim Makokel'!"

459

"Indeed I do. Good old Jim!"

*   *   *   *   *

Years afterwards Jim was still a driver, working when necessary, fighting when possible, and enjoying intervals of lordly ease at his kraal where the wives and cattle stayed and prospered.

HIS · DUTY

And Jock?

But I never saw my dog again. For a year or so he lived something of the old veld life, trekking and hunting; from time to time I heard of him from Ted and others: stories seemed to gather easily about him as they do about certain people, and many knew Jock and were glad to bring news of him. The things they thought wonderful and admirable made pleasant news for them to tell and welcome news to me, and they were heard with contented pride, but without surprise, as "just like him": there was nothing more to be said.

One day I received word from Ted that he was off to Scotland for a few months and had left Jock with another old friend, Tom Barnett—Tom, at whose store under the big fig tree Seedling lies buried; and although I was glad that he had been left with a good friend like Tom, who would care for him as well as any one could, the life there was not of the kind

461

to suit him. For a few months it would not matter; but I had no idea of letting him end his days as a watch-dog at a trader's store in the kaffir country. Tom's trouble was with thieves; for the natives about there were not a good lot, and their dogs were worse. When Jock saw or scented them, they had the poorest sort of luck or chance: he fought to kill, and not as town dogs fight; he had learnt his work in a hard school, and he never stopped or slackened until the work was done; so his fame soon spread and it brought Tom more peace than he had enjoyed for many a day. Natives no longer wandered at will into the reed-enclosed yard; kaffir dogs ceased to sneak into the store and through the house, stealing everything they could get. Jock took up his place at the door, and hungry mongrels watched him from a distance or sneaked up a little closer when from time to time he trotted round to the yard at the back of the building to see how things were going there.

All that was well enough during the day; but the trouble occurred at night. The kaffirs were too scared to risk being caught by him, but the dogs from the surrounding kraals prowled about after dark, scaven-ging and thieving where they could; and what angered Tom most of all was the killing of his fowls. The yard at the back of the store was enclosed by a fence of close-packed reeds, and in the middle of the yard stood the fowl-house with a clear space of bare ground all round it. On many occasions kaffir dogs had found their way through the reed fence and killed fowls perching about the yard, and several times they

462

had burgled the fowl-house itself. In spite of Jock's presence and reputation, this night robbing still continued, for while he slept peacefully in front of the store, the robbers would do their work at the back. Poor old fellow! They were many and he was one; they prowled night and day and he had to sleep sometimes; they were watchful and he was deaf; so he had no chance at all unless he saw or scented them.

There were two small windows looking out on to the yard, but no door in the back of the building; thus, in order to get into the yard, it was necessary to go out of the front door and round the side of the house. On many occasions Tom, roused by the screaming of the fowls, had seized his gun and run round to get a shot at the thieves; but the time so lost was enough for a kaffir dog, and the noise made in opening the reed gate gave ample warning of his coming.

The result was that Tom generally had all his trouble for nothing; but it was not always so. Several times he roused Jock as he ran out, and invariably got some satisfaction out of what followed; once Jock caught one of the thieves struggling to force a way through the fence and held on to the hind leg until Tom came up with the gun; on other occasions he had caught them in the yard; on others, again, he had run them down in the bush and finished it off there without help or hindrance.

That was the kind of life to which Jock seemed to have settled down.

He was then in the very prime of life, and I still

463

hoped to get him back to me some day to a home where he would end his days in peace. Yet it seemed impossible to picture him in a life of ease and idleness —a watch-dog in a house sleeping away his life on a mat, his only excitement keeping off strange kaffirs and stray dogs, or burrowing for rats and moles in a garden with old age, deafness, and infirmities growing year by year to make his end miserable. I had often thought that it might have been better had he died fighting —hanging on with his indomitable pluck and tenacity, tackling something with all the odds against him; doing his duty and his best as he had always done— and died as Rocky's dog had died. If on that last day of our hunting together he had got at the lioness, and gone under in the hopeless fight; if the sable bull had caught and finished him with one of the scythe-like sweeps of the scimitar horns; if he could have died—like Nelson—in the hour of victory! Would it not have been better for him—happier for me? Often I thought so. For to fade slowly away; to lose his strength and fire and intelligence; to outlive his character, and no longer be himself! No, that could not be happiness!

Well, Jock is dead! Jock, the innocent cause of Seedling's downfall and death, lies buried under the same big fig tree: the graves stand side by side. He died, as he lived—true to his trust; and this is how it happened, as it was faithfully told to me:

It was a bright moonlight night—think of the scores we had spent together, the mild glorious nights of the Bushveld!—and once more Tom was roused by a clatter of falling boxes and the wild screams of fowls in the yard. Only the night before the thieves had beaten him again; but this time he was determined to be even with them. Jumping out of bed he opened the little window looking out on to the fowl-house, and, with his gun resting on the sill, waited for the thief. He waited long and patiently; and by-and-by the screaming of the fowls subsided enough for him to hear the gurgling and scratching about in the fowl-house, and he settled down to a still longer watch; evidently the kaffir dog was enjoying his stolen meal in there.

"Go on! Finish it!" Tom muttered grimly; "I'll have you this time if I wait till morning!"

So he stood at the window waiting and watching, until every sound had died away outside. He listened intently: there was not a stir; there was nothing to be seen in the moonlit yard; nothing to be heard; not even a breath of air to rustle the leaves in the big fig tree.

Then, in the same dead stillness the dim form of a dog appeared in the doorway, stepped softly out of the fowl-house, and stood in the deep shadow of the little porch. Tom lifted the gun slowly and took careful aim. When the smoke cleared away, the figure of the dog lay still, stretched out on the ground where it had stood; and Tom went back to bed, satisfied.

*   *   *   *   *

The morning sun slanting across the yard shone in Tom's eyes as he pushed the reed gate open and made

 his way towards the fowl-house. Under the porch where the sunlight touched it, something shone like burnished gold.

He was stretched on his side—it might have been in sleep; but on the snow-white chest there was one red spot.

And inside the fowl-house lay the kaffir-dog—dead.

Jock had done his duty.

THE END

NOTES

SNAKE stories are proverbially an 'uncommercial risk' for those who value a reputation for truthfulness. Hailstorms are scarcely less disastrous; hence these notes!

MAMBA.—This is believed to be the largest and swiftest of the deadly snakes, and one of the most wantonly vicious. The late Dr. Colenso (Bishop of Zululand) in his Zulu dictionary describes them as attaining a length of twelve feet, and capable of chasing a man on horseback. The writer has seen several of this length, and has heard of measurements up to fourteen feet (which, however, were not sufficiently verified); he has also often heard stories of men on horseback being chased by black mambas, but has never met the man himself, nor succeeded in eliciting the important facts as to pace and distance. However that may be, the movements of a mamba, even on open ground, are, as the writer has several times observed, so incredibly swift as to leave no other impression on the mind than that of having witnessed a magical disappearance. How often and how far they 'travel on their tails,' whether it is a continuous movement, or merely a momentary uprising to command a view, and what length or what proportion of the body is on the ground for support or propulsion, the writer has no means of knowing: during the Zulu war an Imperial officer was bitten by a mamba *while on horseback* and died immediately.

HAILSTORMS.—Bad hailstorms occur every year in South

Africa, but they do not last long (ten minutes is enough to destroy everything that stands). The distances are immense, and the area of disturbance is usually a narrow strip; hence, except when one strikes a town, very few people ever witness them. This summer hailstorms were more general and more severe in the Transvaal than for some time past. A bad storm baffles description. The size of the hailstones is only one of the factors—a strong wind enormously increases the destructiveness; yet some idea may be gathered from the size of the stones. The writer took a plaster cast of one picked up at Zuurfontein (near Johannesburg), in November 1906, which measured $4\frac{1}{2}$ inches long, $3\frac{1}{2}$ wide and $1\frac{1}{8}$ inches thick—a slab of white ice. In the Hekpoort Valley (near Johannesburg) and in Barberton, about the same date, the veld was like a glacier; the hail lay like snow, inches deep, and during the worst spells the general run of the hailstones varied in size from pigeons' eggs to hens' eggs; but the big ones, the crash of whose individual blows was distinctly heard through the general roar, are described as 'bigger than cricket balls' and 'the size of breakfast cups,' generally with an elongation or tail—like a balloon. Sheep and buck were killed, and full-grown cattle so battered that some were useless and others died of the injuries; wooden doors were broken in, the panels being completely shattered; corrugated iron roofs were perforated, and in some cases the hailstones drove completely through them. The writer photographed a portion of a roof in Barberton which had suffered thus, and saw plaster casts—formed by pouring plaster of Paris into the indentations which two hailstones had made in a flower bed—in diameter equalling, respectively, tennis and cricket balls.

Near Harrismith, O.R.C., in 1903, two herd boys with a troop of about a hundred goats and calves were caught by the hail. The boys and all the stock, except one old goat, were killed.

GLOSSARY

Note.—*The spelling of Cape Dutch and native names is in many cases not to be determined by recognised authority. The pronunciation cannot be quite accurately suggested through the medium of English. The figures of weights and measurements of animals are gathered from many sources, and refer only to first-class specimens. The weights are necessarily approximate.*

AASVOGEL (D), a vulture (*lit.* carrion bird).

ANTBEAR, AARDVARK (D) (*Orycteropus Afer*).

ANT-HEAP, mound made by termites or 'white ants.' Usually formed by one colony of ants; about two to four feet in base diameter and height, but often in certain localities very much larger. The writer photographed one this year near the scene of the Last Hunt, eighteen feet base diameter and ten feet high, and another in Rhodesia which formed a complete background for a travelling waggonette and six mules. In both cases these mounds were 'deserted cities,' and trees, probably fifty to one hundred years old, were growing out of them.

ASSEGAI (*pro.* ass-e-guy) (N), native spear.

BAAS (D), master.

BANSELA (*pro.* baan-sé-la) (N), a present.

BEKER (*pro.* beaker) (D), a cup.

BILLY, a small tin utensil with lid and handle, used for boiling water.

BUCKSAIL, tarpaulin used for covering transport waggons, which are known as buck-waggons.

469

BUFFALO, Cape buffalo (*Bos Caffer*). Height, 5 ft. 6 in.; weight, possibly 1,000 lbs.; horns, 48 in. from tip to tip, and 36 in. each in length on curve.

BULTONG or BILTONG (*pro.* biltong) (D), meat cut in strips, slightly salted, and dried in the open air.

BUSHBUCK, a medium-sized but very courageous antelope (*Tragelaphus scriptus*). Height, 3 ft.; weight, 130 lbs.; horns (male only), 18 in.

BUSHVELD, properly BOSCHVELD (D), bush country; also called Low Veld and Low Country.

CANE RAT (*Thryonomys swinderenianus*).

CETYWAYO (*see* KETSHWAYO).

CHAKA, properly TSHAKA (N), the first of the great Zulu kings and founder of the Zulu military power.

DASSIE (*pro.* daas-ey) (D), rock-rabbit; coney (*Procavia (Hyrax) capensis*) (*lit.* little badger).

DINGAAN, properly DINGAN (E) (N), the second of the great Zulu kings; brother, murderer, and successor of Chaka.

DISSELBOOM (D), the pole of a vehicle.

DONGA (N), a gully or dry watercourse with steep banks.

DOUGHBOYS, scones; frequently unleavened dough baked in coals; also, ash-cakes, roaster cookies, stick-in-the-gizzards, veld-bricks; &c.

DRIFT (D), a ford.

DUIKER (*pro.* in Eng. dyker, in Dutch dayker) (D), a small antelope found throughout Africa (*Cephalophus grimmi*). Gross weight, 30 to 40 lbs.; height, 28 in.; horns, 5½ in. (*lit.* diver, so called from its habit of disappearing and reappearing in low scrub in a succession of bounds when it first starts running).

GO'WAY BIRD, the grey plantain eater (*Schizorbis concolor*).

HARTEBEESTE (*pro.* haar-te-beast) (D), a large antelope, of which there are several varieties, varying in gross weight from 300 to 500 lbs. Height, 48 in.; horns, 24 in.

HIGHVELD, properly HOOGEVELD (D), high country; the plateau, about 5,000 to 6,000 ft. above sea-level.

HONEY BIRD, the honey-guide (several species; family, *Indicatoridæ*).

HONEY-SUCKER, sunbird (sever&l species; family, *Nectariniidæ*).

HORSE-SICKNESS, a lung infection prevalent during summer in low-lying parts; generally fatal; caused by microbes introduced in the blood by some insect.

IMPALA (N), an antelope (*Æpyceros melampus*); habitat, Bushveld; weight, 140 lbs.; horns, up to 20 in., straight.

IMPI (*pro.* impey) (N), an army or body of armed natives gathered for or engaged in war.

INDUNA (*pro.* in-doó-nah) (N), a head-man, captain, or chief, great or petty.

INKOS (*pro.* in-kós—'os' as in verbose) (N), chief; used as a term of respect in address or salutation.

INSPAN, properly ENSPAN (D), to yoke up, harness up, or hitch up.

ISANDHL'WANA, also 'SANDHL'WANA, incorrectly ISANDULA (*pro.* saan-shle-waá-na), meaning 'the little hand,' the hill which gave the name to the battle in which the 24th Regiment was annihilated in the Zulu War, 1879.

KAFFIR CORN, sorghum.

KAHLE (*pro.* kaa-shle, corrupted in kitchen Kaffir to 'gaashly') (N), gently, carefully, pleasantly, well. 'Hamba kahle,' farewell, go in peace. 'Hlala (*pro.* shlala) kahle,' farewell, stay in peace.

KEHLA (*pro.* keh-shlaa) (N), a native of certain age and position entitled to wear the head ring. Dutch, *ring kop*—ring head.

KERRIE or KIRRIE, native sticks used for fighting, frequently knobbed; hence, knob-kerrie.

KETSHWAYO (*pro.* ketsh-wý-o), incorrectly CETEWAYO, fourth and last of the great Zulu kings.

KLIPSPRINGER (D), a small antelope, in appearance and habit rather like chamois (*Oreotragus saltator*) (*lit.* a rock-jumper).

KLOOF (D), a gorge.

KNEEHALTER (D), to couple the head to one foreleg by a reim or strap attached to the halter, closely enough to prevent the animal from moving fast.

KNOORHAAN, commonly but incorrectly KOORHAAN or KORAAN (D), the smaller bustard (*lit.* scolding cock).

KOODOO, properly KUDU (N) (*Strepsiceros capensis*). Habitat, rugged bushy country. Height, 5 ft.; weight, 600 lbs.; horns, up to 48 in. straight, and 66 in. on curve.

KOPJE (*pro.* copy) (D), a hill (*lit.* a little head).

471

KRAAL (*pro.* in Eng., crawl) (D), an enclosure for cattle, sheep, &c., a corral; also a collection of native huts, the home of a family, the village of a chief or tribe.

KRANS (D), often spelt KRANTZ (German) (D. *krans.* a circlet or crown), a precipitous face or coronet of rock on a hill or mountain.

LAGAVAAN, a huge water lizard, the monitor. Cape Dutch, *lagewaan* (pure Dutch, *laguaan*) (*Varanus niloticus*). Maximum length up to 8 ft.

LOOPER, round shot for fowling-piece, about four times the size of buck shot.

MARULA, in Zulu UMGANO, a tree which furnishes soft white wood, which is carved into bowls, spoons, &c.; fruit eaten or fermented for drink (*Sclerocarya caffra*).

MEERKAT (D), a small animal of the mongoose kind (properly applied to *Suricata tetradactyla*, but loosely to several species).

MIDDLEVELD, properly MIDDELVELD (D), the mixed country lying between the Highveld and the Bushveld.

NEKSTROP (D), the neck-strap, or reim, which, attached to the yoke-skeys, keeps the yoke in place.

NIX (D), nothing (from D. *niets*).

ORIBI (N), a small antelope (*Ourebia scoparia*). Weight, 30 lbs.; height, 24 in.; horns, 6 in.

OUTSPAN, properly UITSPAN (D), to unyoke or unharness; also the camp where one has outspanned, and places where it is customary or by law permitted to outspan.

PANDA, properly 'MPANDE (N), the third of the great Zulu kings.

PARTRIDGE, PHEASANT, names applied somewhat loosely to various species of francolin.

PAUW (*pro.* pow) (D), the great bustard (*lit.* peacock).

PEZULU (N), on top, up, above.

POORT (*pro.* pooh-rt) (D), a gap or gorge in a range of hills (*lit.* gate).

QUAGGA, zebra (correctly applied to *Equus quagga*, now extinct, but still applied to the various species of zebra found in South Africa).

REIM (*pro.* reem) (D), a stout strip of raw hide.

472

REIMPJE (*pro.* reempy) (D), a small reim.

RIETBUCK, properly (D) RIETBOK (*pro.* reet-buck), reed buck (*Cervi-capra arundinum*). Height, 3 ft. 6 in.; gross weight, 140 lbs.; horns, male only, up to 16 in.

SABLE ANTELOPE (*Hippotragus niger*; Dutch, *zwaart witpens*). Habitat, bushveld. Height, 4 ft. 6 in.; weight, 350 lbs.; horns, up to 48 in. on curve.

SAKUBONA (N), Zulu equivalent of 'Good day.'

SALTED HORSE, one which has had horse-sickness, and is thus considered immune (as in small-pox); hence 'salted' is freely used colloquially as meaning acclimatised, tough, hardened, &c.

SCHANS (*pro.* skaans) (D), a stone or earth breastwork for defence, very common in old native wars.

SCHELM (D), a rascal; like Scotch skellum.

SCHERM (*pro.* skarem) (D), a protection of bush or trees, usually against wild animals.

SJAMBOK (*pro.* in English shambok, in Dutch saam-bok) (D), tapering rawhide whip made from rhinoceros, hippopotamus, or giraffe skin.

SKEY (*pro.* skay), a yokeskey; short for Dutch *jukskei*.

SLOOT (D), a ditch.

SPAN (D), a team.

SPOOR (D), footprints; also a trail of man, animal, or vehicle.

SPRINGBUCK, properly SPRINGBOK (D), a small antelope (*Antidorcas (Gazella) euchore*). Habitat, high veld and other open grass country. Height, 30 in.; weight, up to 90 lbs.; horns, 19 in. (*lit.* jumping buck).

SPRUIT (*pro.* sprait; also commonly, but incorrectly, sproot) (D), a stream.

SQUIRREL, or TREE RAT, native name 'MCHINAAND (*Funisciurus pallia-tus*).

STEMBUCK (Cape Dutch, *stembok* or *steinbok*, from the pure Dutch *steenbok*, the Alpine ibex), a small antelope (*Raphicerus campestais*). Height, 22 in.; weight, 25 lbs.; horns, 5 in.

STOEP (*pro.* stoop) (D), a raised promenade or paved veranda in front or at sides of a house.

TAMBUKI GRASS, also TAMBOOKIE, and sometimes TAMBUTI (N), a very rank grass; in places reaches 15 ft. high, and stem diameter ¼ in.

473

TICK, or RHINOCEROS, BIRD, the 'ox-pecker' (*Buphaga Africana*).
TIGER. In South Africa the leopard is generally called a tiger; first so
described by the Dutch—*tijger*.
TOCK-TOCKIE, a slow-moving beetle, incapable of flight. Gets its
name from its means of signalling by rapping the abdomen on
the ground (*tenebrionid* beetle of the genus *Psammodes*).
TREK (D) (*lit.* to pull), to move off or go on a journey; a journey, an
expedition—*e.g.*, the Great Trek (or exodus of Boers from
Cape Colony, 1836-48); also, and commonly, the time, distance,
or journey from one outspan to another.
TREK GEAR, the traction gear, chain, yokes, &c., of a waggon. The
Boer pioneers had no chains, and used reims plaited into a stout
'rope'; hence *trek-touw*, or pulling-rope.
TSESSEBE, an antelope, one of the hartebeeste family (*Damaliscus
lunatus*; Dutch, bastard hartebeeste). Height, 48 in.; weight, 300
lbs.; horns, 15 in.
TSETSE FLY, a grey fly, little larger than the common house-fly, whose
bite is fatal to domesticated animals.
TWIGGLE, little people's word for the excited movement of a small
dog's tail, believed to be a combination of wriggle and twiddle.

UMFAAN (N), a boy.
UMGANAAM (N). my friend.
UMLUNGU (N), the native word to describe a white man.

VELD (*pro.* felt) (D), the open or unoccupied country; uncultivated
or grazing land.
VLEI (*pro.* flay) (D), a small, shallow lake, a swamp, a depression
intermittently damp, a water meadow.
VOORLOOPER (D) (*lit.* front walker), the leader, the boy who leads the
front oxen; the *pat'-intambu* (Zulu for 'take the reim').
VOORSLAG (*pro.* foor-slaach) (D) (*lit.* front lash or skin), the strip of
buck hide which forms the fine end of a whip-lash.

WATERBUCK (*Cobus ellipsiprymnus*; Dutch, *kring-gat*). Height 48 in.;
weight, 350 lbs.; horns, males only, 36 in.
WILDEBEESTE (*pro.* vill-de-beast) (D) (*lit.* wild cattle), the brindled
gnu, blue wildebeeste (*Connochaetes taurinus*). Height, 4 ft. 6 in.;
weight, 400 lbs.; horns, 30 in.
WILD DOG, the 'Cape hunting dog' (*Lycaon pictus*).

474

WOODEN ORANGE, fruit of the klapper (a species of *Strychnos*).

WOLF, the usual name for the hyena, derived from *tijger-wolf*, the pure Dutch name for the spotted hyena.

YOKESKEY, the wooden slat which, coupled by nekstrops, holds the yoke in place.